CW00924026

RHETORIC
IN
CLASSICAL
HISTORIOGRAPHY

FOUR STUDIES

A.J. Woodman

Routledge
Taylor & Francis Group

LONDON AND NEW YORK

© 1988 A.J. Woodman

Reprinted 2003
by Routledge
2 Park Square, Milton Park, Abingdon, Oxfordshire OX14 4RN
711 Third Avenue, New York, NY 10017

First issued in paperback 2014

Routledge is an imprint of the Taylor and Francis Group, an informa business

British Library Cataloguing in Publication Data

Woodman, A.J.
Rhetoric in classical historiography
1. Rome — Historiography   2. Greece —
Historiography
I. Title
907′.2037   DG205
ISBN 0-7099-5256-2

Published in the USA in 1988 by
Areopagitica Press

ISBN 13: 978-0-7099-5256-5 (hbk)
ISBN 13: 978-0-415-76004-1 (pbk)

Typeset by Leaper & Gard Ltd, Bristol

Contents

Contents

To Dorothy

ficta uoluptatis causa sint proxima ueris

Prologue

No discussion of classical historiography can proceed very far before encountering the two contradictory beliefs which R.F. Atkinson mentions in his book *Knowledge and Explanation in History* (1978):

> From outside one tends to think of history as continuing from classical times to the present day; but many professional historians seem rather to think that their subject underwent a major change around the beginning of the nineteenth century. It may even be thought that history 'proper' *began* about that time. (p. 14)

Among classical scholars it is, somewhat paradoxically, professional historians who tend to hold the former view, the latter being held by literary specialists. Yet despite the conceptual chasm which separates them, neither group argues its case. Literary scholars, whose principal concern is not usually with historical texts, feel no need to do so, while most historians seem constitutionally opposed to all questions of historiographical theory and, if pressed, take refuge in allusions to the authority of Thucydides and Cicero.

It is true that Thucydides holds a unique and formidable position in any debate concerning classical historiography. On the evidence of his preface and narrative alike he is commonly believed to have intended and produced the equivalent of a modern work of 'scientific' history. 'In his conception of what is required of a writer of history', runs a typical comment, 'he is nearer to the twentieth century AD than he is to the fifth BC.' Yet in the first Study I point to some of the obvious practical difficulties involved in writing narrative history, and I question whether Thucydides' preface and its famous statements of method are in fact to be understood in the ways which are commonly supposed. Similarly the narrative itself, when one of its most admired sections is analysed in detail, is shown to have different qualities from those associated with 'scientific' history. I am of course aware that numerous other scholars in recent years have queried the reputation which Thucydides has traditionally enjoyed, but there is clear and ample evidence that his work still suffers from widespread and mistaken preconceptions. If I have asked some of the right questions (and even if I have not always suggested the right answers), it becomes more likely that one can investigate other areas of classical historiography on their own terms and without risking the automatic response: 'But what about Thucydides?'

Antonius' speech in Book 2 of Cicero's *De Oratore* is just such an area. In this speech, which is our fullest and most important Roman source for the theory of classical historiography, Cicero is assumed by scholars to have put forward criteria for historical writing with which all modern historians would agree. Indeed, a distinguished modern historian and classical scholar has recently stated that 'Cicero is not expressly advocating a type of historical exposition different from that commonly employed by modern political historians'. Yet in the second Study I demonstrate that such assumptions are based on an equal disregard for the context and the argument of the passage. When analysed in detail, Antonius' observations are revealed to derive wholly from rhetorical prescriptions for the invention of material (*inuentio*) which were fundamental to forensic oratory in the ancient world. If my analysis is correct, it means that there is no theoretical basis whatsoever for the view that classical historiography resembles its modern namesake. Historiography was regarded by the ancients as not essentially different from poetry: each was a branch of rhetoric, and therefore historiography, like poetry, employs the concepts associated with, and relies upon the expectations generated by, a rhetorical genre.

An example of this phenomenon is the style in which history is written. Cicero had prescribed what he considered the appropriate style, but his younger contemporary Sallust, while illustrating many of the great orator's other historiographical prescriptions, signally failed to implement those which relate to style. In the third Study I argue that style was used by historians to denote the attitude which they adopted towards their material. Sallust, writing recent history in a time of civil war, was unable to adopt the kind of optimistic attitude which Cicero had taken for granted, but instead preferred to be seen as imitating the critical attitude associated with his stylistic model, Thucydides. Livy, writing later, is generally thought to have reacted against Sallust and returned to the ideals of Cicero; but a close analysis of his preface reveals that he too was writing during the civil wars and thus had no more cause than Sallust for optimism. On the contrary, his original plan was to contrast a Sallustian treatment of Rome's decline with a Ciceronian account of the glorious early republic. Yet since Livy's long career lasted the length of Augustus' principate, he had the opportunity of appreciating the practical benefits of the Augustan programme, to which he became an enthusiastic convert. This conversion is demonstrated by the change which he introduced into the plan of his history, extending it to deal with Augustus' reign in the same encomiastic style which he had used for the early republic.

Both Sallust and Livy were available for imitation by subsequent Roman historians, and it has often been thought that Sallust proved the more popular choice; yet the political atmosphere of the first century AD was such that Sallustian pessimism was dangerously open to misinterpretation and hence best avoided. Even Tacitus in the preface to his *Histories*, as I show in the fourth Study, did not openly espouse the style and attitude of Sallust but instead was more concerned to emphasise that his work exhibited all the exciting topics and dramatic techniques which had been prescribed for historiography by Cicero. Tacitus begins the *Annals*, however, by calling attention to his Sallustian style; and though in the narrative of Book 1 he gives every impression of trying to repeat the success story of the *Histories* (thereby providing an excellent example of classical historiography in action), this turns out later to be merely a device designed to shock readers out of their complacency. In Book 4 he maintains that, given the nature of Tiberius' reign, he is unable to write history at all in the conventional sense but has been compelled to adopt an alternative format. Yet this too turns out to be a device, since Tacitus subsequently resorts to the further alternative of 'metahistory', in which he provides, in a metonymic or metaphorical form, precisely the elements of conventional historiography which he had earlier professed to exclude.

In an Epilogue I draw together the main threads of the preceding arguments and attempt to place classical historiography, and the discussion thereof, in an appropriate generic context.

Each of the four Studies was written (and is intended to be read) as an independent contribution to the understanding of classical historiography, but it will be clear from the above synopsis that there are also links between them and that some themes are developed from one Study to the next. I should perhaps add that the Studies are not intended to constitute a comprehensive treatment of the authors or issues discussed, and that the absence of certain aspects does not necessarily mean that I do not believe in them or do not consider them important. By a similar token I hope that readers will be prepared to make allowances for any bibliographical shortcomings: the scholarly literature on the five authors is extensive, and that on such subjects as the history of historiography, the philosophy of history, and narrative discourse even more so. There comes a point at which one must simply call a halt, otherwise nothing would ever get written at all; but I realise that in so doing there will be relevant items which I have missed.

Many of the arguments presented in this book are either illustrated by, or depend upon the detailed analysis of, passages of Greek or Latin texts. In the hope that the subject might be accessible to a wider readership than simply professional classicists, all the central passages have been translated into English. I have taken a great deal of trouble in trying to get these translations right, and I like to think that on at least some occasions I am presenting readers with the only correct translation they are likely to have seen. Mistakes and misconceptions will, however, remain; and for these I apologise in advance.

All four of these Studies enjoyed a previous existence in oral form, when they were delivered as papers to various audiences up and down the country. Their publication gives me the chance to thank all those who invited me to speak on such occasions, as well as those who volunteered comments afterwards. Two or three pages of the fourth Study have already appeared in a fuller version in a book published by Cambridge University Press, to whom I am grateful for their permission to reproduce the material here.

During the writing of the book I have been offered bibliographical and other help by David Bland, Jocelyn Core, Roger Scott and Richard Stoneman, to all of whom I am obliged for their kindness. I have also pestered shamelessly other friends and colleagues either by sending them drafts to read and criticise or by asking for their help with problems and questions. Apart from one notable exception they have all responded with prompt and unfailing generosity, among them Charles Brink, John Davies, Alan Douglas, Sir Kenneth Dover, Ian DuQuesnay, Denis Feeney, the late Colin Macleod, Stephen Oakley, Jeremy Paterson, Jonathan Powell, Peter Rhodes, Robin Seager, Anne Sheppard, John Smart, Robert Tannenbaum, Robin Waterfield,

David West and Hayden White.

I am especially indebted to Ronald Martin, John Moles and Peter Wiseman for allowing me to take repeated advantage of their friendship and learning; and I should like also to take this opportunity of acknowledging how much I have profited from conversations with John Bramble, Ian DuQuesnay and David West at various points during the past twenty years.

A.J.W.
University of Durham
September 1986

1
Preconceptions and Practicalities: Thucydides

Preliminary

'Herodotus is to us the "father of history", as he was to Cicero',
writes Momigliano, the doyen of Greek and Roman historiographical scholarship.[1] Does this mean that Herodotus 'invented'
historiography? The ancients believed that he imitated Homer,[2]
which suggests that in some sense Homer was regarded as his
predecessor. But if Homer was his predecessor, does this mean
that it is Homer, and not Herodotus, who is the real 'father of
history'? Not according to Momigliano:[3]

> As the Greeks had a long tradition of epic poetry before
> they began to write historical prose, it is tempting to take
> Homer as a predecessor of the historians ... Herodotus
> may seem to encourage us in this direction. But the Greeks
> themselves, and the Romans, knew that there were two
> differences between history and epic poetry: history was
> written in prose, and was meant to separate facts from
> fancies about the past.

Thus it is on the grounds that Herodotus, like modern historians,
wrote in prose and dealt in facts rather than fancies, that
Momigliano accepts him as the 'father of history'. Most scholars
would probably agree.[4] Yet even on the assumption that these
grounds are adequate and wholly true, which we shall see is not
the case, they do not explain the ancient view, which Momigliano
effectively ignores, that Herodotus imitated Homer.[5]
Modern scholars who ignore the views of the ancient literary
critics, perhaps seeing them as illustrating the amiable naivety by

which the critics themselves are traditionally characterised, come up against the programmatic evidence of Herodotus' own text.[6] Just as Homer at the beginning of the *Iliad* 'attracted his readers' attention by the greatness of his proposed theme',[7] so did Herodotus in the preface at the beginning of his history:

Ἡροδότου Ἁλικαρνησσέας ἱστορίης ἀπόδεξις ἥδε, ὡς μήτε τὰ γενόμενα ἐξ ἀνθρώπων τῷ χρόνῳ ἐξίτηλα γένηται, μήτε ἔργα μεγάλα τε καὶ θωμαστά, τὰ μὲν Ἕλλησι, τὰ δὲ βαρβάροισι ἀποδεχθέντα, ἀκλεᾶ γένηται, τά τε ἄλλα καὶ δι' ἣν αἰτίην ἐπολέμησαν ἀλλήλοισι.

Herodotus of Halicarnassus has presented his findings here lest human events should eventually be forgotten through the lapse of *time* and lest the *great* and admirable achievements presented by both *Greeks* and *barbarians* should be unglorified, both in *other respects* and as regards the reason why they *waged war* on *each other*.[8]

'Unglorified' is an allusion to *Iliad* 9.189,[9] where Achilles' singing of the 'glorious deeds of men' (κλέα ἀνδρῶν) points to the encomiastic character which Homer's own epic poetry was thought to possess;[10] and Herodotus' last clause reproduces in an indirect form the question which Homer asked the Muse in a direct form at *Iliad* 1.8, 'Which of the gods set these two on a collision course to battle?'[11] The statement which Homer made at *Odyssey* 1.3, that the hero 'saw the cities of many men' (πολλῶν δ'ἀνθρώπων ἴδεν ἄστεα), is echoed by Herodotus at the end of his preface, where he says that he himself 'investigated the cities of men' (1.5.3 ἄστεα ἀνθρώπων ἐπεξιών).[12] Much later in his work, when he reached the point where the Persian expedition against Greece is about to be launched, Herodotus inserted a second preface in which he re-emphasised his subject and introduced an unfavourable comparison of an earlier expedition in the opposite direction, that of the Greeks against Troy (7.20.2-21.1):[13]

For [γάρ], of the expeditions about which we know, *this amounted to the greatest indeed* by far [πολλῷ δὴ μέγιστος οὗτος ἐγένετο]: that of Darius ... seemed insignificant by comparison ..., as did that of the Atreidae against Troy and that of the Mysians and Teucrians before the Trojan War ... All these armies together, with others like them, would not have

equalled the army of Xerxes. There was not a nation in Asia
that he did not take with him against Greece.

It would therefore seem that Herodotus wanted his own work to
be seen in terms of Homer's work, and his own subject in terms
of Homer's subject.

Of course many scholars would be prepared to accept this
conclusion, believing it harmless enough. After all, what does
Herodotus' imitation consist of? 'There are many Homeric words
and phrases in Herodotus', says D.A. Russell, 'but the judgement
[that Herodotus imitated Homer] might just as well be based,
say, on Herodotus' battle scenes and heroic temper, his methods
of narrative and digression, his frequent use of direct speech, his
dialect, or his rhythms.'[14] From a historical point of view these
manifestations of imitation do indeed seem harmless. But only at
first sight. Let us look at some of them more closely.

It is a commonplace of modern (and of some ancient) theory
that language profoundly affects the narration of historical facts
and that style is inseparable from historical interpretation.[15] It is
even said that no history exists apart from narrative.[16] Thus the
'many Homeric words and phrases in Herodotus' begin to
assume more significance. What about battle scenes? If they are
in some sense Homeric, does this mean that Herodotus believed
that history repeats itself, and, if he does, what implications does
this have for his work as history?[17] At the very least, Homeric
battles in Herodotus can only mean that the battles he describes
are less historical, less true, and more universalised.[18] 'Methods of
narrative' is a vague phrase, but if we were assured that A.J.P.
Taylor had adopted his 'methods of narrative' from *Paradise Lost*
we would presumably become very worried indeed. If by
Herodotus' 'frequent use of direct speech' is meant his putting
into the mouths of historical characters words which they did not
utter (and it cannot be denied that he does this),[19] it is being
recognised that he is presenting as true something which is not or
was not the case.[20] This recognition has profound implications for
the difference between our own and Herodotean historiography,
which, though obvious, are almost never acknowledged.[21]
Finally, rhythms. Herodotus often echoes the rhythms of poetry,
and some passages of his prose can actually be turned into verse
without too much difficulty;[22] this suggests a deeper and more
intimate affinity between history and poetry than any we might
care to contemplate today. In short, Herodotus' imitations of

Homer betoken something absolutely fundamental about the nature of his narrative.

The implications of Herodotus' imitation of Homer are rarely faced by scholars, either because they ignore the imitation itself, as we have already seen, or because they merely pay lip-service to it.[23] In which case let us remember another accepted fact: that Herodotus regarded Homer as a historical source and his narrative as in some sense a true record of events which actually took place.[24] Now it has to be acknowledged that modern scholars too admit that there is some kind of reality lying behind the Homeric poems; but theirs is a radically different stance from that which Herodotus adopted.[25] If Herodotus regarded Homer as history (which he did), that has far-reaching implications for the nature of his own history. It does not mean that he did not distinguish between true and false, which is a distinction to be found in Homer;[26] but it does mean that he did not distinguish between the narratives of epic and history and hence between the realism of the former and the reality which we today associate with the latter.[27]

Despite these points it will still be maintained that Herodotus is the 'father of history'. So let us consider a final set of arguments. Herodotus' work embraces accounts of visits to foreign lands and descriptions of the natural phenomena, monuments and customs to be found there. These accounts and descriptions give every impression of being based on autopsy, yet O.K. Armayor has argued convincingly, from archaeological and other evidence, that there are many occasions where Herodotus is most unlikely to have seen what he claims to have seen and indeed may never have made the requisite journeys in the first place. Rather, he has adapted his information from the literary tradition.[28] Armayor's approach, similar to that of Fehling a few years earlier, has recently received strong support from a detailed investigation of Herodotus' epigraphical interests by S. West.[29] There is therefore a discrepancy between Herodotus' apparent method and the method which he actually followed; and the fact that he is able to present the latter in terms of the former argues for an attitude towards historical writing which is totally alien to everything we take for granted today. If he were a modern historian he would be taken to court for false pretences under the Trades Descriptions Act and sued for damages.[30] But that is of course the whole point. He is *not* a modern historian. When Cicero called Herodotus the 'father of history' he meant that he was the founder of the genre as it was known to Cicero; and while Cicero undoubtedly had in mind the fact that Herodotus wrote in prose, he can hardly have been thinking of our modern, 'scientific' historiography, which did not come into being until last century.

But surely, it will be said, this is to forget Herodotus' younger contemporary, Thucydides? 'In his conception of what is required of a writer of history he is nearer to the twentieth century AD than he is to the fifth BC.'[31] Remarks like this, which can be found in almost any of the standard works in which Thucydides is discussed,[32] have created the impression that he at least can safely be regarded as the first 'scientific' historian. Thucydides has thus exercised a unique influence on the way in which scholars have regarded all other ancient historians, Roman as well as Greek. He is commonly believed to have set standards of objectivity, accuracy and truth against which all subsequent historians should be judged but which none was ever able to match. And despite some recent reappraisals of his alleged objectivity,[33] he can still be said by T.P. Wiseman in 1979 to be 'unique' and to have 'set himself a standard of accuracy unparalleled in the ancient world'.[34]

Yet a moment's thought should remind us just how unusual it is to talk about a classical author in these terms. When we think of classical authors, we normally think about them in relation to their literary tradition, which in Thucydides' case would mean in relation to Herodotus and (as we have just seen) Homer. That he is usually treated instead as an exception is exceptionally curious. What is the explanation for it?

Preface

Part one (Chapter 1)

Thucydides' preface occupies the first 23 chapters of Book 1, and, as we shall see, it falls into various parts. The first of these parts is the introduction, of which the text and a translation follow:

Θουκυδίδης Ἀθηναῖος ξυνέγραψε τὸν πόλεμον τῶν Πελοποννησίων καὶ Ἀθηναίων, ὡς ἐπολέμησαν πρὸς ἀλλήλους, ἀρξάμενος εὐθὺς καθισταμένου καὶ ἐλπίσας

μέγαν τε ἔσεσθαι καὶ ἀξιολογώτατον τῶν προγεγε-
νημένων, τεκμαιρόμενος ὅτι ἀκμάζοντές τε ἦσαν ἐς
αὐτὸν ἀμφότεροι παρασκευῇ τῇ πάσῃ καὶ τὸ ἄλλο
Ἑλληνικὸν ὁρῶν ξυνιστάμενον πρὸς ἑκατέρους, τὸ μὲν
2 εὐθύς, τὸ δὲ καὶ διανοούμενον. κίνησις γὰρ αὕτη
μεγίστη δὴ τοῖς Ἕλλησιν ἐγένετο καὶ μέρει τινὶ τῶν
3 βαρβάρων, ὡς δὲ εἰπεῖν καὶ ἐπὶ πλεῖστον ἀνθρώπων. τὰ
γὰρ πρὸ αὐτῶν καὶ τὰ ἔτι παλαίτερα σαφῶς μὲν εὑρεῖν
διὰ χρόνου πλῆθος ἀδύνατα ἦν, ἐκ δὲ τεκμηρίων ὧν
ἐπὶ μακρότατον σκοποῦντί μοι πιστεῦσαι ξυμβαίνει οὐ
μεγάλα νομίζω γενέσθαι οὔτε κατὰ τοὺς πολέμους οὔτε
ἐς τὰ ἄλλα.

Thucydides of Athens wrote the account of the *war* which
Athens and Sparta *waged* against *each other*, having begun at
its outbreak in the expectation that it would be a *great* war
and more worthy of record than those in the past, seeing
that both sides went into it at the peak of readiness and that
Greece in general was lining up with one side or the other,
2 some at once, others intending to do so in their turn.[35] *For
this indeed amounted to the greatest* upheaval to affect the
Greeks and many of the *barbarians* and thus (one might
3 almost say) a very large part of mankind.[36] For though it
was impossible to draw clear conclusions about the preceding and still earlier periods on account of the *time* span
involved, nevertheless, on the basis of such evidence as I can
trust from this long-distance view, I believe that they were
not great either in wars or in *other respects*.

Though the precise logic of the paragraph is still disputed after
almost two and a half thousand years,[37] the italicised words and
phrases, which are borrowed directly from one or other of the two
passages of Herodotus quoted above, make it clear that
Thucydides wishes his own work to be seen in terms of that of
Herodotus.[38] And just as Herodotus had emphasised the greatness of his proposed theme, so does Thucydides — only more so:
he first states a two-fold expectation in his opening sentence, and
then re-states each element of that expectation in his second and
third sentences respectively. This quadruple emphasis on the size
of the war suggests that the Augustan critic Dionysius was quite
right when, in his essay *On Thucydides*, he described this opening
paragraph as an example of rhetorical magnification (αὔξησις,

amplificatio);[39] and the point is proved by the fact that Thucydides attributes to the Peloponnesian War a global dimension which it, unlike the Persian Wars, clearly did not warrant.[40] So far from being disengaged or objective, Thucydides has deployed standard rhetorical exaggeration in order to demonstrate the superiority of his own work and subject over those of Herodotus.

The two complementary statements of Thucydides' second and third sentences are each illustrated, though in reverse order, in the second and third parts of his preface respectively (i.e. in 2-21.1 and 21.2-23.3).[41] That is to say: in the second part he demonstrates to his own satisfaction the negative statement that earlier periods of Greek history were 'not great either in wars or in other respects', and in the third part the positive statement that 'this was the greatest upheaval to affect the Greeks' etc.

Part two (2-21.1)

Much of 2-21.1 is devoted to a survey of ancient history,[42] in the course of which Thucydides naturally gives considerable space (chapters 9-11) to the Trojan War, which he, like Herodotus, regarded as historical. (This means that we can apply also to Thucydides what was said about Herodotus on p. 4 above.) Since by reading Homer one would rapidly form the impression that earlier times *were* great, particularly in wars, Thucydides argues (10.3) that 'as a poet he (Homer) embroidered his description to make it more impressive' (ἐπὶ τὸ μεῖζον ... κοσμῆσαι). Thus he tries to depreciate the scale of the Trojan War by alleging that Homer employed the rhetorical technique of embellishment or 'embroidery', for which κοσμεῖν is the technical verb.[43] Thucydides' anxiety to depreciate Homer suggests that it was natural to regard him, no less than Herodotus, as a predecessor.[44] This is exactly what we should expect. Yet his qualification that Homer wrote 'as a poet' suggests that Thucydides himself regarded the embellishment of poetry as being foreign to the writing of history and hence that he did not after all regard Homer as a genuine predecessor. That this dilemma is only apparent, however, can be seen from the end of this part of the preface.

Throughout the second part of the preface Thucydides employs an extremely rigorous technique of argument. His procedure is first to propose a thesis, then to give proof(s) or illustration(s) of that thesis, and finally to re-state the thesis as if to say 'Q.E.D.'[45] An example of this technique is 20-21.1, which opens with this 'thesis':

> Such, I conclude, was the nature of ancient history [τὰ μὲν οὖν παλαιὰ τοιαῦτα ηὗρον], although it is difficult to place equal trust in every item of evidence [τεκμηρίῳ πιστεῦσαι].

After illustrating this thesis in the passage which follows (20.2-3), Thucydides then re-states it, as is clear from the verbal correspondences, in a longer form at 21.1:

> Yet if someone decided, on the basis of the above evidence [τεκμηρίων], that the nature [τοιαῦτα] of events was as I have described, he would be quite correct: he would not be placing more trust [πιστεύων] either in the panegyrics of poets, who embroider their subject matter to make it more impressive [ἐπὶ τὸ μεῖζον κοσμοῦντες], or in logographers, whose compilations are aimed at audience entertainment rather than truth and whose subject matter is unprovable and because of the time factor has largely achieved the status of untrustworthy legend, but would have considered that my conclusions [ηὑρῆσθαι], based as they are on the clearest available evidence [σημείων], are satisfactory, given that they concern ancient history [ὡς παλαιά].

The very fact that this is a re-statement means that a section of argument has come to an end and that a break should be observed at 21.1; and from the reference to '*ancient* history' in both the thesis and its re-statement it is clear that 20-21.1 constitutes an epilogue to the survey of ancient history which Thucydides has just provided in the immediately preceding chapters (2-19).[46]

Now since 20-21.1 is methodological in nature and is separated from another methodological section in chapter 22 by only a single sentence (viz. 21.2), some scholars, failing to observe the break after 21.1, have treated chapters 20-2 as a single passage and called them the 'chapters on method'.[47] In this way Thucydides' negative statements about poetic technique at 21.1 have been aligned with his positive statements about his own technique in chapter 22, and together they have been taken as a programmatic assertion on Thucydides' part that in his narrative of the Peloponnesian War he himself will refrain from poetic techniques since they are foreign to the writing of history.[48] (And since this stance is not adopted by Herodotus but is in keeping with our modern notions of 'scientific' historiography, Thucydides emerges from this extrapolation as the first modern historian.) Yet this whole hypothesis is based on a false assumption.

We have just seen that 21.1 is explicitly integrated with the survey of ancient history which began in chapter 2; and this is virtually proved by the fact that the criticism of poets at 21.1 is expressed in identical terms to those used in the criticism of Homer at 10.3 (ἐπὶ τὸ μεῖζον ... κοσμῆσαι). The criticism of poetry at 21.1 is therefore an integral part of Thucydides' larger attempt to denigrate the achievements of ancient history, which in turn is part of his overall attempt to magnify the Peloponnesian War; being formally quite unconnected with the main narrative of the Peloponnesian War, 21.1 cannot therefore be used as a programmatic statement of how Thucydides will describe that war. It is no doubt true that he wishes his readers to *infer* from both 10.3 and 21.1 that in his main narrative he will refrain from the embellishments of poetry;[49] but that is simply because he wishes to suggest that the greatness of his own war does not require such embellishments and to distract attention from the embellishment which, as we shall see below, he does indeed employ.[50] Thus the dilemma which was raised at 10.3 above is only apparent: it cannot be argued from any passage in the second part of the preface that Thucydides was *in fact* averse to poetic techniques or did not regard Homer as his genuine predecessor in the genre.

Part three (21.2-23.3)

We must now consider the third part of the preface, in which Thucydides turns to illustrate the other statement which he made in his introductory paragraph, namely that 'this was the greatest upheaval to affect the Greeks' etc. He begins at 21.2 with a transitional sentence which concludes, perhaps significantly, by reproducing the hexameter rhythm of an all but complete line of epic verse:[51]

To return to the present war: although men always reckon

that their own war is the greatest [μέγιστον] while they are fighting it, but after demobilisation tend to magnify the past, nevertheless to those who judge the present war simply on the basis of its events [ἀπ᾽ αὐτῶν τῶν ἔργων], it will be seen to have been greater than any predecessor [δηλώσει ὅμως μείζων γεγενημένος αὐτῶν]. (-ı- ∪ ∪ı--ı- ∪ ∪ı- ∪ ∪ı--)

Now Thucydides is about to list a selection of the war's constituent 'events' at 23.1-3, and his use of the word αὐτῶν, which I have translated as 'simply', suggests that they are self-evident in a way that the events of earlier history, which depend on different sorts of 'evidence' (τεκμήρια), are not.[52] Nevertheless, the truth of his statement about the greatness of the war depends upon the credibility of the detailed narrative by which those events are described: therefore, in much the same way as he defended his account of ancient history in an epilogue at 20-21.1, so his summary of the greatness of the war at 23.1-3 is here introduced by a kind of prologue in chapter 22 where he explains the method he has followed in writing the narrative of the Peloponnesian War.

Chapter 22 is naturally extremely important because it is the *only* occasion on which Thucydides discusses his method of writing contemporary history:

As for the numerous speeches which individuals made, either in the prelude to the war or during the war itself, it was difficult for me to recall the actuality of what was said [τὴν ἀκρίβειαν αὐτὴν τῶν λεχθέντων] when I heard it myself, and also for those who reported to me from various places; but the speeches have been rendered in accordance with what I thought each person would have said (namely, that which was generally necessary [τὰ δέοντα] given their circumstances at the time), keeping as closely as possible to the general gist [τῆς ξυμπάσης γνώμης] of what was actually said [τῶν ἀληθῶς λεχθέντων].

2   As for the events which took place during the war, on the other hand, I did not consider it right to describe them either on the basis of what I learned from just anybody or in accordance with what I thought, but from personal experience and after investigating with as much accuracy [ἀκριβείᾳ] as
3   possible each event reported by others.[53] It was a fairly troublesome process because those who were present at the

various events did not make the same reports about the same things: it depended upon an individual's prejudice for either
4 side or his memory. And for audience purposes the non-legendary aspect of my work will perhaps seem less entertaining; but if anyone, wanting a realistic view both of the things which took place and of those which one day (given human nature) are destined to take place again in more or less the same fashion, should judge my work useful, that will be enough. My history is not a one-off performance but a possession for posterity.

Although numerous scholars have already subjected almost every word of this chapter to the most minute analysis, I nevertheless believe, as may be clear from my translation, that crucial sections are still not properly understood. I shall therefore go through the chapter section by section.

22.1 Speeches. The account which Thucydides gives of his speeches is one of the most discussed and controversial passages of Greek literature.[54] Numerous scholars, convinced that Thucydides is a unique figure, credit him with the unique achievement of reproducing more or less exactly what a given speaker actually said.[55] Indeed D. Kagan, whose detailed study of the Peloponnesian War is still in progress, not only uses Thucydides' speeches as a more or less exact record of what a speaker said, but has even stated that 'Thucydides claims to present the most accurate account possible of what was actually said in speeches'.[56] Yet Kagan's willingness to believe in Thucydides' infallibility has led him to omit from his paraphrase of 22.1 the very words by which Thucydides makes it clear that this is *not* his claim. The historian claims only to have kept as closely as possible to the ξύμπᾶσα γνώμη of what was actually said. What do these words mean?

I believe that G.E.M. De Ste Croix has produced an interpretation which accounts for all the apparent difficulties. He has argued, on linguistic and other grounds, that ἡ ξυμπᾶσα γνώμη should be translated as 'general gist' and that Thucydides means 'something that can be expressed in a single sentence', representing the 'main thesis' of a speech which is otherwise completely invented by Thucydides.[57] It is relevant to note that modern psychologists who have conducted memory experiments have come to draw a distinction between 'verbatim recall' and 'memory for the gist of what was said', the former being beyond, and the latter within, the capabilities of normal individuals.[58] Since the former corresponds exactly with Thucydides' expression 'the actuality of what was said', which he acknowledges to be beyond both himself and his informants, it is tempting to believe that the latter corresponds to that which Thucydides says is within his powers. If this is so, it provides strong support for the translation of ἡ ξύμπασα γνώμη as 'general gist'.

De Ste Croix's narrow interpretation of these words has not won general acceptance, most scholars wanting them to include at least some of the arguments used by the original speaker;[59] yet modern experience again shows that more generous interpretations are unlikely to be right. Ulric Neisser, for example, has compared the testimony which John Dean (ex-President Nixon's former counsel) gave before the Watergate Committee with the tape-recordings of what he is known to have said on the relevant occasions. The results are extremely interesting:[60]

> Analysis of Dean's testimony does indeed reveal some instances of memory for the gist of what was said on a particular occasion. Elsewhere in his testimony, however, there is surprisingly little correspondence between the course of a conversation and his account of it ... Comparison with the transcript [of the meeting between Nixon and Dean on 15 September 1972] shows that hardly a word of Dean's account [of that meeting] is true. Nixon did not say *any* of the things attributed to him here ... Nor had Dean himself said the things he later describes himself as saying ... His account is plausible, but entirely incorrect ... Dean cannot be said to have reported the "gist" of the opening remarks; no count of idea units or comparison of structure would produce a score much above zero.

Such evidence shows that we should not place an optimistic interpretation even on the 'general gist'.

Now it is of course true that some quite staggering feats of memory are sometimes attributed to the ancients on the basis of statements which appear in their works, and that through living in an oral culture Thucydides no doubt possessed powers of memory superior to our own.[61] Yet modern scholars tend to look with scepticism on the ancients' claims to prodigious recall, regarding them rather as examples of a rhetorical motif,[62] and

Thucydides for his part expressly tells us that he and his inform-ants did *not* find it easy to remember speeches. My own view, therefore, is that De Ste Croix's interpretation is more realistic than those of his critics and that, although there are doubtless differences between one speech and another depending on the oral evidence available to Thucydides,[63] the majority of each speech in his work is the creation of the historian himself.[64]

This conclusion raises a more general issue. While scholars will continue to disagree on the precise meaning of 22.1 and on the extent to which Thucydides reproduces the actual speech of others, it is generally assumed that (in Fornara's words) he 'held that verbatim speeches would have been best'.[65] Yet how many modern historians, with whom Thucydides is supposed to have so much in common, would include speeches of Thucydidean length in their works?[66] How many ancient historians did? Tacitus, one of the few who are thought to approach Thucydides in reliability, was happy to reproduce verbatim the occasional *bon mot* but refrained from reproducing verbatim a full speech of the emperor Claudius.[67] It must be remembered that speeches feature so prominently in Thucydides' work not simply because oratory was important in contemporary public life but also because, as is generally recognised, speeches play a significant role in the epic of Homer.[68] Thus, if Thucydides included lengthy speeches composed by someone else, he would be denying himself the chance, which all the evidence suggests that he wanted, of rivalling Homer in a major area of his work.[69] Verbatim speeches and classical historiography are a contra-diction in terms.[70] As far as I know, the only historian who included verbatim speeches was Cato — and it is significant that they were *his own* speeches.[71]

It is of course true that rivalry with Homer would be satisfied if Thucydides merely invented speeches, whereas we have already seen that he claims to have reproduced the 'general gist' of what was actually said. That this is a remarkable claim to make will become evident if we consider what he says in chapter 22 as a whole. On the assumption that ἀκριβείᾳ at 22.2 is to be under-stood subjectively of the historian's own 'accuracy' or 'care',[72] it will be seen that the words 'actuality' (ἀκρίβειαν in its objective sense) and 'actually' (ἀληθῶς) are found only in 22.1, where Thucydides discusses speeches, and not in 22.2-4, where he discusses events and where, as has rightly been observed, he speaks not of 'accounts that agree with the reality' but simply of 'accounts that agree with each other'.[73] If I am right to maintain that verbatim speeches were not considered an ideal, this apparent emphasis on the reality of speeches is striking and requires an explanation.

Thucydides' lifetime coincided with the rise of the sophistic movement, whose protagonists championed the importance of *logos* ('speech' or 'language') at the expense of reality.[74] Gorgias in particular maintained that the language we use to describe reality is not the same as the reality itself, and that, when we communicate, we communicate language not reality.[75] It has been generally accepted, in antiquity as well as today, that at least the style of Gorgias made its mark on that of Thucydides,[76] and it may be that in Chapter 22 we can detect his philosophical influence too. It would be consonant with sophistic theory for Thucydides to have believed that a speech was potentially repeatable by a historian in a way that actions were not, because both speaker and historian shared the common medium of language: provided that a historian had a perfect memory of a given speech, or of course a transcript of it, he could exactly reproduce that speech in his work. There is thus a sense in which the speeches in a historian's work are potentially more 'real' than the actions, a potentiality which Thucydides, influenced (perhaps unconsciously) by the sophists, acknowledges by his use of the words 'actuality' and 'actually'.[77] Yet it must be emphasised that he is acknowledging no more than a potentiality: its realisation would depend upon his having a perfect memory, which he denies, upon the availability of transcripts, which from his silence on the subject we may discount,[78] and above all upon a belief that verbatim speeches were the ideal, which I have argued was not the case.

It follows from the above that if one of Thucydides' readers happened to get hold of a transcript of a speech which also appears in his work, he would have (as it were) two versions of the 'same' speech: the original and Thucydides'. Yet this is true of many of the speeches in the ancient historians.[79] The Greeks and Romans were capable of accepting reality and the representation thereof each on its own terms, no matter how much the latter 'misrepresented' (as we see it) the former.[80] A good example is Tacitus' version of Claudius' published speech, mentioned above; similarly the Athenians at Sparta are made by Thucydides to boast in terms which conflicted with evidence they saw every day of their lives with their own eyes.[81] This 'bi-focal' capacity of the ancients is so fundamentally alien to modern historical thought that we often fail to come to terms with it or recognise the chasm between classical and modern historiography which it implies.[82]

22.2-3 Events. Having described his method of composing speeches, Thucydides next explains how he has written his narrative of events: 'from personal experience and after investigating with as much accuracy as possible each event reported by others'. The distinction made here between autopsy and the testimony of other eyewitnesses is a further reminder of his indebtedness to Homer, who had drawn the same distinction in the *Odyssey*. At 8.489-91 the hero addresses the singer Demodocus and says: 'it is remarkable how well you sing the story of the Achaeans' fate and of all their achievements, sufferings and toils. It is almost as though you had been present yourself or listened to someone else <who was>'.[83] But in the case of Thucydides there are difficulties associated with each part of his famous statement.

First, there are occasions in his work where it is virtually certain that he is *not* relying on personal experience despite giving the impression of having done so. For example, it was argued many years ago by L. Pearson that Thucydides' geographical digressions (such as 1.46.4ff. and 2.96-7) do not result from autopsy but derive from existing geographical writings.[84] He pointed out that such digressions can be traced back through Hecataeus and Herodotus to Homer, that in Thucydides their character is usually mythological or legendary, and finally that they are often irrelevant to Thucydides' main theme. From these observations Pearson concluded that Thucydides introduced such extraneous material because it was the kind of thing which he knew would provide entertainment for his readers. In a remarkable example of the preconceptions with which students of Thucydides are affected, Gomme not only dismissed Pearson's arguments by saying that 'the opposite conclusion seems more likely *in a writer like Thucydides*' but also admitted that his own hypothesis of autopsy was 'not made more likely by a mistake here made [by Thucydides] and by the obscurities in the whole account'.[85] Some years after Pearson, Dover produced evidence on Thucydides' Sicilian material which, in Westlake's words, 'established almost beyond doubt that it is based on a written source'.[86] Yet Gomme again objected by begging the question at issue: 'It is not at once apparent that Thucydides here, *contrary to his practice everywhere else when narrating contemporary events*, was using a written source'.[87]

Since Thucydides himself gives us no sign on these occasions that his method has changed, we cannot know how often he followed a different method from that stated at 22.2. But that he sometimes did adopt a different method should not in itself cause any surprise: it is often forgotten that in this very same chapter (22.4) he claims to have excluded legendary or mythical material from his work but that that claim is not borne out by the subsequent narrative.[88] And in case this example is not thought to be good evidence,[89] we can always refer to Herodotus for comparison (above, p. 4).

As for the second part of Thucydides' statement, that he wrote 'after investigating with as much accuracy as possible each event reported by others', he adds to it the following:

> It was a fairly troublesome process because those who were present at the various events did not make the same reports about the same things: it depended upon an individual's prejudice for either side or his memory.

It will be observed that the emphasis is entirely upon the difficulty of the process rather than on the results achieved (the imperfect tense of ηὑρίσκετο contrasts strikingly with the perfect ηὑρῆσθαι at 21.1).[90] But what scale of difficulty is Thucydides referring to? One way of answering this question is by examining the narrative which this process produced.

Thucydides' narrative, as Dover has remarked, 'sustains an almost unvarying level of magisterial assurance'.[91] There is only a single further occasion where Thucydides refers to the difficulty of acquiring accurate information (7.44.1), and only a single occasion where he gives two sides of an issue and is evidently unable to make up his own mind (2.5.4-7).[92] Though we might have expected him to argue towards conclusions on the basis of evidence received, there is only a single occasion where he uses the word 'evidence' (τεκμήριον) with reference to the narrative he is writing,[93] and very few occasions where he uses the 'thesis — proofs — thesis' type of argument which was frequent in the preface.[94] De Ste Croix has argued that Thucydides 'shows some uncertainty about the facts he relates, more often, perhaps, than is generally realised';[95] yet many of his examples will not stand up to closer examination. Some, for example, are cases where the historian uses such expressions as 'it is said' (λέγεται); but after a careful investigation Westlake concluded that these expressions 'should *not* be interpreted, as modern scholars tend to assume, as though in every instance their sole function was to convey uncertainty'.[96] Again, some expressions of apparent uncertainty seem to be used, not to indicate real uncertainty at all, but to tone down hyperbole;[97] and often those that do betray uncertainty are concerned with trivial matters. 'If these are data about which Thucydides felt less sure than about others', remarks Dover again, 'it seems to follow that he felt quite sure about almost everything.'[98]

At this point we are perhaps reminded of Macaulay, who (in Peter Gay's words) 'does seem to know everything — a posture that tempts skeptical readers to wonder how much he really knows'.[99] And indeed it has been rightly observed, again by Dover, that 'it is disturbing to find that in those few cases where we can actually consider what Thucydides says in the light of demonstrably independent evidence ..., the usual outcome is not renewed confidence but *doubt*'.[100] But the fact is that for the vast majority of Thucydides' material there is no such independent evidence with which his narrative can be compared; and this happy circumstance, coupled with his authorial assurance, has discouraged most of his readers from scepticism and persuaded them that his narrative is almost entirely reliable.[101] Thus Lesky, for example, while admitting that 'a careful scrutiny of testimony was necessary since *even among eye-witnesses* ... reports varied widely', has stated that '*unqualified accuracy*' was '*frequently attainable*'.[102] But although they are entirely characteristic of modern scholarship, Lesky's words (and particularly those I have italicised) reveal an alarming ignorance of the difficulties which are involved in the process mentioned by Thucydides at 22.3.

In a pioneering work, which was published after his death and to which classical scholars have paid little attention, an American lawyer and amateur ancient historian, T.S. Jerome, reported on tests which European psychologists (including W. Stern) had conducted on eyewitnesses in the early years of this century. His report is extremely interesting:[103]

> It will appear from these and similar experiments that erroneous testimony was given in simple matters of direct, personal observation by witnesses who were not influenced by any conscious preëxisting emotion or prepossession and who were actuated by a desire to give an exact and truthful narra-

tive. Yet the results were not encouraging. It is evident, as scholars who have conducted or studied such experiments have shown, that good faith, the desire to tell the truth, and the certainty that the testimony is true, as well as the opportunity to secure correct information, and the absence of prepossessions, are far from affording adequate guarantees that the truth will be told. The most honest witness may misstate; the worst may tell the truth. Entirely faithful testimony is not the rule but rather the rare exception. If such then are the distortions which appear in testimony when there is a desire to give a precise and accurate narrative, we cannot be surprised at any result where the feelings are less scientific in character.

Subsequent, more sophisticated, experiments by F.C. Bartlett in the 1930s, for example, and by R. Buckhout in the 1970s have only served to confirm these results.[104]

The difficulties of remembering are greatly increased during wartime, which generates special circumstances of its own:[105]

Men advanced and fought in a self-drugged state. The upset in body chemistry produced by a state of high fear long sustained gave strength to eliminate a calculating response for a limited time. This would explain too the difficulty in recalling battle details afterwards, even of comprehending the elation of battle a day afterwards. Crozier wrote more truthfully than he knew when he observed that 'God is merciful and it almost seems as though he chloroforms us on these occasions'. ... A battle ... seldom left anything of detail. Kipling remarked at the time that 'men could give hideous isolated experiences of their own, but no man could recall any connected order of events'. Andrews carried a reporter's notebook into Neuve Chapelle battle. He had been a journalist in civilian life. When he came later to look at his battle impressions, he saw that his sweat had smeared the pencil and he found it impossible to remember what had happened. In his own words, he had gone through the battle 'like a sleepwalker'. All that remained, as for most combatants, were the brilliantly limelighted vignettes set in a confused, timeless grey sea of fear.

Robert Graves resorts to paradox to express the same feelings:[106]

The memoirs of a man who went through some of the worst

experiences of trench warfare are not truthful if they do not contain a high proportion of falsities. High-explosive barrages will make a temporary liar or visionary of anyone; the old trench-mind is at work in all over-estimation of casualties, 'unnecessary' dwelling on horrors, mixing of dates and confusion between trench rumours and scenes actually witnessed.

These views are corroborated by almost everything which Phillip Knightley discovered when he researched into the history of war-reporting. He records, for example, that a *Sunday Times* reporter during the Second World War later wrote as follows of his experiences:[107]

> In the nature of things it was difficult, if not impossible, for any man on the spot to write a balanced account of events as they were taking place. Some saw, others listened, and often the events men saw did not match the things to which men listened. Inevitably, prejudices were fed, and I believe that it was impossible for a general reader of a newspaper to form a balanced view of the progress of the war. I'm certain that readers of *The Times* in 1854 had a damned sight better view of the Crimean War than readers of *The Times* in 1939-45 did of the Second World War.

Yet William Howard Russell, who actually covered the Crimean War for *The Times*, also despaired of collecting reliable information to send back home.[108] And the experience of these two reporters is repeated time and again in Knightley's brilliant book: even professionals find it almost impossible to record accurately incidents which they witnessed with their own eyes.

This is not to deny that 'oral history', which is what Thucydides was recording and which (by one of those curious circles of history) is now extremely fashionable, can be both important and successful. As John Keegan remarks in his well known study of *The Face of Battle*, '"allowing the combatants to speak for themselves" is not merely permissible but, when and where possible, an essential ingredient of battle narrative and battle analysis.'[109] An outstanding modern example is *The First Day on the Somme* by Martin Middlebrook, who sought out and interviewed 526 British and 20 German survivors in order to write his account of a single day's battle in July 1916. But, as is clear from the formidable appendices and other lists at the end of his book, Middlebrook also had at his disposal all those other sources which, as Keegan reminds us,[110] are essential to supplement oral reports: official state and regimental records, newspapers, private diaries, a scholarly bibliography — to say nothing of map-tracings, pictures, photographs, and personal acquaintance with the terrain.[111] Indeed it was principally because these other sources were available to Middlebrook that he was able to place some order upon his interviewees' answers, which 'collectively depict almost indecipherable chaos'.[112] It is interesting to note that when Middlebrook later came to compile his oral evidence for *The Kaiser's Battle*, in which he recounts the first day of the German spring offensive in 1918, the claims which he makes for his method of writing seem, at least to me, more circumspect than those he had made seven years earlier for his account of the Somme.[113]

Another example is the well known American reporter Theodore H. White, who covered the war in Asia during the Second World War. He too admits that it is advisable to be close to the action:[114]

I was following the reporter's trade in 1944, and a young reporter in a war is best advised to get as close to the sound of guns as possible; the closer he gets to combat and the in-tight view of battle conditions, the more useful his dispatches.

But White is also aware of the limitations of this approach:[115]

Almost all the story ... was unknown to me at the time. I have written it from the documents, archives, letters and memoirs that professional historians have uncovered in the thirty-five years since. And few sequences illustrate better the usefulness of history than the understanding it has brought to the chain of events I reported episodically in the summer of 1944. The connection between events and decisions is the domain of the historian. But the true connection becomes clear only years after the events tumble over the participants. Thus I am grateful to the historians who have come since and clarified what to me was a summer of absolute bewilderment.

Yet the clarification for which White is grateful presupposes that the official documents, upon which historians and others base their accounts, are themselves accurate. This, of course, is often not so:[116]

> Communiqués are issued at headquarters which are inevitably some way from the scene of the fighting. The staff at them do not always know what is going on when a battle of movement is in progress and subordinate commanders sometimes have reasons for being slow to tell them. Figures of losses are built up from reports by individual units, who have in the heat of battle many other things to think about besides checking accurately the effect of their actions ... Double or even multiple counting is all too easy. Even today some facts are in dispute.

Sometimes indeed the participants falsify information intentionally. It seems that Haig persevered with his action at Ypres in 1917 because he believed the false reports and statistics which were knowingly fed to him by his intelligence section.[117]

It also happens regularly that participants in an action, aware of their inability to recall the totality of what occurred, themselves invent material in order to impose upon their fragmented recollections precisely the kind of coherence which Theodore White sought from later historians. The following case is typical:[118]

> It was found that the average number of specific points recalled by any individual was only 8.4 per cent of the total recorded. However, the really remarkable thing about these recalled points was that, on average, no less than 42 per cent of them were substantially incorrect. A large variety of errors and confusions appeared. Happenings were reported which had never taken place at all or which had taken place on some other occasion and were wrongly recalled as having taken place on this particular [occasion]. ... In short, what was recalled was not only fragmentary but also distorted, and much was recalled which, in fact, had never happened. ... It may be said that the recall of stories and events is rarely accurate. There are omissions, transpositions, and additions resulting from interpretation, from the individual's making the account conform to his standards of intelligibility. Thus, recall is often less a matter of literal reproduction than of the imaginative construction of fragmentary recall into a coherent whole.

Such invented material characteristically tends towards the conventional and the cliché; it constitutes an appeal to the common background of the person who is trying to remember and of the person who is seeking to know what happened.[119] This leads me to think that when Thucydides said that 'those who were present at the various events did not make the same reports about the same things', he meant not only that informants reported differently about the same things but also that they gave the same reports about different things. And Paul Fussell, in a rightly praised book, has shown how eyewitnesses in a society which is deeply familiar with literature will, in order to help express such memories as they have, often resort to their knowledge of appropriate war literature which they share with their questioners.[120] Keegan has argued that the same is true of military historians themselves:[121]

> Battles are extremely confusing; and confronted with the need
> to make sense of something he does not understand, even the
> cleverest, indeed pre-eminently the cleverest man, realising his
> need for a language and metaphor he does not possess, will
> turn to look at what someone else has already made of a
> similar set of events as a guide for his own pen.

This of course explains why we so often experience a sense of *déjà vu* when reading the battle accounts of the ancient historians.

I have dwelt on this subject at some length in order to emphasise that oral historiography is an exceptionally difficult process which requires severe and rigorous procedures in order to minimise the errors to which, as even its devotees admit, it is prone.[122] It is reasonable to assume that Thucydides, when writing his history of the Peloponnesian War, experienced this difficulty; and it may be that through living in an oral culture he was instinctively aware of some of the safety procedures.[123] Yet his six hundred pages of narrative, as we have already seen (above, pp. 16-17), show hardly any sign of this difficulty; nor do they show much preoccupation with the documentary evidence which modern writers regard as an essential check on oral contributions and which, as is generally recognised, did not come into its own until the nineteenth century.

In the light of the difficulties experienced by modern military writers I conclude that Thucydides' narrative cannot be as accurate as is usually thought. What seems to have happened is that Thucydides has eliminated almost all traces of the difficulties he encountered and in so doing has created an *impression* of complete accuracy, in order to enhance the credibility of a narrative which is intended to demonstrate that the Peloponnesian War is the greatest of all. Yet he has thereby misled the majority of modern scholars, who have mistaken an essentially rhetorical procedure for 'scientific' historiography at its most successful.[124] The extent of this misconception can be gauged from the usual interpretations of the next section of Thucydides' preface, where τὸ σαφές is translated by Lesky as 'complete accuracy' and by Dover as 'the truth'.[125]

22.4 Audience. I begin with the text and a partial translation of the first sentence of this section:

καὶ ἐς μὲν ἀκρόασιν ἴσως τὸ μὴ μυθῶδες αὐτῶν ἀτερπέστερον φανεῖται· ὅσοι δὲ βουλήσονται τῶν τε γενομένων τὸ σαφὲς σκοπεῖν καὶ τῶν μελλόντων ποτὲ αὖθις κατὰ τὸ ἀνθρώπινον τοιούτων καὶ παραπλησίων ἔσεσθαι, ὠφέλιμα κρίνειν αὐτὰ ἀρκούντως ἕξει.

And for audience purposes the non-legendary aspect of my work will perhaps seem less entertaining; but if anyone, wanting to view τὸ σαφές of the things which took place and of those which one day (given human nature) are destined to take place again in more or less the same fashion, should judge my work useful, that will be enough.

Thucydides begins by disavowing the legendary or fabulous, and I believe that this disavowal provides the key to the interpretation of the rest of the sentence (cf. μέν ... δέ). Since it was above all Herodotus who became famous for purveying *mythoi*,[126] and since Thucydides' preface is written in rivalry of Herodotus, it seems natural to understand Thucydides' disavowal as an emphatic statement that his work is not like that of Herodotus.[127] Thucydides is claiming that by rejecting *mythoi* he has applied to his work the rationalising process which came to be expected of all ancient historians and which had already started with Hecataeus and Herodotus himself.[128] But this does not necessarily prepare us for an assertion that his own work is 'completely accurate' or 'true', as a comparison with 21.1 will reveal. There Thucydides complained that the logographers, of whom

23

Herodotus was one,[129] composed their works with a view to audience entertainment rather than truth and that as a result their works had achieved the status of legend or myth (τὸ μυθῶδες). Here at 22.4, however, though the vocabulary is otherwise very similar to that at 21.1, the contrast with legend or myth is conspicuously *not* 'the truth' (τὸ ἀληθές).[130] The reason for this emerges in the second part of the sentence. It will be noticed that Thucydides there speaks not only of 'the things which took place' but also of 'those which ... are destined to take place again in more or less the same fashion'; and it is difficult to see how these latter can be 'true' or 'accurate' in the sense that is generally meant, since they have not yet happened. Yet they, no less than the things in the past, are governed by τὸ σαφές,[131] which therefore assumes an extra dimension, taking it into the realm of the hypothetical.

There are thus three categories of events in Thucydides' sentence: the mythical, legendary or fabulous (which is disavowed), the past and the hypothetical (both of which are embraced); and these three bear a striking resemblance to the familiar rhetorical division of narrative literature into the 'historical' (ἱστορία, *historia*), the 'realistic' (πλάσμα, *argumentum*) and the 'mythical', 'fabulous' or 'legendary' (μῦθος, *fabula*).[132] According to this tripartite division, what distinguishes both the historical and the realistic from the third category is the notion of probability (τὸ εἰκός);[133] and since Thucydides also distinguishes his third category from the other two (μέν ... δέ), it may be that he too saw the distinction in terms of probability. It is true that the noun εἰκός itself is not used, but probability is clearly implied by the phrases μελλόντων ... ἔσεσθαι ('are destined to take place') and κατὰ τὸ ἀνθρώπινον ('given human nature'). It is also true that this tripartite division is usually thought to be post-Aristotelian;[134] but we know that rhetorical handbooks existed in the early fifth century and that they championed precisely the notion of probability (even at the expense of truth).[135] Given Herodotus' predilection for *mythoi* and Thucydides' own evident determination to reject them, it is not hard to see how he came to produce the formulation expressed at 22.4. His statement there guarantees that he is providing his future audience, not with the entertainment which conventionally derived from the mythical or legendary and which they could get from Herodotus, but with τὸ σαφές of two categories of events which are linked by the notion of probability. What, then, is τὸ σαφές?

In the late first or early second century AD Plutarch discussed the concept of imitation (μίμησις) in terms of a comparison between poetry and painting which the lyric poet Simonides had allegedly made in the late sixth or early fifth century BC.[136] As an example of what he means, Plutarch chooses to discuss historiography, saying that the most powerful historian is one who, by vividly representing emotions and characters, makes his narrative like a painting:

> Take Thucydides, for instance. In his writing he is constantly striving for this vividness [ἐνάργειαν], wanting to turn his readers into spectators, as it were, and to reproduce in their minds the feelings of shock and disorientation which were experienced by those who actually viewed the events.

Plutarch thus regarded Thucydides as an exponent of literary imitation and as an expert in that particular form of it by which a narrative is made as realistic or lifelike as possible. To this form of heightened or vivid description the ancients gave a variety of technical names, such as ἐνάργεια, ὑποτύπωσις, *demonstratio*, *euidentia* and *sub oculos subiectio*.[137] Plutarch was not alone in this opinion of Thucydides, who is singled out as a master of vivid writing not only by later rhetoricians but also by the Augustan critic Dionysius in the first century BC.[138] The same is likely to be true of the historian Duris, who flourished in the late fourth century BC and who wrote in a famous fragment that the historians Ephorus and Theopompus 'did not match the things which took place [τῶν γενομένων]: they did not indulge in imitation [μιμήσεως] or narrative entertainment [ἡδονῆς]'.[139] Though the precise interpretation of this criticism is disputed,[140] Duris sees to be accusing his predecessors of failing to make their narratives sufficiently realistic or true to life. In other words, he seems the description of 'the things which took place' in terms of imitation; and since Duris is thought to have modelled his own work on that of Thucydides,[141] and since he couples τῶν γενομένων and 'entertainment' exactly as Thucydides does at 22.4, it may be that he was thinking of the passage of Thucydides, that he interpreted it in terms of 'realism' rather than 'truth', and that he was criticising Ephorus and Theopompus for not having written their histories in accordance with precisely Thucydidean practice.

Of course it cannot be inferred conclusively from any later author either that Thucydides saw himself as an exponent of this heightened form of literary imitation or that he intended this particular sentence of his preface to allude to it. And since Plutarch's references to Simonides may be apocryphal, we cannot even be certain that the concept of imitation had been given theoretical expression before Thucydides started to write his history of the Peloponnesian War.[142] On the other hand, we have seen that the usual interpretations of τὸ σαφές are inadequate and that another way of looking at the sentence is required. And it will be recalled that there is in *Odyssey* 8 a passage which presupposes the idea of narrative imitation and with which Thucydides was almost certainly familiar (above, p. 15).[143] Although it is true that σαφήνεια is not one of the terms which later became common to describe the quality of vivid imitation which Thucydides' readers detected in his work, it is linked with ἐνάργεια by two late rhetoricians as if the two terms were synonymous;[144] and since appealing to the sense of sight is the characteristic feature of ἐνάργεια,[145] it will be observed that the verb which Thucydides uses in his sentence is σκοπεῖν ('see' or 'view'), its almost literal sense being activated by the express contrast with ἐς μὲν ἀκρόασιν ('for audience purposes'). His readers are thus guaranteed the superior experience of 'sight over sound' (see p. 15 and n. 83), an *imitation* of the experiences on which the narrative is based, but enhanced through its having been structured and shaped by the author himself.

What implications does this interpretation have for Thucydides' work as a whole?[146] Earlier in this same chapter Thucydides drew a distinction between events which he experienced himself and those which were reported to him by others (22.2). Although he never gives us any indication of how many, or indeed which, events fall into each category,[147] it is natural to assume that more of his narrative is based on reported evidence than on autopsy and hence, as he says himself (22.3), on evidence which he found conflicting. And modern experience shows that Thucydides is also likely to have been uncertain even about those events in which he participated himself (above, pp. 17ff.). It therefore seems reasonable to assume that there were certain events about which the historian felt confident and that these formed the 'hard core' (so to speak) of his narrative; equally, there were major areas of his narrative for which the evidence was conflicting or doubtful. It was presumably in these latter areas that Thucydides resorted to the principle of probability.

Historians in later centuries were also confronted by a hard core of apparently reliable knowledge which they were required to elaborate into a coherent and attractive narrative; and to achieve this process of elaboration they had at their disposal a set of rules based on their own and their readers' expectations of what was likely to have happened in a given situation.[148] I am not of course suggesting that in writing 22.4 Thucydides was influenced by some lost and hitherto unsuspected predecessor of the works *On Historiography* which are attributed to the later writers Theophrastus and Praxiphanes;[149] but in any of the innumerable cases of doubt in his narrative, Thucydides was able to provide a probable scenario based on what was likely to happen again in the future, which in turn was based on his own knowledge of what had happened in the past.[150] Such a procedure would help to explain the presence in his work of recurring patterns,[151] the archetypal nature of the speeches, characters and events[152] — in short, the almost indefinable characteristic of his work which has given it its universal appeal.

It should be noted, however, that this tendency towards the universal does not mean that 'the probable' does not extend to details.[153] Detailed events were regarded as an essential component of vivid description (ἐνάργεια)[154] and hence as providing 'the flavour of authenticity without which history would not be itself and could not teach its lessons'.[155] Let us take as example the battle in the Great Harbour at Syracuse in 413, which Thucydides describes at 7.70-1.[156] It is clear from his account that the battle in such a constricted area was extremely confusing; it was thus one of those episodes for which certain information was unreliable. Yet Thucydides' description is extremely detailed and is generally hailed as a masterful instance of vivid writing. How did the final narrative come into being? No doubt this is one of the episodes for which Thucydides had some eyewitness information; but J.H. Finley has observed that not only the general structure of Thucydides' account, but also several of its details, bear a striking resemblance to passages in the tragedies of Aeschylus and Euripides.[157] If Finley is correct, it follows that Thucydides was able to make his description even of details convincing because the tragedians had served to confirm for his contemporary audience how battles in the past had progressed and how men in battle had behaved;[158] hence his audience will have been persuaded that these circumstances were likely to hold true both for the present and any future wars.[159] But 'true' on this interpretation is not, of course, equivalent to 'historically true'.[160]

Yet we should not automatically assimilate τὸ σαφές, isolated from its context, to our modern notions of historical truth; rather we should see Thucydides' graphic account of probable events (τὸ σαφὲς ... τῶν μελλόντων ... κατὰ τὸ ἀνθρώπινον ... ἔσεσθαι) in the terms which he himself states at 1.22.4, namely as the alternative to the discredited mythologised form of narrative which he rejects (τὸ μυθῶδες).[161] His own narrative has seemed true and reliable to scholars precisely because he was successful in making it both vivid and probable — in a word, realistic;[162] but the circumstantial detail and the magisterial assurance are both equally misleading. No doubt modern historians of the fifth century BC should be concerned primarily with attempting to identify the hard core of his narrative; but the task is supremely difficult because there are few, if any, criteria for drawing the line, and in the nature of the case 'the things which took place' are almost indistinguishable from 'those which one day (given human nature) are destined to take place again in more or less the same fashion'.[163]

23.1-3 The Peloponnesian War. From Thucydides' reference at 22.4 to the non-legendary aspect of his work it has often been assumed that he is denying the entertainment value of his narrative as a whole. 'Pleasure in narration for its own sake is rigorously excluded', says Lesky.[164] Yet the diminution in entertainment is stated to be only apparent ('will *perhaps seem* less entertaining')[165] and is restricted to the historian's exclusion of the legendary, mythical and fabulous from his work. We must infer that he *did* expect his work to be entertaining in all other respects,[166] which is certainly the impression we derive from 23.1-3, where he returns to the thesis which he earlier stated at 21.2, namely that the present war is the greatest of all.

Here is what he says:

> Of earlier events the greatest [μέγιστον] that took place was the Persian War, which was nevertheless decided in a couple of sea- and land-battles; but the present war's duration was greatly [μέγα] protracted, and disasters [παθήματα] befell Greece in the course of it which are unparalleled over a similar period.
>
> For never had so many cities been captured and abandoned — some by barbarians, others by the Greek combatants, while still others were re-settled; never had there been so

many refugees or dead — some in the war itself, others through revolution; and as for ancient folk-tales, so very rarely confirmed by events, they ceased to be incredible — about earthquakes, which were extremely violent over a wide area, and about solar eclipses, which were more frequent than any revealed by the records of former times, and there were great droughts, resulting in famines and in that which caused most damage and extensive destruction: the apocalyptic plague.[167]

All these <disasters> mounted a combined and simultaneous attack in this war.

As is clear from my edentation, the section exemplifies 'ring-composition', and from the generalised references at the beginning and end, not to mention the long list in between, it is clear that Thucydides saw the Peloponnesian War in terms of the disasters and sufferings which it brought. This is above all the perspective of epic poetry, in which war and its attendant sufferings are the staple ingredients.[168] Homer begins the *Iliad* by saying 'Goddess, sing of the wrath of Achilles ..., which brought the Achaeans so much suffering'; and the *Odyssey* begins with an account of its hero, 'Many were the sufferings which he experienced'. Homer mentioned sufferings in the overtures to his poems because it was a subject which fascinated and appealed to his audience. Thucydides is following Homeric practice and for the same reason. In so doing he reveals himself as a true successor to Homer and also, as his biographer Marcellinus observed, as a rival.[169]

In order to emphasise the unprecedented nature of the suffering and disasters, and in particular to contrast them with those in Homer, Thucydides has devoted all his compositional skill to the magnification of this section — an analogous technique to that for which he earlier criticised poets in general and Homer in particular.[170] The effect is achieved partly through the listing itself, since 'a great chain or series is of its essence impressive',[171] partly through the employment of polysyndeton, which 'is more conducive to grandeur [and] the use of the same connective suggests infinite size',[172] and partly through the contents of the list. Thucydides has been particularly careful with the items he places at the three key points in his passage, the beginning, middle and end. He begins by referring to the number of cities captured. No doubt ultimately influenced by the fall of Troy, the motif of the 'captured city' became one of the commonest in later historiography and is regularly used as an opportunity for vivid writing.[173] There is, however, evidence that this had already become a rhetorical motif even by the time of Homer,[174] something on which Thucydides will later capitalise metaphorically in Book 7.[175] By beginning his list with this motif, Thucydides sets the tone for what follows. In the middle of the list he mentions folk-tales and natural disasters: the former, often handed down from one war to the next, brilliantly encapsulate within a single phrase the quintessential unreality of war;[176] the latter allude to the belief, common in ancient times, that natural and human disasters went hand in hand.[177] The climax of the list is the plague, ἡ ... νόσος, where 'the nine words that intervene between the first article and its noun probably set a syntactical record'.[178] It is no coincidence, as has been remarked in this context, that plague too has Homeric precedent, in the opening scene of the *Iliad*.[179]

Few 'blurbs' can have been composed more thoughtfully than this, yet, as Kitto has rightly remarked, 'many scholars, though they have read it, have not believed it, being so certain that Thucydides really meant something quite different'.[180] The reason for their certainty of course lies in their assumption that Thucydides is a modern or 'scientific' historian. Thus Fornara has written as follows:[181]

> When a writer attempts to invest his history with significancies external to it, and, in addition, strives for literary brilliance, the magnification of his subject must follow. Wars are greater than ever, battles more fierce, the sacks of cities more violent, commanders more brave, tragedies deeper.

These words read almost like a paraphrase of Thucydides' passage, yet Fornara is in fact talking about the later historians Clitarchus and Duris: it never occurs to him that his comment is precisely applicable to Thucydides. But despite the neglect it has received, this is one of the most important sections of Thucydides' preface. It demonstrates that he, like Homer, is writing a 'disaster narrative' of the most vivid and dramatic type.

It is a feature of many blurbs that their seductive promises are not fulfilled between the covers, but the Augustan critic Dionysius rightly noted that Thucydides 'sometimes makes the sufferings appear so cruel, so terrible, so piteous, as to leave no

room for historians or poets to surpass him'.[182] Dionysius'
spontaneous linking of 'historians or poets' should not be lost on
us:[183] he is saying that Thucydides has realised his ambition of
achieving Homeric status and of himself becoming the model to
which subsequent authors will aspire. And indeed throughout his
narrative, at the appropriate moments, Thucydides reminds his
readers of the unprecedented sufferings and disasters which 'his'
war entailed:[184]

> 'This day will be the start of great disasters [μεγάλων κακῶν]
> for the Greeks' (2.12.3, spoken by a Spartan ambassador).
> [This statement, which 'reflects the symbolic importance of all
> that happens',[185] echoes several in Homer, who was also
> echoed by the 'epic' Herodotus and by Virgil.[186]]
> No one up to that time had ever seen a greater conflagration
> arise, at least, not one produced by human agency (2.77.4)
> Every form of death [πᾶσα ... ἰδέα ... θανάτου] was there:
> everything that normally happens in such situations took
> place, and still worse besides (3.81.5)[187]
> Nothing did the Athenians so much harm as this or so
> reduced their strength for war. In the regular army no less
> than 4,400 hoplites and 300 cavalry died of it (the plague),[188]
> and among the general mass of the people no one ever
> discovered how many the deaths were. It was at this time too
> that there occurred the many earthquakes in Athens, Euboea
> and Boeotia, particularly in the Boeotian city of Orchomenus
> (3.87.2-4)
> This disaster amounted to the greatest indeed [πάθος γὰρ
> τοῦτο ... μέγιστον δὴ ... ἐγένετο] of those in this war ever to
> affect a single Greek city in a comparable number of days.[189] I
> have not written down the total of dead because the reported
> figure is beyond belief, given the size of the city (3.113.6)
> It was the greatest battle which had taken place for a very long
> time among Greek states, and it was fought between their
> most distinguished cities ... As for the Spartans' own losses it
> was difficult to discover the truth (5.74.1-3)
> The general confusion was very great and there was every form
> of destruction ... The disaster which befell the entire city was
> greater than any other, more sudden and more terrible (7.29.5)
> Such was the disaster of Mycalessus, which, given its size,
> endured suffering as great as any in the war (7.30.4)
> Though it is difficult to speak with accuracy, the total number

of prisoners was not less than seven thousand. This action was the greatest of the war, and, in my opinion at least, of Greek history, the culmination of glory for the victors and of disaster for the victims (7.87.4-6)

Such statements hardly seem characteristic of the cold and 'scientific' historian whom we meet in the pages of many scholarly writings: on the contrary, they are designed to re-emphasise the point made in the third section of Thucydides' preface, namely that the Peloponnesian War is the greatest war of all.

Plague

The climax of the sufferings and disasters listed by Thucydides at 1.23.1-3 is the plague which struck Athens in 430 BC and which the historian describes in the central section of Book 2. The description provides an excellent opportunity for us to observe how a substantial portion of his narrative accords in practice with what he said in the preface.

Thucydides was not of course the first Greek writer to feature a plague in his work. We have already noted that in the opening scene of the *Iliad* the Greeks are suffering from a plague which has been sent by Apollo as a result of the hybristic behaviour of Agamemnon — though it is not until he has compounded his guilt a second time that the actual word ὕβρις is used of him (1.203, 214). Though Homer does not describe the plague at length (1.43-54), it is clearly a terrible enough disaster to turn Achilles' thoughts towards going home (1.61): 'if together war and plague are to subdue the Achaeans' (εἰ δὴ ὁμοῦ πόλεμός τε δαμᾷ καὶ λοιμὸς Ἀχαιούς). The presence of this brief plague description in the *Iliad* may suggest that more extended descriptions were to be found in the so-called 'epic cycle', a collection of epic poems which were written in the seventh and sixth centuries BC to supplement or continue the Homeric poems. Though the surviving fragments admittedly give no sign of it, these epics were in general far less restrained than those of Homer,[190] and we do know that in early near-eastern literature, with which Greek has much in common, accounts of plagues (often legendary in character) occur regularly.[191] At any rate, plague features in the story of the Athenian hero Theseus[192] and also, very prominently, in Sophocles' *Oedipus Tyrannus* (though the exact date of the play is uncertain).[193]

There is also a rather different context in which plague occurs in earlier literature. Hesiod in his *Works and Days*, after a section (213-24) in which he warns that retribution (δίκη) will always follow hybristic behaviour (ὕβρις), develops a comparison between the just and the unjust: the city of the former will enjoy innumerable blessings (225-37), but that of the latter will suffer 'famine and plague together' (λιμὸν ὁμοῦ καὶ λοιμόν) and their army will be destroyed (238). M.L. West's commentary on this passage makes it clear that such pairings of blessings and sufferings are again a regular feature of early near-eastern literature,[104] and they also recur in Aeschylus' *Supplices*, where the chorus prays that Argos will escape war and plague and will enjoy peace and fertility (esp. 659-62, 678-87).

Thus by Thucydides' time there was an established connection between war, plague and ὕβρις, and it was conventional for writers to juxtapose blessings and sufferings including war and plague. If we now turn to Thucydides' own account, we read that when the Spartans were about to invade Attica in 431, Pericles gave the Athenians the same advice as before:[195] they should come into the city from the countryside and guard it, bringing their rural property with them (13.2).[196] The Athenians took his advice (14) but found it hard, because they had long been used to living in the country. Thucydides then embarks on an antiquarian digression (15-16), which stands in marked contrast to the surrounding narrative because it is one of the few places outside Book 1 where he employs argumentation of the 'thesis — proofs — thesis' type.[197] The purpose of the digression is to demonstrate the antiquity of the Attic way of life and hence to heighten the emotion of the upheaval. 'It was sadly and reluctantly that they now abandoned their homes and the temples time-honoured from their patriotic past, leaving behind what each man regarded as his own city' (16.2).[198] Thucydides returns to the main narrative at 17.1ff., remarking that many of the incoming countrymen had to settle in the temples and shrines of the heroes, and later among the Long Walls and at Piraeus (17.3). Though the reader is as yet unaware of it, these chapters 13-17 constitute Act One of a remarkable drama.[199]

The following chapters describe the remainder of events for the year 431.[200] As Thucydides begins his narrative of the winter of 431/0, he tells us (34.1-7) that it was an annual custom to give a public burial to those who had died in the war. The accompanying funeral speech was on this occasion delivered by Pericles, into whose mouth Thucydides puts a whole series of fine-sounding sentiments, among them the following: the Athenians have a great respect for law, especially unwritten law (37.3); they conduct regular sacrifices (38.1); Athens is a great centre of imported goods from abroad (38.2); the Athenians know how to use wealth properly (40.1, 42.4); they are individually self-sufficient (τὸ σῶμα αὔταρκες) in the most varied forms of activity (41.1); they believe in a sense of decency (43.1) and honour (44.4 'The love of honour alone is ageless, and ... it is not so-called "gain" but honour which gives the greater satisfaction'). So ends Act Two.

No sooner does Thucydides make Pericles finish speaking (46.2), than the plague strikes Athens (47.3):

> We know, because Thucydides tells us, that an *epitaphios* was delivered every year during the war: this is the only one that he ever mentions; the others were carved away. Then, the speech was delivered, say, in March; the plague broke out in, say, July. What happened in the interval? We may guess: one or two debates in the Assembly, certain dealings with allies or neutrals, some financial or administrative measures — small beer perhaps, but beer nevertheless. A different historian might have diligently recorded all this: the Epitaphios (one out of twenty in his complete work), then a lot of detail, and finally the plague. He would have set down 'what happened', but it would look entirely different; it would lack the arresting perspective that we find in Thucydides.[201]

Thucydides describes the plague from its outset, listing the symptoms and giving a detailed account of the effects it produced. We are first told (48.1) that the plague was imported from abroad, like the goods of which Pericles has just been made to boast; and it appeared first at Piraeus, precisely the place where, as a result of the policy which Thucydides made Pericles emphasise earlier (13.2), the countrymen had been compelled to settle. Indeed, Thucydides later states (52.1) that the general removal of people from the countryside to the town made matters much worse; and the temples, where (as we have already been told) they had been forced to take refuge, were now full of the dead and dying (52.3). No one proved self-sufficient (σῶμα ... αὔταρκες ... οὐδέν) against the disease (51.3);[202] men became indifferent to written law and to its unwritten equivalent, fear of the gods (53.1, 4);[203] they abandoned religious practices and all sense of decency (52-3); they used their wealth for self-indulgence (53.1-2); and they disregard honour (53.3 'No one was keen to concern himself with so-called "honour" ... but immediate satisfaction, or whatever gained such satisfaction, became honourable').

Thus the plague in Act Three dramatically and ironically overturns everything of which Thucydides made Pericles boast in the funeral speech in Act Two. It is as if Thucydides in these two juxtaposed sections has 'realised' and therefore magnified the blessings and sufferings which, as we saw above, were paired together by earlier authors. The historian has presented his readers with a dramatic reversal (περιπέτεια), like that of a tragedy;[204] and the analogy with drama is sustained by the language which Thucydides has used to describe the plague and which, as Parry has shown, is drawn, at least partly, from tragic poetry.[205]

Thucydides concludes Act Three in chapter 54: 'Such was the character of the disaster [πάθει] from which, once it had struck, the Athenians were suffering' — the use of the word πάθος reminding us of the blurb at 1.23.1-3 and that the plague was the climax of the disasters (παθήματα) listed there. Thucydides then continues by mentioning a prophecy, the wording of which was disputed, and an oracle (54.2-5). He treats the linguistic dispute in a dismissive manner (54.3), which only prompts the question why he has mentioned it.[206] The reason is that the prophecy, in one of its versions (ἥξει Δωριακὸς πόλεμος καὶ λοιμὸς ἅμ' αὐτῷ, 'There will come a Dorian war and a plague with it'), recalls the words of Achilles in *Iliad* 1 already quoted (above, p. 32, the synonymous ἅμ' αὐτῷ, 'with it', having taken the place of ὁμοῦ, 'together').[207] By this means Thucydides directs his readers' attention towards Homer and invites them to see his own account of the Athenian plague and its sequel in Homeric terms. Finally, after this brief but important diversion, Thucydides repeats in different words the sentence with which chapter 54 began: 'This is what happened in connection with the plague'. Since these words self-evidently constitute a concluding formula, it comes as something of a surprise to learn much later (at 3.87, during his account of 427/6) that on its first appearance the plague lasted two years and in fact dragged on until 426.[208] By thus confining his main account to chapters 47-54 of Book 2, Thucydides has avoided potential anti-climax and has successfully given the impression that the Athenians were struck by a single shattering blow in the summer of 430.

It is clear from Thucydides' account that Pericles' policy of removing people from the countryside, which was so heart-breaking at the start, contributed to the virulence of the disease. Are readers therefore to infer that Pericles' praise of Athens in the funeral speech was a demonstration of ὕβρις, which, as earlier authors had made clear, required retribution — in this case the plague?[209] It is this question which Thucydides answers in Act Four (chapters 59-65).

We are first told (59) that people did indeed start to blame Pericles, but he is then given a long speech (60-4), during the course of which he is made to say (61.3-4): 'That which happens suddenly and unexpectedly and contrary to all expectation takes hold of one's mind, and this is what has happened to you, especially with regard to the plague. Yet . . . you should be willing to undergo even the greatest accidents [ξυμφοραῖς]'.[210] Thus Pericles is made to maintain that there are some things for which men simply cannot calculate, and the plague is one of them. The historian then tells us that eventually the people were won round and even re-elected Pericles as general (65.1-4); but this is quickly followed by an announcement of his death in the following year and an obituary notice (65.6-13).

Since Thucydides' history is almost invariably a year-by-year account of events, he ought to have reserved Pericles' death and obituary notice for the appropriate point in his narrative of the following year; but he places it here because it provided the ideal opportunity to demonstrate that in his opinion Pericles could not be blamed for the events of 430. It is significant that the first virtue of Pericles which he singles out for praise is his foresight (65.6 πρόνοια), adding that whenever the leader saw his people over-confident with ὕβρις, his policy was to bring them back to their senses (65.9): from this it may be inferred that if Pericles habitually curbed the ὕβρις of others, he is unlikely to have been guilty of it himself. Thus the tragedy described in Book 2 is to be contrasted with that described in Books 5-7, where the Sicilian Expedition follows disastrously on the Melian Dialogue. It is doubly ironical that Pericles is the man of foresight undone by unforeseeable disaster, while Nicias, one of the main protagonists in the Sicilian Expedition, is the believer in chance who is at the mercy of the miscalculations of others.[211]

Although we have hitherto concentrated on the literary back-ground and tragic context of Thucydides' plague, it must be acknowledged that his account of the plague has often been taken as one of the best examples of his allegedly 'scientific' historiography.[212] At first sight this seems reasonable enough. His account is one of only two places in his whole history where he vouches for the autopsy to which he referred at 1.22.2;[213] his concern that as a result of his account future readers will not remain in ignorance seems to tally closely with his statement at 1.22.4;[214] and the account of the symptoms which he gives in chapter 49 is extremely detailed. Yet each of these points may be countered in its turn. The historian begins his account with a statement which sets the tone for what follows and which seems anything but 'scientific' (47.3-4):

> No pestilence of such extent nor any scourge so destructive of human life is on record anywhere. For neither were doctors able to cope with the disease ... nor did any other human art avail. The supplications made at sanctuaries, or appeals to oracles and the like, were all futile, and at last men desisted from them, overcome by the disaster [τοῦ κακοῦ].

This example of rhetorical magnification clearly belongs with Thucydides' other 'disaster statements' already mentioned (above pp. 31-2): it employs the familiar magnifying device of the comparison (σύγκρισις),[215] in this case with the virulence and destructive power of former diseases, and it involves the familiar antithesis of the human and the divine.[216] Again, we know from modern experience how qualified the advantage of autopsy can be; and although an epidemic obviously poses different problems from the reporting of a battle, Thucydides does tell us that the disease affected people in different ways (51.1): therefore it too will have been difficult to report. Finally, it is notorious that despite Thucydides' detailed account and his evident concern for future readers, modern scholars have failed to identify the plague with any single disease known today.[217] Can Thucydides' description therefore be called 'scientific' or not?

In an attempt at answering this question let us look at the important paragraph at 50.1-51.1, which (like chapter 54: see above, p. 35) characteristically exemplifies Thucydidean ring-composition but which uncharacteristically mentions the word 'evidence' (τεκμήριον):[218]

For the character of the disease was too powerful to describe [κρεῖσσον λόγου]. In general its impact on each individual was too hard for human nature to bear, and in one aspect in particular it showed very well that it was different in kind from any normal disease. For birds and quadrupeds which usually come into contact with man either did not approach the many bodies lying unburied or else were killed if they tasted them. As evidence there was, first, the obvious scarcity of such birds, which were simply not seen either around the corpses or anywhere else; and dogs for their part, being domestic animals, provided a better view of what happened. Thus the disease (I pass over [παραλιπόντι] many other of its abnormal features and the way it happened to affect each individual differently in comparison with another) was like this as regards its general character [τοιοῦτον ἦν ἐπὶ πᾶν τὴν ἰδέαν].

This paragraph illustrates two forms of the familiar magnifying device known as the 'inexpressibility motif': the event in question is 'beyond describing',[219] and it has many other aspects which the author will 'pass over'.[220] The reference to quadrupeds and dogs also assists the rhetoric by providing a possible allusion to Homer, in whose plague, as has been remarked, mules and dogs are affected.[221] Yet there is an inherent paradox in all this. In saying that the plague was too powerful to describe, Thucydides is attributing to himself the kind of limitation in descriptive technique which Duris later attributed to Ephorus and Theopompus (above, p. 25): that is, he has been unable to find words to match the events which took place.[222] But how can this be, since in the immediately preceding chapter he has produced a vivid and detailed description of the plague which has compelled universal admiration?[223]

In the case of events as difficult to report as the plague, the practice of all but the most modern historians, including Thucydides himself, was to supplement their own hard core of knowledge by reference to some pre-existing account (see above, pp. 22, 27). For Thucydides' purposes the natural source of reference was medical literature, and it is indeed well established, both from his vocabulary and from his general method of describing the plague, that he was familiar with the medical writers. His day-by-day account of the disease, and particularly his allusion to 'the critical period' (49.6), bears much similarity to the work known as *Epidemics*; and his emphasis on prognosis

(48.3) seems akin to the beginning of the work known as *Prognosticon*.[224] It therefore seems possible that Thucydides, confronted by more than the usual difficulties of reporting, resorted to the medical writers for help — in just the same way as Procopius later resorted to Thucydides himself to help his description of the plague which struck Byzantium in AD 540.[225] If this is correct, it would of course explain why modern scholars have failed to identify the plague at Athens from the account which Thucydides provides.[226]

It will of course be objected that such a practice is unthinkable for a 'scientific' historian like Thucydides; but consider the case of Lucretius, who also describes the plague at Athens at the end of his sixth book. Most of Lucretius' account follows Thucydides closely, but lines 1182-96 are based on well known medical sources which have nothing to do with the plague at Athens.[227] Page has objected that this 'is an extraordinary procedure for a scientific writer',[228] but that of course depends upon what is meant by 'scientific': as if to illustrate further the preconceptions by which modern scholars are affected, Gomme attributes to Lucretius a 'rhetorical method and *lack* of scientific interest' in comparison with Thucydides.[229] The fact is that Thucydides and Lucretius are both rhetorical, and we have seen that Thucydides, like Lucretius, aims to make his account of the plague as impressive as possible. At the same time Thucydides also aimed, in accordance with his statement at 1.22.4, to provide a graphic account which would hold true for future plagues, as he confirms at 51.1 by saying that the plague 'was like this as regards its general character'. Each of these aims Thucydides will have been able to fulfil simultaneously by resorting to medical literature for the appropriate details.[230]

Despite the impression created by Thucydides of an unprecedented and major disaster, the plague has (perhaps surprisingly) left no trace at all on any independent piece of evidence or inscription.[231] Is this the result of mere chance? Or has Thucydides magnified the plague out of all proportion to its real significance? Whatever the reason, modern scholars are thereby presented, in an acute form, with the question of the extent to which his narrative reflects reality.[232]

If the analysis given in this section is anything like correct, the extent of that reflection is considerably limited. And although this limitation might be found alarming by modern scholars, the ancients themselves would not have given it a second thought. In his essay on Thucydides the Augustan critic Dionysius asked the following question:[233]

> As for the much talked-of funeral speech, which Thucydides recounted in his second book, for what reason is it placed in this book rather than in another?

'It seems', says Dover, 'that he would have regarded the answer "Because Pericles delivered it in the winter of 431, and not at any other time" as frivolous.'[234] Exactly so; but that is because his expectations of Thucydides' history were different from those of modern historians. It must however be admitted that Thucydides' narrative in this book is so powerful that the possibility of there being other answers to Dionysius' question appears to have occurred even to the literal-minded Gomme:[235]

> The deep contrast between the sunlit description of Athens in the Funeral Speech and this of the sufferings and demoralisation of the very next summer ... does not prove that the speeches and events did not take place, and in the order in which he gives them.

And though Gomme naturally dismissed the possibility without further consideration, as we see, the really interesting thing is that it should ever have crossed his mind in the first place.

Posterity

One of the points which Dionysius makes about Thucydides is that the historian is hostile towards Athens. His fullest statement of this view occurs in his comparison of Herodotus and Thucydides in the *Letter to Pompey*:[236]

> For all writers of history the first and most essential task of all is choosing a noble subject and one which will please their readers [ὑπόθεσιν ... καλὴν καὶ κεχαρισμένην τοῖς ἀναγνωσομένοις]. In this Herodotus seems to me to have succeeded better than Thucydides ... The second task of historiography is knowing where to begin and how far to proceed. In this respect too Herodotus seems much more judicious than Thucydides [who] starts with the incipient decline of the

Greek world, something which should not have been done by a Greek and an Athenian ... In his malice [φθονερῶς] he finds the overt causes of the war in the conduct of his own city, although he might have found many other grounds for its outbreak. He might have begun his narrative ... with the magnificent achievements of his country immediately after the Persian War ... and described them with all the enthusiasm of a patriot ... I will mention one other feature of the treatment of subject-matter, a feature which in all histories we look for no less than any of those already mentioned. I mean the attitude [διάθεσιν] which the historian himself adopts towards the events he describes. The attitude of Herodotus is fair throughout, showing pleasure in the good and distress at the bad. But that of Thucydides is severe and harsh and proves that he had a grudge against his native country because of his exile. He recites a catalogue of her mistakes, going into them in minute detail; but when things go according to plan, he either does not mention them at all, or only like a man under compulsion.

Although we cannot know for certain whether other ancient critics held a similar view,[237] it is not difficult to see how the view itself came to be held.

Greek thought often expressed itself in terms of opposites,[238] one manifestation of which is the pair ἔπαινος and ψόγος, praise and blame (in Latin *laus* and *uituperatio*). It has recently been argued that 'the opposition of praise and blame [was] a fundamental principle in the archaic Greek community',[239] and indeed we are told by Plutarch that the ancient Spartans used praising poetry to celebrate those whose character and behaviour were socially acceptable and to glorify those who had died for their city, and critical poetry to denigrate those whose behaviour was unacceptable or who had proved cowardly in war.[240] Whether or not this is true for ancient Sparta, Plato certainly recommended a similar system for his utopia;[241] and Aristotle, discussing the origins of poetry, divided it into the two basic types of praise and blame.[242] The same two are of course extremely familiar as divisions of epideictic literature in general.[243]

Now historiography was itself a form of epideictic,[244] and it is clear from Dionysius' own work of history that he envisaged the genre as essentially encomiastic (*Roman Antiquities*, 1.1.2-3, 2.1):[245]

[Historians] ought first of all to choose noble [καλάς] and

elevated subjects ... Those who use material which is trivial or base or unworthy of serious study, either because they crave attention and want to make a name for themselves or because they want to show off their rhetorical skill, are neither admired by posterity for their fame nor praised for their eloquence ... That I have indeed chosen a noble [καλήν] and elevated ... subject will not in my opinion require any lengthy argument ... For if anyone turns his attention to the successive supremacies both of cities and of nations ..., he will find that the supremacy of the Romans has far surpassed all those that are recorded from earlier times, not only in the greatness of its empire and the splendour of its achievements ...

Similarly Polybius, who at the start of his history says that the historian should exclude from his work the prejudice which he would normally show towards his friends and country in everyday life (1.14.4-5), later contradicts himself by admitting that historians should after all display partiality to their own countries (16.14.6).[246] Lucian too, in *How to Write History*, takes for granted the nobility (τὸ κάλλος) of the historian's subject-matter (45); and from the amount of space which he devotes to the topic of praise (7-14) it seems that he, like Dionysius, expected works of history to have an encomiastic slant.[247] This did not of course mean that criticism should be entirely absent from the genre. On the contrary, Polybius said that historiography embraces both praise and criticism (10.21.8 κοινὸς ὢν ἐπαίνου καὶ ψόγου), and historians regularly praised or criticised this or that character as they saw fit:[248] indeed, they could not do otherwise, since one of the principal functions of historiography was to furnish examples of behaviour which readers should imitate or avoid and which therefore required writing up in the appropriate manner.[249] The important thing, as Lucian makes clear (59, cf. 9), was to avoid excess whether in praise or criticism.

It is easy to see how Herodotus fitted into this background by the time Dionysius came to write. By stating in his preface that his aim was to honour the great and admirable achievements of men, Herodotus made explicit an aspect of his work which in Homeric epic remained implicit (above, p. 2); and while he portrays both sides in the conflict with sympathy in the Homeric manner,[250] he singles out Athens as the saviour of Greece (7.139.5).[251] It was therefore natural for Herodotus to be regarded, as he is by Dionysius, as an encomiastic historian.[252] But this immediately leaves a question-mark over Thucydides. Since Herodotus and Thucydides were regarded as the twin founders of historiography,[253] they each attracted the same kind of attention as was conventionally paid to founders of all types.[254] And since another manifestation of the Greek love of opposites was the σύγκρισις, or 'comparison of famous authors', there was considerable incentive to compare Herodotus and Thucydides with each other.[255] And given that Herodotus had already pre-empted (as it were) the role of encomiastic historian, it was almost inevitable that Thucydides should be assigned, as he is by Dionysius, the role of critical historian. After all, as Immerwahr has rightly observed, Thucydides' preface differs strikingly from Herodotus' in that praise is nowhere mentioned as one of the themes of his work.[256]

Since the borderline between praise and flattery was notoriously thin,[257] praise was usually regarded as incompatible with truth.[258] This explains why encomiastic poets are so keen to emphasise the truth of what they say.[259] Praise was also liable to provoke the envy (φθόνος, *inuidia*) of one's readers, as Thucydides makes Pericles point out in his funeral speech, in words which are later echoed by Sallust.[260] No doubt each of these corollaries of praise contributed to Herodotus' well known reputation as a liar.[261] Criticism, on the other hand, was regarded as a function of free speech (παρρησία, *libertas*),[262] and hence as a medium for arriving at the truth.[263] Thus the Hellenistic historian Theopompus, who is universally acknowledged by ancient readers to have been critical,[264] is said by Dionysius, whose hero he was, to have reached the truth through his criticism.[265] It was of course always possible, as Sallust again pointed out, that criticism was prompted by an author's malicious intent (also φθόνος, *inuidia*).[266] This explains why satirists, belonging to a critical genre, conventionally disclaim malice.[267] Thus the borderline between malice and criticism was also thin, as Tacitus acknowledged in the preface to his *Histories* when he wrote that 'malice gives a false impression of free speech' (1.1.2 'malignitati falsa species libertatis inest', *libertas* being equivalent to criticism, as we have just seen). This no doubt explains why Dionysius could reasonably differ from other readers in his estimations of Theopompus and Thucydides. Everyone agreed that the former was critical; but whereas others believed that he had gone too far through malice,[268] Dionysius maintained that he had thereby been truthful. Everyone except Dionysius agreed that

Thucydides was the best Greek historian and hence, no doubt, the most truthful, since truth was regarded as a primary virtue;[269] but while this suggests that others also regarded him as in some sense critical, Dionysius was able to attribute his criticism to malice.[270]

I have gone into this matter in some detail because the ancient response to Herodotus and Thucydides helps to illustrate the response of readers today, when the same kinds of ambiguity are present. Modern scholars have often believed that Herodotus intended his work as a praise of Athens,[271] and in any case the generally encomiastic nature of his preface cannot be gainsaid. Conversely, Thucydides is thought by many modern scholars to have executed his work in a state of profound pessimism and to have exhibited towards Athens, his native city, an attitude that is either strikingly impartial or downright critical.[272] An extract from De Ste Croix is typical:[273]

> He ruthlessly applied to his own city, Athens, to which he was deeply devoted, the same analysis in terms of power politics as that which he applies to other cities — perhaps in an even more merciless way, because it is usually the Athenians who are in the foreground, and he views them with the same dispassionate eye as everyone else.

Thus in modern times too the two historians are thought to have adopted quite different attitudes towards their respective subjects, and it is in this perceived contrast that Immerwahr rightly saw one of the explanations for Thucydides' reputation. 'For Herodotus, praise is a mainspring of historical thought, but in Thucydides this element is much harder to discern. Modern scholarship has therefore seen in him the origin of "scientific" history.'[274] Yet this is still not the whole story. I have been using the word 'critical' to describe the attitude which both ancient and modern readers have attributed to Thucydides; but this word, which hitherto has been a convenient synonym for 'hostile', is of course ambiguous in English and the other major European languages. 'Critical' can also mean 'discriminating', the ambiguity no doubt arising precisely because a 'critic' (in the sense of an opponent) is assumed to have gone through a preliminary process of 'discrimination' in order to reach his hostile judgements. This ambiguity is similar to, though not identical with, that discussed above with reference to Dionysius' judgement on

Theopompus. I believe that modern readers, misled by the critical slant of Thucydides' work (which Dionysius detected) into thinking that he is a 'critical historian' like themselves, have read into his famous preface an anachronistically 'scientific' interpretation for which there is, as we have seen, very little evidence.

The contrast between Herodotus and Thucydides extends also to their styles, as Hermogenes, writing about style in the second century AD, makes plain:[275]

> In approaching Thucydides, I have one preliminary point to make clear. That I mention him after Herodotus and the others carries no implication that I regard him as their inferior in literary skill and capacity ... I ... placed Herodotus first among the historians because he is more panegyrical and more charming not only than Thucydides but than any other practitioner in this manner. Of Thucydides indeed, it might be doubted into which category he falls: he is as much forensic and deliberative as panegyrical.

Slightly earlier, Quintilian described Herodotus' style as 'attractive, lucid and flowing' and that of Thucydides as 'condensed, abbreviated and highly pressurised'.[276] Similarly Cicero said that the former 'flows along like a calm stream without any choppiness', while Thucydides is so compressed 'that almost every word contains a full statement: he is so exact and concise that you do not know whether to say that his material is made brilliant by its expression or the other way round'.[277] It is this compression on which Dionysius comments in his essay on Thucydides (24), before proceeding to other well known characteristics of his style:[278]

> The most conspicuous and characteristic features of the author are his efforts to express the largest number of things in the smallest number of words, and to compress a number of thoughts into one, and his tendency to leave his hearer still expecting to hear something more, all of which things produce a brevity that lacks clarity. To sum it up, there are four instruments (as it were) of Thucydidean diction: poetic vocabulary, great variety of figures, harshness of sound combination, and swiftness in saying what he has to say. Its qualities are solidity and compactness, pungency and harshness.

And once again it is interesting to note that these verdicts have their parallels today. In his book on Greek prose style, for example, J.D. Denniston chose the words 'effortless', 'flow' and 'suppleness' to describe Herodotus, while for Thucydides he used 'stiffness', 'compression' and 'boldness'.[279] R.G. Collingwood was even more forthright about Thucydides, whose style he described as 'harsh, artificial, repellent. In reading Thucydides I ask myself, What is the matter with the man, that he writes like that? I answer: he has a bad conscience'.[280]

It will be clear that Collingwood has drawn from Thucydides' style a conclusion about Thucydides as an historian. This is common practice. Peter Gay has written an excellent book, dealing with such historians as Gibbon and Ranke, which 'may be read as an extended critical commentary' on the principle that 'the style is the man'.[281] Thus 'the dramatic devices shaping Ranke's prose reveal his implicit conformity and conservatism',[282] while Gibbon's decision to model himself on Tacitus reveals his 'decisive rejection of the Christian view of the world' and 'a kind of discriminating disenchantment'.[283] The style of A.J.P. Taylor, to take a contemporary illustration, has been said by one of his colleagues to reflect 'the dissenting qualities of his own personality'.[284] It is thus hardly surprising that G.R. Elton has stated the general rule that 'what a writer is, both as a man and as an historian, will appear in his style of writing'.[285]

So was Collingwood right to deduce from Thucydides' style that 'he has a bad conscience'? Elton, having stated the general rule, also warns that wrong conclusions can be drawn from stylistic evidence, and he points to two fallacies in particular:[286]

A good many scholars seem to have thought that the more readable their colleagues were the less they merited consideration. Difficult things, 'real problems', could not be dealt with in lucid or attractive language but required obscure technical terms and a style which reflected the agonising processes of thought that had gone into their analysis. Any historian who expressed himself well and showed some respect for the remarkable possibilities of the English language was automatically assumed to have achieved ease of expression by sliding over the difficulties of the matter. Perhaps he was not even aware of them; perhaps he had deliberately sacrificed depth and accuracy to his ambition to become a publisher's dream; it was hard to say which failing deserved the more severe censure ... It seems to have been the fashion to think that only a particularly austere and even repulsive style of writing could entitle the historian to the name of scholar, and some men appeared to reserve a special vocabulary and syntax for the occasions on which they wished to claim that distinction.

On the one hand we have 'lucid', 'attractive' and 'ease of expression'; and on the other 'obscurity', 'austere' and 'repulsive'. It is remarkable how Elton's two extremes are described in terms which exactly mirror those used to describe Herodotus and Thucydides by ancient and modern readers alike. I believe that modern readers, misled by Thucydides' difficult style into thinking that his approach to historiography was the same as their own, have interpreted his narrative in anachronistically 'scientific' terms which, as we have seen from our analysis of one of its allegedly most 'scientific' sections, it does not warrant. His ancient readers, blissfully unaware of the rise of 'scientific historiography' in the nineteenth century, naturally made no such mistake.

Notes

Modern scholarship on Thucydides continues to increase at an enormous rate: in addition to the works listed by Luschnat, for example, at least half a dozen books in English alone have appeared since 1980. I admit that I have been selective in the face of such a bibliography, but I should mention that I have found particularly stimulating the work of Parry (1957), Kitto pp. 257-354 and Macleod pp. 52ff., especially pp. 140-58. There are also some excellent but brief remarks in Lloyd-Jones pp. 137-44.

1. Momigliano (1978) p. 1. Cf. Cic. *Leg.* 1.5.
2. Dion. *Ep. Pomp.* 3 (2.379 Usher), [Long.] *Subl.* 13.3; cf. F. Jacoby, *RE* 2A.502.
3. Momigliano (1978) p. 2.
4. E.g. R.G. Collingwood, M.I. Finley, K. von Fritz and M. Grant, quoted by Drews pp. 43 and 165-7. Other examples are G.E.M. De Ste Croix ('Herodotus', *GR* 24 (1977) pp. 130-48) and Press (e.g. p. 31). In fairness, however, it must be added that M.I. Finley (1985) came to adopt a more realistic view of classical historiography than that illustrated by Drews's reference.
5. The standard work on Homer and historiography is Strasburger (1972); for various other statements of the relationship between poetry and historiography see e.g. Norden (1958) pp. 38-41 and 91-5, Walbank (1960) pp. 221-8.

6. In what follows I assume that the practice and purpose of literary borrowing were the same for Herodotus as they were for later authors. This seems a reasonable assumption to make in the light of the evidence of e.g. the lyric poets.

7. Quint. 10.1.48 'operis sui ingressu ... auditorem ... intentum proposita rerum *magnitudine*... fecit'.

8. The clumsiness of the latter part of my translation reflects the difficulty of a controversial passage of Greek. For a full discussion see Drexler pp. 3ff.; more briefly, Drews pp. 187-8.

9. See e.g. Stambler p. 210.

10. For the ancient view of Homeric epic as encomium see Feeney pp. 147-8 with references.

11. See Fornara p. 77. Homer's question continued to be reproduced by epic writers, e.g. Virg. *Aen.* 1.*8*, Luc. 1.*8*. For other questions in Homer and Herodotus (but not, however, this one) see Lang pp. 37ff.

12. For the continuation of Herodotus' preface to chapter 5 see Immerwahr (1966) pp. 17-19 and 80-1.

13. For this passage as a second preface see Immerwahr (1966) pp. 63-4 and 129-30.

14. Russell (1964) on [Long.] *Subl.* 13.3.

15. For a summary of these points, see the introduction to Cameron (1988); see also e.g. Fussell pp. 169ff., Gay *passim*, Mink (especially pp. 134-5, 144-5, 147), Dray pp. 27ff., H. White (1980), McCullagh pp. 91ff. for various aspects. Note too the interesting remarks of Gossman p. 32 on footnotes: 'The division of the historiographical page [into text and evidence] is a testimony to the discontinuity between past "reality" and the historical narrative; and those historians who have wished to create the greatest impression of continuity between their text and reality have in fact taken care to eliminate the telltale scar separating the two parts of the page'. Footnotes were not of course used by ancient writers, for some of whose views see pp. 14-15, 24.

16. For various views on this subject see e.g. Carr pp. 7ff., Elton pp. 71ff., Atkinson pp. 10-11, 51ff.

17. The cyclic view of history is perhaps to be found in Hesiod, *WD* WD 174-5.

18. For the Homeric nature of Herodotus' battles see e.g. De Romilly (1967) pp. 112-15. (By 'less true' I of course mean less true in modern terms.)

19. It does, however, seem to be denied by Fornara pp. 162-7.

20. Herodotus characteristically introduces speeches with ταῦτα or τάδε, i.e. 'these (words)'.

21. Further remarks on this at pp. 14-15.

22. See e.g. Myres pp. 93-5, who transforms Hdt. 1.7-94 into a 'tragedy'. ('To bring these [embryonic iambics] to birth, I have adventured slight metrical transpositions': p. 94 n. 1.) Aristotle, however, remarked that 'one could turn Herodotus' work into verse and it would be just as much history as before' (*Poetics* 1451b 2-4). For epic as the parent of both history and tragedy see especially Walbank (1960).

23. Much of the evidence for Herodotus' imitation of Homer is in *RE* 2A. 502-4. See also Stambler pp. 210-11 (though she proceeds to make

some good points in support of her general view that Hdt. is essentially different from Homer).

24. See e.g. Gabba (1981) pp. 52-3 and (1983) pp. 27-8. It is of course true that Herodotus can also adopt a 'rationalising' approach to his material, e.g. at 3.122.2; but this should be taken no more seriously than Hecataeus' famous dismissal of *his* predecessors' *logoi* ('accounts'), which certainly does not prevent his repeating the kind of material which he appears to criticise (see e.g. Fornara pp. 4ff.). Such attitudes are an aspect of literary imitation and rivalry, and came to be an accepted pose of the historian (see e.g. Dion. *Thuc.* 5). See in general Howie, and the brief remarks of Breisach p. 20.

25. See e.g. the excellent papers of J.K. Davies, 'The reliability of the oral tradition', and J.B. Hainsworth, 'The fallibility of an oral heroic tradition', in Foxhall and Davies pp. 87-135. They conclude that any historical kernel to the *Iliad* is slight indeed.

26. E.g. *Od.* 19.203 (see Adkins (1972a)).

27. Fornara pp. 134-5 rightly remarks: 'The need for imaginative recreation and inferential elaboration from the facts was the necessary consequence of the demands placed on all subsequent historians by Herodotus when he decided, following Homer, to present events with verisimilitude. Everything from needful circumstantial detail to the virtual reproduction of the thoughts of leading figures was injected into the historical narrative, often on mere grounds of probability ... In this fashion, the requirements of the medium resulted in the fusion of the factual basis of the record with its imaginative reenactment by the writer. The process here described is irrelevant to the categories of "fact" and "fiction", "truth and falsity", "honesty and dishonesty", so often applied to the discredit of the ancients.' [However, these excellent points are utterly at variance with the general thesis of Fornara's book, which is that during the past 2,500 years 'history has altered but little' (p. 200). See e.g above, n. 19.] Hainsworth (in Foxhall and Davies p. 111) rightly observes that 'fiction is a sophisticated concept, too difficult for the Singers of Tales, for whom truth is opposed to falsehood'.

28. See Armayor (1977-8), (1978), (1978a), (1978b), (1978c), (1980) and (1985), a most impressive series of papers. There is also much of interest in Kazazis.

29. Herodotus' 'reassuring air of coherence undoubtedly derives in part from the *illusion of autopsy*... His authoritative manner creates the presumption that he speaks of what he has himself observed. What we have seen of his procedure ... should make us cautious in dealing with other passages which give the impression of first-hand observation, where we have no such control' (S. West (1985) p. 302, my italics). See also Fehling (1971).

30. Cf. the case of one C. Jones, whose account of the Khmer Rouge in Cambodia in the *New York Times* was subsequently proved to have been fabricated (*The Times* 22.2.1982).

31. L.E. Lord, *Thucydides and the world war* (1945) p. 216, quoted by Stahl p. 12.

32. As is also remarked by M.I. Finley (1985) pp. 47-8, paralleling Ranke, whose famous statement that the historian should aim to say

'how it really was' is now thought to be borrowed from Thuc. 2.48.3 (p. 116 nn. 4-5); see further Bann pp. 8-31, and, for another parallel between Th. and Ranke, see p. 17 and n. 98.

33. See Wallace, V.J. Hunter (1973), Connor (1977) and (1984) p. 6.

34. Wiseman (1979) p. 41 (quoting M.I. Finley in support!).

35. For δὲ καί = 'in turn' see Denniston (1959) p. 305. Classen and Steup render καί as 'wenigstens'.

36. For μέρος τι indicating something extensive or large, also at 1.23.3, Connor (1984) p. 31 n. 30 refers to Poppo and Stahl on 4.30.3.

37. The main problems are these. (a) What is the subject of the second sentence and what are the meanings of κίνησις, γάρ and ἐγένετο in this context? See e.g. Hammond pp. 129-33 and Erbse p. 45 with n. 7. I have assumed that Th. is drawing a distinction between his preliminary work (ἀρξάμενος κτλ.), which is explained at some length by τεκμαιρόμενος and ὁρῶν, and his writing the final version of his history (ξυνέγραψε), which is explained by γάρ. I thus agree with Erbse that αὕτη is the subject of the sentence (which makes good sense of δή: see Denniston (1959) p. 209) and that κίνησις refers to the war (which is supported by the repetition of 'barbarians' at 1.23.1-3, where the present sentence is expanded: see pp. 9 and 28). Hammond pp. 130-2 maintains that κίνησις does not refer to the war, but that is because he regards κίνησις γάρ κτλ. as parallel to τεκμαιρόμενος κτλ., a view forced on him by his mistaken assumption (p. 129) that ἐλπίσας κτλ. is Th.'s main contention. His point that otherwise the second sentence results in 'a puerile *vaticinium post eventum*' (p. 133 n. 1) is met by making γάρ explain ξυνέγραψε. As for ἐγένετο, I am attracted by the neglected suggestion of Parry (1957) p. 208 n. 13 that it means 'amounted to' (see LSJ s.v. I.2.a), a meaning which I have also adopted in my rendering of Hdt. 7.20.2 (p. 2) and Thuc. 3.113.6 (p. 31).

(b) In the third sentence to what does πρὸ αὐτῶν refer, and what are the periods of time alluded to? I myself do not find it difficult to refer αὐτῶν to the Peloponnesian War (*contra* Erbse p. 47), but scholars have object to this interpretation (i) on the grounds that events of 510-435 BC cannot be described as 'impossible to find out about on account of the time span involved', and (ii) because in his account of the Pentecontaetia (1.89-118) Th. nowhere mentions any such impossibility. See Gomme (1945) p. 91. Yet neither of these objections can reasonably be sustained. (i) At 1.20.2 Th. goes out of his way to say that people have consistently failed to recover the truth of an event of 514, which precedes 510 by a mere four years. (ii) Though it is true that nowhere in 1.89-118 does Th. mention the impossibility of recovering the truth, this precisely reflects his practice in the history as a whole, where the difficulties mentioned at 1.22.3 are hardly ever mentioned thereafter (see pp. 16-17, 23).

38. See Schadewaldt p. 50 n. 1 (also p. 59 n. 1), Parry (1957) pp. 93-5, Strasburger (1972) pp. 13-14, Erbse pp. 45-6, Cagnazzi pp. 197-204. The fact that the Pentecontaetia begins at the point at which Herodotus' work left off (479 BC) is a further indication of the relationship between the two authors. But none of this makes any impression on Gabba (1983) p. 6 ('even the link with Herodotus [does] not indicate a conscious desire to follow a model or continue the work of a predecessor'). By beginning his

history with his own name and origin, Th. is also following in the footsteps of Herodotus (and of Hecataeus before him); but Th. characteristically omits the demonstrative pronoun which the two earlier historians had employed (see Fehling (1975) pp. 61-2): he thereby achieves variation and perhaps also authority ('*the* account ...'). For conscious rejection of this tradition (by Arrian) see Moles (1985) p. 164 and n. 13.

39. *Thuc.* 9 with Pritchett ad loc. That Th.'s first paragraph serves as a magnification of his theme was seen by Schwartz pp. 168-72 and some others (cf. Luschnat 1203), but it is denied without argument by Gomme (1945) pp. 89 and 140, and seems no longer fashionable. Yet, as Herkommer p. 167 points out, the key words in an *amplificatio* are μέγας in Greek and *magnus* in Latin, and the former occurs three times in chapter 1. It is also profitable to recall (a) the techniques which Th. himself uses to achieve *amplificatio* in his speeches and which are directly comparable to those used here (see e.g. Macleod p. 230); (b) those used by other historians to achieve their own *amplificatio*, e.g. Plb. 1.2.1, Sall. *J.* 5.1. For *amplificatio* in general see Cic. *Or.* 125; Lausberg 1.234-5, Herkommer pp. 39 n. 7, 164-8.

40. See, briefly, Gomme (1945) p. 91. Th.'s treatment of the Persian Wars is, conversely, to dismiss them as being over in no time, in merely two sea- and land-battles (1.23.1). 'He is thus announcing himself as the rival of Herodotus' (Lloyd-Jones p. 141).

41. It can be argued that 23.4-6, which is usually regarded as the final part of the preface and with which I am anyway not concerned, is rather the start of the main narrative. My view of the preface's structure is similar to, but not identical with, that proposed by Hammond; for a different suggestion again, see Connor (1984) p. 30 n. 29.

42. The so-called 'Archaeology' (chapters 2-19).

43. For contemporary examples of κοσμεῖν in this sense see Eur. *Med.* 576, Aristoph. *Frogs* 1005, 1027. In general, Lausberg 2. 50-1.

44. 'He is announcing himself as the rival of Homer' (Lloyd-Jones p. 141). Since successive examples of γάρ are a feature of both Homer and Herodotus (see Denniston (1959) p. 58), and since Th. uses γάρ four times in 1.1.2-2.2, it may be that he is recalling a recognisable mannerism of both authors.

45. See Hammond pp. 127-36.

46. So too Hammond p. 134. He rightly points out that 20-21.1 is in fact an elaboration of the phrase 'on the basis of such evidence [τεκμηρίων] as I can trust [πιστεῦσαι]' at 1.1.3, where *ancient* history was indeed the subject under discussion (see p. 7). The verbal correspondences between 1.1.3 on the one hand, and the thesis at 20.1 and its re-statement at 21.1 on the other, make the link quite clear.

47. So e.g. Immerwahr (1960) p. 277 (1973), pp. 18 and 20 (1985), p. 444; V. Hunter (1982) pp. 287-8. Lesky first says that chapters 20-2 'form a close unity', then (correctly) that only chapter 22 is the 'chapter on method' (pp. 459 and 473).

It is admittedly arguable whether 21.2 is prospective (as I believe) or retrospective (as Erbse p. 64 believes, linking it with chapter 19): in themselves the words ὁ πόλεμος οὗτος ... δηλώσει ὅμως μείζων γεγενημένος αὐτῶν [sc. τῶν ἀρχαίων] could look either way. But if the second part of the preface is not regarded as ending until 21.2, it follows that the beginning of the third part at 22.1 is intolerably abrupt (καὶ ὅσα μὲν λόγῳ εἶπον ...). There is no such problem if the third part is regarded as beginning with καὶ ὁ πόλεμος οὗτος at 21.2. In addition, the words ἀπ' αὐτῶν τῶν ἔργων σκοποῦσι at 21.2 constitute an anticipation of 22-23.3 (see pp. 9-10; also Gomme (1945) p. 139). I have not seen an edition of Th. which prints a paragraph break after 21.1 (though Parry (1957) pp. 7-8 does so by implication): most editors seem content simply to follow the traditional chapter divisions.

48. See e.g. Lesky (last n.), Usher p. 28, Gentili and Cerri p. 140.

49. It has been argued (e.g. by Connor (1984) pp. 27-32) that the 'Archaeology' is 'an exhibition of a new technique of analysis ... Thucydides intends a new kind of history. His approach is not that of the poets' (pp. 29, 31). But see my next remarks.

50. See pp. 28-30, 32-40.

51. Connor (1984) p. 29 notes that the sentence concludes with an 'heroic clausula'.

52. For the self-evidential character of Th.'s main narrative see pp. 16-17, 22-3. In the preface τεκμήριον occurs at 1.2, 20.1 and 21.1; τεκμηριόω at 3.3 and 9.3; σημεῖον at 6.2, 10.1 and 21.1; μαρτύριον at 8.1. Parry (1957) p. 96 counted 23 phrases describing the 'process of intellectual discernment' in chapters 1-21.

53. Some scholars take the phrase 'after investigating with as much accuracy as possible each event' as referring also to the events which Th. experienced himself (see Gomme (1945) pp. 142-3). But I think that (a) Th. would in that case have written περὶ ἑκατέρων, and (b) the structure of the sentence is against it: in contrast with speeches at 22.1, Th. at 22.3 seems to exclude himself from the difficulties of bias and memory, and since ἐπιπόνως εὑρίσκετο clearly refers to ὅσον δυνατὸν ... ἐπεξελθών, I infer that this last phrase is restricted to <τὰ> παρὰ τῶν ἄλλων. Thus οὐδ' ὡς ἐμοὶ ἐδόκει, ἀλλ' οἷς τε αὐτὸς παρῆν alone forms the two central elements of a chiasmus.

54. In addition to works cited below see e.g. Luschnat 1162-83, Schneider pp. 143-54, Wilson. For a list of Th.'s speeches and a bibliography thereon see Stadter (1973).

55. So Gomme (1945) pp. 140-1, endorsed by Dover (1973) pp. 26-7; other examples are given by De Ste Croix p. 296 and Kagan (1975) pp. 71-9.

56. Kagan (1975) p. 74, thereby repeating the statement which he had made in *The Outbreak of the Peloponnesian War* (1969) ix, and which had already been corrected by De Ste Croix p. 296. (Kagan's other books are *The Archidamian War* (1974) and *The Peace of Nicias and the Sicilian Expedition* (1981).) By also ignoring De Ste Croix, Fornara p. 144 makes the same mistake ('[Th. asserts] that he will supply "the actual words"').

57. De Ste Croix pp. 7-11, a discussion of fundamental importance (my quotations come from pp. 9-10). Since the word γνώμη is regularly used in a technical sense — the 'motion' of a speaker (see Dover (1981) p. 394, with examples), a key question is the meaning of the adj. ξυμπᾶσα, as De Ste Croix p. 9 insists. See also below, n. 59.

58. Neisser p. 141, referring to the work of Bartlett.

59. Thus Fornara p. 144 (who of course does not mention De Ste Croix), Wilson. Dover (1981) pp. 394-5 seems to agree with De Ste Croix's contention that, on the basis of the linguistic evidence, ξύμπᾱς signifies a whole as distinct from its parts, i.e. the 'general gist' as distinct from the individual arguments used to support it; but he finally argues against this view on the grounds that it leaves little room for the degrees of fidelity suggested by the words 'keeping as closely as possible to ...'. But this point is met if we remember that the general gist has to be extracted from a complete speech by inference: it is therefore a matter of interpretation and may be very different from, or 'as close as possible to', the general gist intended by the original speaker. Dover's point is also met by De Ste Croix p. 8 n. 9 and by my remarks on memory which follow.

60. Neisser pp. 142, 147.

61. One of numerous scholars to make this point is Dover (1981) p. 394. See also below, n. 123.

62. See Lockyer, who deals with Plato, Xenophon, Cicero, the elder Seneca, Gellius, Athenaeus and Macrobius.

63. See De Ste Croix p. 8 n. 9.

64. I thus agree entirely with M.I. Finley (1985) pp. 13-14, who appositely remarks: 'Certainly that is how they were understood in antiquity [sc. as inventions]: witness the discussion in his long essay on Thucydides (chapters 34-48) by Dionysius of Halicarnassus, the most acute and most learned of ancient critics and himself a prolific composer of speeches for his multi-volume *Roman Antiquities*' (cf. also p. 56). See also below, n. 79.
The consequence of De Ste Croix's position, as he himself remarks (11), is that 'we can never be sure that any particular argument used in a speech, or any particular statement made in it, can be attributed to the actual speaker, or was necessarily true ... We can seldom be sure that we know how extensive the "general gist" is, and therefore we may often not be able to decide how much of a speech represents what was actually said, and how much is Th.'s own formulation of the issues'.

65. Fornara p. 143. The statement of Dover (1981) p. 395 that 'accurate recollection is always desirable and invention ... always a *pis aller*' is almost, but not quite, the same thing. Yet this hardly squares with those sections of Th.'s work (5.25-83, 8.7-109) which both quote documents verbatim and lack speeches, and which on other grounds are thought by Dover himself to be less revised than the rest of the work (p. 393). The natural inference is that Th.'s procedure was to move *from* the verbatim (assuming he could recapture it) *towards* free composition.

66. 'An authentic dialogue between Napoleon and Alexander I, had it been preserved in shorthand, will not be "stuck" in the account. The historian will most usually prefer to talk about this dialogue; if he quotes it verbatim, the quotation will be a literary effect, designed to give life — let us say *ethos* — to the plot, which would bring history thus written close to the historical novel' (Veyne p. 5, who is of course talking about a hypothetical case of *genuine* dialogue). Churchill in his account of the Second World War often quotes extensively from (his own) speeches, though never (I think) a whole speech; yet he repeatedly makes it clear that he is not writing a proper history but supplying the material upon which

proper histories might be based (i.e. like Julius Caesar, cf. Cic. *Brut.* 262).

67. For *bons mots* see *Ann.* 14.59.3, 15.67.2-3; for the re-casting of Claudius' speech see 11.24. The fact that Tac. was able to reproduce five of the emperor's main points (see Miller (1956)) is explained by his using a transcript.

68. See e.g. Strasburger (1972) pp. 38-9. Conceivably, it may be due to Homer, in whom the heroic ideal is said to be 'a speaker of words and a doer of deeds' in that order, that Th. in chapter 22 discusses speeches before events (*Iliad* 9.443, to which Lesky p. 474 draws attention). In his *Encomium of Helen* (8) Gorgias famously described *logos* ('speech', 'language') as δυναστής ('chief', 'master', 'lord'): see Parry (1957) pp. 44 and 88.

69. For his rivalry of Homer see pp. 7, 9-10, 28-30, 32ff. Scholars often suggest stylistic homogeneity as the main reason why ancient historians put their own words into the mouths of their characters (see e.g. Norden (1958) pp. 88-91).

70. This is exactly the opposite conclusion from that of Fornara in his chapter on the subject (pp. 142-68). Fornara bases his thesis on the assumption that 'the Thucydidean principle of 1.22 seems to have governed the practice of the historians, both Greek and Latin, whether they dealt with ancient or with modern times' (167), yet he himself mistranslates that passage of Th. (see above, n. 56), and his chapter is otherwise riddled with mistaken assumptions and misuses of evidence (too numerous to refute here, but for one example see below, n. 79). Polybius (36.1.7) said that historians should record 'what was actually said' (τὰ κατ' ἀλήθειαν ῥηθέντα), but Walbank (1965) pp. 7-8, to whom Fornara pp. 157-8 omits to refer, has rightly argued that this phrase is his equivalent to Th.'s τῆς ξυμπάσης γνώμης.

71. See Liv. 45.25.3 'I will not insert a copy <of the speech> of this prolix orator by mentioning what he said [*non inseram simulacrum uiri copiosi, quae dixerit, referendo*]: the original survives, incorporated in Book 5 of the *Origins*'. Gabba's comment on this ('The most accurate reports of speeches are to be found in Cato, who inserted his own speeches in his historical writing') is an interesting illustration of modern preconceptions (1983, p. 7).

72. Schneider p. 139 n. 311 has said that the word 'sich nicht auf die Methode der Untersuchung, sondern auf die Übereinstimmung ihres Ergebnisses mit der Wirklichkeit bezieht', but the translation of 22.2 on which this is based ('wie sich jedes einzelne genau verhielt') does not seem to me to tally with Th.'s Greek. Classen and Steup ad loc., on the grounds that ἀκριβείᾳ must mean the same at 22.2 as it does at 22.1, say that the word must 'von der genauen Wahrheit, dem genauen Sachverhalt, nicht aber subjektiv von der Sorgfalt des Th. verstanden werden'; but once again, though I sympathise with their reasoning, I do not see that their rendering fits the Greek.

73. Parry (1957) p. 103.

74. See Parry (1957) pp. 18, 20, 82-3; Guthrie (1971) pp. 44-5, 176ff. Kerferd p. 78 states the matter very well: 'What people thought and said was beginning to be more important than what was actually the case. In its extreme form this leads to the doctrine that there are no facts and no

truth ... What happened in the fifth century BC hardly went as far as this. What did emerge however was a realisation that the relationship between speech and what is the case is far from simple. While it is likely that fifth-century thinkers all were prepared to accept that there is and always must be a relationship between the two, there was a growing understanding that what is very often involved is not simply a presentation in words of what is the case, but rather a representation, involving a considerable degree of reorganisation in the process.'

75. See Parry (1957) pp. 46-7, Guthrie (1971) pp. 198-9 and 272-3, Kerferd pp. 80-1.

76. References in Rittelmeyer pp. 25-9, Guthrie (1971) p. 223, Dover (1973) pp. 12-13.

77. I am not of course denying that there is in Th.'s narrative a close relationship between speeches and events and that he often uses the latter to reveal the excellence or inadequacy of the former, as appropriate.

78. The first author to circulate transcripts of forensic speeches is thought to have been Antiphon (c. 480-411 BC).

79. I say 'many', not 'all', because innumerable speeches in the ancient historians do not, of course, represent a speech that was actually delivered. This is clear from Dion. (see nn. 64 and 233), Cic. *Or.* 66 'interponuntur etiam contiones et hortationes', Gran. Licin. 36 A-B 'contiones inserit' (of Sallust), Quint. 10.1.101 'T. Liuium ... in contionibus supra quam enarrari potest eloquentem'. These uses of *interponere* and *inserere* put a rather different complexion on Fornara's statement that 'the general inclination today is to dismiss most of the speeches inserted (a tell-tale word!) by the Greco-Roman historians ... on the ground that they are mere rhetorical constructions' (p. 142, with a promise that he himself will take 'a much more positive view'). And almost everything that Fornara says about Livy's speeches (pp. 151-2 and 160-1) is invalidated by Quintilian's statement, which he actually quotes (p. 152 n. 10, though in H.E. Butler's misleading translation).

80. So too M.I. Finley (1985) p. 14: 'It is untenable that every single practitioner [of history] was indifferent to the fact that he was a falsifier ... Thucydides must have had something more in mind than just crude deception of his readers when, in the short statement of method in his first book, he wrote the awful part-sentence (1.22.1) that has exercised commentators for perhaps two centuries ... We start from the wrong premise by assuming that Greeks and Romans looked upon the study and writing of history essentially as we do.' See too pp. 15-17.

81. At 1.73.4 Th. makes the Athenians say that they 'faced the barbarian alone at Marathon'; yet in the painting of the battle, which was clearly displayed in the Stoa Poikile in the Athenian Agora, the Plataeans are correctly shown as assisting them. See Walters for discussion.

82. Gabba (1983) p. 49 remarks that 'it was legitimate for a historian to reconstruct in *his* work a speech probably delivered by a politician, with some approximation to reality' and he uses this to explain the proliferation of literary *forgeries*. The implications for historiography itself are ignored! On the other hand, Collingwood pp. 30-1 (to whom M.I. Finley (1985) pp. 14-15 rightly refers) is much more realistic; but he is almost a lone voice.

83. See also *Od.* 3.93-5 — 4.323-5; Lloyd p. 425. Thus it cannot be claimed (as it is e.g. by Momigliano (1966) pp. 130-1, 135, 214-15, and Usher pp. 28-9) that Th.'s statement at 1.22.2 is an epoch-making assertion of the primacy of contemporary historiography. Momigliano (1978) p. 5 seems tacitly to have realised this. The common belief that 'eyes are more reliable than ears', which is closely allied to what is said by Homer and Th., is regularly alluded to by Herodotus (e.g. 1.8.2) and seems also to have been mentioned by Heraclitus before Th. (see Walbank on Plb. 12.27.1). See also Avenarius pp. 78-9, Herkommer pp. 87ff.

84. Pearson (1939). For this as the technique of the modern *novelist* see e.g. Georges Simenon (quoted in *The Sunday Times* 16.5.1982) and W.H. Davies and Anthony Burgess (quoted in Woodman (1983a) p. 116).

85. Gomme (1945) pp. 179-80.

86. Westlake (1977) p. 361, referring to K.J. Dover, *Maia* 6 (1953) pp. 1-20, and also to R. van Compernolle, *Étude de chronologie et d'histori-ographie siciliotes* (1960) pp. 437-500. The conventional nature of the wording at Th. 6.2.2 (for other examples of which see e.g. Avenarius pp. 163-4 and Norden (1959) pp. 167-8) makes the hypothesis of a written source virtually certain.

87. Gomme (1956) p. 389.

88. See Wardman.

89. Cf. also the argument of M. Pohlenz concerning Th.'s speeches, that the historian began by trying to reproduce speeches as closely as possible to what was actually said but ended up by diverging quite radically from them. This suggestion, initially rejected by Dover (1973) p. 27, seems to be treated with more sympathy by Dover (1981) pp. 398-9.

90. It is of course true that results are implied by the following sentence, but I think it is significant that they are there presented from the point of view of Th.'s *audience* and not as an achievement of the historian himself: see pp. 23ff., especially 27.

91. Dover (1973) p. 29.

92. The example at 8.87 is different because Th. there does make up his own mind. Whether he would have eliminated the alternative possibilities in a final draft of Book 8 (see n. 65 above) must of course remain uncertain. For cases of uncertainty over numerals, which perhaps form a special category (e.g. 5.68.2), see Rubincam; also below, n. 188.

93. Viz. 2.50.2 (see pp. 37-8). Significantly, the word is used in anti-quarian digressions at 2.15.4 and 6.28.2; of the five other examples, four (1.34.3, 73.5, 2.39.2, 3.66.1) are in speeches (1.132.5 is irrelevant). τεκμαίρεσθαι occurs in a speech (3.53.2; 4.123.2 is irrelevant); σημεῖον occurs twice in speeches (2.41.4 and 42.1; 1.132.1 is irrelevant); μαρτύριον occurs in speeches (1.33.1, 73.3, 3.11.4, 53.4, 6.82.2).

94. See Hammond p. 137, Katičič p. 195 (but cf. n. 30).

95. De Ste Croix p. 8 n. 9, where he nevertheless accepts the con-clusion of Westlake (1969) pp. 153-60 that Th. never uses ὡς εἰκός — 'probably' as if to indicate lack of confidence in a statement; the phrase — 'naturally'.

96. Westlake (1977) pp. 345-62 (the quotation from p. 362, my italics).

97. See Grant p. 84. Examples are 3.87.2-4 and 5.74.1-2 (quoted on p. 31).

98. Dover (1973) p. 31, another interesting parallel with Ranke (see M.I. Finley (1985) pp. 48-9). The self-assured nature of Th.'s narrative has been commented on by numerous scholars (e.g. Parry (1972) p. 48, De Ste Croix p. 7) and is one of the ways in which he may be compared with Herodotus (cf. e.g. Gomme (1945) p. 142). Indeed Rosenmeyer has said that 'Herodotus is the Father of History ... in that he makes a proud show of his tentativeness, his occasional irresolution in the face of a bewildering mass of materials pressing for recognition and winnowing' (p. 36, continuing 'A work of poetry, on the other hand, ... will persuade us to go along with its charms only if it offers its structure as authoritative and complete', evidently not thinking of the implications of this comparison for Th.). See also below, n. 124.

99. Gay p. 118; but then Macaulay is an 'honorary novelist' (*The Times* 14.2.1985). Gay in fact proceeds to Macaulay's defence (see also Atkinson pp. 15-16), but he was certainly capable of invention: for an example based on an ode of Horace see Crump pp. 151-2.

100. Dover (1973) p. 4.

101. 'There is surprisingly little immediate evidence for the famed accuracy of Ranke, almost none for Thucydides' (M.I. Finley (1985) p. 51).

102. Lesky p. 474.

103. Jerome pp. 33-4.

104. Bartlett; Buckhout (= Neisser pp. 116-25).

105. Winter pp. 181, 189. His references are to: F. Crozier, *Brass Hat in No-man's Land* (1930); R. Kipling, *Souvenirs of France* (1933); W. Andrews, *Haunting Years* (1929). For the opposite, the case of an exceptional memory of the Great War (A.C. Aitken, *Gallipoli to the Somme* (1963)), see Neisser pp. 419-20; and cf. also Fussell p. 327.

106. *But It Still Goes On* (1931) pp. 32-3, quoted by Fussell p. 207. The ancients did not, of course, have to contend with shell-shock, but I think the general point still stands.

107. Knightley p. 317 and n.

108. Knightley pp. 9-10.

109. Keegan p. 31.

110. Keegan p. 32.

111. Middlebrook (1971) pp. 317-56.

112. Keegan p. 262.

113. Middlebrook (1978) pp. 10-12.

114. T.H. White (1979) p. 172. On the difficulties of even getting close to the action in the Falklands War see e.g. *The Times* 21.7.1982.

115. T.H. White (1979) p. 172. See also Robert Kee, *The Listener* (1971) p. 208, quoted by Fussell p. 311.

116. Balfour p. 172 on the Second World War. According to Professor P. Nailor, a member of the Ministry of Defence Advisory Panel on Public Records, 'the real problem is getting historians to use primary sources' (*The Times* 19.2.1980)!!

117. Wolff pp. 185-6. And of course officials can also twist or falsify the information which they give to reporters and historians: for an example from the Falklands see *The Times* 22.7.1982.

118. I.M.L. Hunter (1978) pp. 161, 183.

119. I.M.L. Hunter (1978) pp. 148-52.

120. Fussell pp. 169ff., especially p. 173: 'Strictly speaking, it would seem impossible to write an account of anything without some "literature" leaking in. Probably only a complete illiterate who very seldom heard narrative of any kind could give an "accurate" account of a personal experience ... [But actually he] would have had to learn somewhere the principles of sequence and unity and transition and causality.'

121. Keegan pp. 62-3.

122. See Thompson. A reviewer of R.A. Caro, *The Years of Lyndon Johnson* Vol. 1 (1982), concluded that 'oral history is bunk' (*The Times* 10.2.1983).

123. For some distinctions between oral and written historiography see Momigliano (1966) pp. 211ff.

124. 'A special case ... is that where the author seeks to stand aside from his own discourse by systematically omitting any direct allusion to the originator of the text: the history seems to write itself. This approach is very widely used, since it fits the so-called "objective" mode of historical discourse, in which the historian never appears himself. What really happens is that the author discards the human persona but replaces it by an "objective" one; the authorial subject is as evident as ever, but it has become an objective subject. This is the process that Fustel de Coulanges revealingly and rather naively calls the "chastity of history". At the level of discourse, objectivity, or the absence of any clues to the narrator, turns out to be a particular form of fiction, the result of what might be called the referential illusion, where the historian tries to give the impression that the referent is speaking for itself. This illusion is not confined to historical discourse: novelists galore, in the days of realism, considered themselves "objective" because they had suppressed all traces of the *I* in their text' (Barthes pp. 148-9). See also H. White (1980) p. 7, and Gossman p. 21 and n. 27.

125. Lesky p. 459, Dover (1973) p. 43 (comparing Eur. *Helen* 21). Following Pohlenz, Gomme (1945) p. 142 compares Antiochus, fr. 3 Ἀντίοχος ... τάδε συνέγραψε περὶ Ἰταλίης ἐκ τῶν ἀρχαίων λόγων τὰ πιστότατα καὶ σαφέστατα, where, however, the meaning is clearly dictated by λόγων and πιστότατα: it is parts of the λόγοι that are σαφέστατα and it is because of this that they are πιστότατα (see pp. 27-8).

126. See Murray p. 205.

127. As the scholiast on 1.22.4 remarks; see also Gomme (1945) p. 149, Wardman pp. 404-5.

128. See above, n. 24. For example, women appear only infrequently in Th.'s work, but when they do, it is often in an 'irrational' context (see Wiedemann): he perhaps sees them as playing a role which Herodotus would attribute to some god.

129. Gomme (1945) pp. 138-9.

130. See also above, p. 13, on the contrast with 22.1.

131. It has been suggested (see Classen and Steup ad loc.) that the text is defective and that τῶν μελλόντων ... ἔσεσθαι should be governed by some such phrase as ἀγαθοὶ γνώμονες γίγνεσθαι.

132. For this see Walbank (1960) p. 225, Brink on Hor. *AP* 119-30

(intro. n.), 151, 338.

133. Walbank (1960) p. 226.

134. Following Rostagni (reference in Brink on *AP* 119-30), numerous scholars have believed that the division was first enunciated by Aristotle's successor, Theophrastus, although the first actual evidence we have is in the obscure Asclepiades of Myrlea in the first century BC (reference in Walbank (1960) p. 225). (The A scholiast on *Il.* 19.108 categorises this section of Homer's narrative as τὸ ... ὅλον μυθῶδες ... οὐδ᾽ ἀφ᾽ ἑαυτοῦ ... οὐδὲ γινόμενα, which is not unlike Th.'s sequence οὐδ᾽ ὡς ἐμοὶ ἐδόκει ... τὸ μὴ μυθῶδες ... τῶν γενομένων in 22.2-4, but whether the similarity is significant I do not know.)

135. One of the first such handbooks is attributed to Tisias, who according to Plato 'held the probable [εἰκότα] in more honour than the true' (*Phaedr.* 267a). See Guthrie pp. 44 n. 4, 178-81.

136. Plut. *Mor.* 346F-347C. For the similarity to eighteenth-century views see Gossman pp. 16-17.

137. See Lausberg 2.224-31 and Zanker.

138. Dion. *Thuc.* 15 (quoted on pp. 30-1), Theon 118.9 (quoted by Zanker p. 301 n. 15).

139. Fr. 1 Jacoby.

140. See e.g. Scheller pp. 68ff., Ullman p. 38, Strasburger (1975) pp. 78ff., Gentili and Cerri pp. 141ff., Fornara p. 124.

141. Fornara p. 130.

142. Simonides' comparison between poetry and painting is mentioned several times by Plutarch elsewhere and 'its authenticity is widely accepted' (Lucas p. 269 n. 2; cf. also Brink on Hor. *AP* 361-5. intro. n.). Simonides is also said to be responsible for the aphorism 'language is a representation of things' (ὁ λόγος τῶν πραγμάτων εἰκών ἐστι), which is numbered 190 in Diehl's edition. Yet neither appears in the edition of D.L. Page.

143. Odysseus' words '*can characterise a passage as being true*' (Adkins (1972a) p. 17, his italics). For the passage as evidence of μίμησις see Lucas pp. 269-70 (who also notes the relevance of Gorgias) and Harriott pp. 121-2, 143-4. For the attitude adopted by the epic poet himself see Strasburger (1972) p. 20; further references in Gabba (1983) p.35 n. 29.

144. Hermog. 16.32 'The virtues of description are σαφήνεια and ἐνάργεια, since the narrative should enable one almost to see [sc. the events described] when it is read' (δεῖ γὰρ τὴν ἑρμήνειαν διὰ τῆς ἀκοῆς σχεδὸν τὴν ὄψιν μηχανᾶσθαι), Theon 119.27.

145. See Zanker p. 301.

146. 'If vividness or the sense of actually being there is the main source of Thucydides' ability to persuade, I don't see how one can easily distinguish his performance from that of a novelist, who also deludes us into believing that we are live witnesses to the events portrayed in his book ... If he persuades us by vividness, then is there not reason to worry about the durability of his claim on our convictions?' (Robinson p. 21). Exactly so — though Robinson himself argues against any such conclusions.

147. The only exceptions are the plague (cf. 2.48.3) and his own command at Amphipolis (cf. 4.104-7). In the 'second preface' (5.26) he

tells us that as a result of Amphipolis he was banished from Athens for 20 years and so had the chance of seeing things from the Spartan side. We have already seen (p. 15) that some passages of his narrative, which are apparently based on autopsy, are more likely to be based on the literary tradition.

148. This matter is discussed at length in Chapter 2; and compare Kazazis pp. 196-9.

149. For these works see p. 108 and n. 77.

150. Conversely, scholar critics later dismiss the stories of myth on the grounds that nothing could have happened in the past which we do not see still happening today: thus Palaephatus says that such stories are 'too mythical' (μυθῶδες ἄγαν) or 'improbable' (οὐκ εἰκός); the poets have 'elaborated actual occurrences into myth' (*Mythogr. Graeci*, ed. Festa, 23.11-12, 50.6, 8.8-10, 14.8-10). See also Strabo 1.2.8-9.

151. For a particular study of such patterns see Rawlings, who has cleverly argued that the narrative which follows the 'second preface' is the mirror-image (so to speak) of the narrative which precedes it and that this is the very cycle of events alluded to at 1.22.4.

152. For speeches in particular see, briefly, Collingwood pp. 30-1 (Fornara p. 172 is also relevant, but confused); also below, n. 158.

153. Atkinson notes that according to some modern philosophers of history, modern historians 'have to summarise and select, and may accordingly mention individual events and states as representative or typical rather than strictly for their own sakes. They offer imaginative accounts which aim to be both concrete and typical. They aim, *compatibly with the evidence*, to achieve the sort of universality Aristotle allowed to poetry, though not to history' (37). This analysis in some ways resembles the practice of Th., but differs crucially in the matter of the words I have underlined. See further above, pp. 27-8 and nn. 160, 161, 163.

154. Quint. 9.2.40 'sub oculos subiectio tum fieri solet cum res non gesta indicatur sed *ut sit gesta ostenditur, nec uniuersa sed per partes*'.

155. Macleod p. 144. According to Ephorus (fr.9), 'those who give the most accurate account [ἀκριβέστατα] of contemporary events are those whom we consider the most believable'; but since 'accuracy' means no more than 'circumstantial details' (see Schultze pp. 126-7), Ephorus is actually saying no more than the fact (as obvious to Aristotle as to us: see Lucas p. 229) that a detailed account tends to be plausible. Yet plausibility is the vital criterion, for without it history cannot be useful. Hence the usefulness of Th.'s history, to which he refers at 22.4 (ὠφέλιμα), depends upon the details of his narrative. The same is generally true of Homeric narrative: see e.g. Schol. BT on *Il.* 14.226-7.

156. Another example is the plague, which I discuss in detail on pp. 36-40.

157. J.H. Finley (1942) pp. 321-2 (1967), pp. 46-9. The parallels with Aesch. *Pers.* are as follows: with 7.69.2 cf. 403-5 (very striking, and for Aesch.'s ἀγών cf. 68.3), 70.2 cf. 412-13, 70.4 cf. 413-16 (for Aesch.'s ἀρωγή cf. perhaps 62.1), 71.6 cf. 426-7 (and Aesch.'s lines 431-2 are also very 'Thucydidean', cf. 3.113.6, quoted on p. 31). The parallels with Eur. are as follows: with 70.6-7 cf. *Heraclid.* 832-40, *Phoen.* 1145, *Suppl.* 683-93, 702, 711-12; 71.1-4 cf. *Phoen.* 1388-9, *Suppl.* 719-20; 71.4 cf. *Bacch.* 1131ff.

(this last not mentioned by Finley, though it is by Dover ad loc.). These parallels ought to strike the modern reader, whose expectations of history are very different, as odd; but 'especially through the influence of epic and drama Herodotus and Th. set a style followed by almost all ancient historians, which may be called mimetic, that is, they write as if they had been present at the events they describe ... The use of speeches is only the most obvious device of the mimetic method; it reaches into the smallest narrative details and tends to destroy the distinction between "fact" and interpretation' (Immerwahr (1985 pp. 457-8). See also above, p. 3.

158. I think it worth emphasising again that when Th. talks about τὸ σαφές, he does so from his *audience*'s point of view (see also above, n. 90). He himself knew what battles were like, even if he did not exactly know what happened in this one; but the vital thing was that he should present this battle in terms which his audience would readily appreciate. *A fortiori* the same holds good for his speeches. Th.'s debates resemble those in Herodotus and Homer (see Latham) because these authors served to confirm how men speak in such archetypal situations. Again, when putting words into the mouths of Pericles (2.63.2) and Cleon (3.40.4, 37.2), Th. calls to his readers' minds Achilles and Thersites in the *Iliad* (see Cairns (1982)): the comparison is effected by means of linguistic detail, but the point he is making is (in the opinion of himself and his audience) universally true: namely, that this is how men of such character speak and act.

159. In a section of his work devoted to 'history and prophecy', Atkinson writes as follows (p. 61): 'Nomological inference ought to yield rather general conclusions with a high degree of certainty, subject, no doubt, to a variety of other things remaining equal. That we do not in fact enjoy very much in the way of such knowledge, about either the human past or the human future, presumably reflects the present shortage of well established scientific generalisations about human affairs ... As things are, there is little doubt that historians are more concerned with the detail of what *did* happen or was done than with the outline of what *must have* happened.' This statement helps to illustrate Th.'s position by contrast: he was concerned with the *outline* of what *did* happen (which was all that he could recapture) and the *detail* of what *must have* happened (which he could infer from his knowledge of human beings as reflected in both literature and life). See also Kazazis pp. 170-1, and nn. 160-2 below.

160. 'History differs from imaginative literature in offering not truth-likeness or truth to life, but truth; not what might or could have happened, but what did ... Some historians make it a major aim to convey how things presented themselves to participants at the time; and ... more are given to adorning their narratives with what often seems to be rather randomly selected concrete human detail. Nor is there anything exceptionable in this, provided only that the pictures thus vividly painted are adequately evidenced. It is, however, here that there is some danger in stressing resemblances between novels and even narrative history, in holding that history is logically continuous with literature rather than science. A novelist may aim at human credibility, truth to life, and so fail if he does not attain it: but the more significant failure in an

historian would be to supply it in the absence of supporting evidence. He must never attribute to his characters more in the way of motive and intention than the evidence warrants' (Atkinson pp. 6 and 65). Thus one of the major differences between Th. and a modern historian lies in what is meant by 'evidence': a modern historian is reluctant to go beyond his 'hard core' and will only do so when certain fairly well established criteria are fulfilled, but Th. is anxious to expand his 'hard core' on the evidence of normal human behaviour. See also H. White (1982) pp. 123-4; also above, nn. 153 and 158-9, and below, nn. 161, 162, 163. And contrast Momigliano (1984) p. 51.

161. It is in my opinion of great importance that Th. includes the phrase κατὰ τὸ ἀνθρώπινον, 'given human nature', in his statement at 22.4: it expressly provides a guaranteed basis for his extrapolation from the 'hard core' of his material. In the absence of modern concepts such as 'laws of economics' and so on, human nature was the one thing on which he could rely to draw his 'nomological inferences'. See De Ste Croix pp. 29-33.

162. Hence my translation of τὸ σαφὲς ... σκοπεῖν as 'a realistic view' (above, p. 11). I have chosen the word 'realistic' advisedly. Not only does it assist the contrast with τὸ μυθῶδες, which Th. clearly considered *un*realistic, but it also encapsulates the difficulty modern readers have had in their response to Th.'s narrative: see how even Parry (1957) p. 84 can move directly from 'Th.'s firmness and *accuracy in his grasp of what really happened* on a campaign or in a battle is very striking' to 'few writers, ancient or modern, give *so convincing a sense of reality* as he does'.

163. It is of course well known that Aristotle made just such a distinction, in theory, between historians and poets (cf. n. 153, above). At *Poetics* 1451b1ff. Ar. says: 'the essential difference is that the one tells us what happened and the other the sort of thing that would happen. That is why poetry is at once more like philosophy and more worthwhile than history, since poetry tends to make general statements, while those of history are particular. A "general statement" means one that tells us what sort of man would, probably or necessarily, say or do what sort of thing, and this is what poetry aims at, though it attaches proper names; a particular statement on the other hand tells us what Alcibiades, for instance, did or what happened to him' (translated M.E. Hubbard). But this distinction is difficult to maintain in practice, especially in the case of Th., as most readers would agree. Ar. goes on to acknowledge that 'there is no reason why some things that actually happen should not be the sort of thing that would probably happen' (1451b30-2); and though Ar. is there talking about poetry (historical drama), his statement, or at least an extended version of it, seems entirely applicable to Th.'s history as seen by the historian himself. It has to be remembered that Ar., as the title of his work implies, is concerned principally with poetry, not history, and it is accepted that he 'took a low view of history' (Lucas p. 119). See too below, p. 108 n. 77.

164. Lesky p. 472, cf. Fornara p. 120; other examples cited by Grant p. 81.

165. Grant pp. 81-2, Lateiner p. 43 n. 4a.

166. 'He doth protest too much — literary, artistic considerations

were very much on his mind, he wanted his work to be a popular success'
(Grant p. 82).

167. I have borrowed my translation of ἡ λοιμώδης νόσος from
Connor (1984) p. 31 and n. 30, q.v.

168. See Stahl pp. 33-4, Kitto pp. 273-5, Strasburger (1972) pp. 33-4
(who remarks that 'suffering' is a key-word), Parry (1972) pp. 47-52,
Macleod pp. 1-14, 140-58.

169. Marc. *Vit. Thuc.* 35, 37. For some recent discussion of Th.'s
relationship to Homer see e.g. Lloyd-Jones pp. 140-4 and 203-6; also the
works of Latham and Cairns (1982), cited above, n. 158.

170. See above, pp. 7-9. Cf. also Dion. *Demosth.* 39 (1.387 Usher) on
Thuc. 1.23.1-3.

171. Denniston (1959) p. xlv.

172. Demetr. *On Style* 63. Note especially the series οὔτε ... μέν ... δέ
... δέ ... οὔτε ... μέν ... δέ ... τε ... τε ... τε ...

173. See Paul pp. 144-8.

174. See Paul p. 147, quoting *Iliad* 9.593-4, 22.61-2.

175. See Macleod pp. 143-4.

176. See Fussell pp. 115ff., quoting Bloch (pp. 107-8) on how, during
the Great War, 'there arose a prodigious renewal of oral tradition, the
ancient mother of myths and legends'. On our passage see Parry (1957)
pp. 114-15.

177. See e.g. Gabba (1981) p. 56.

178. Parry (1969) p. 116.

179. Luschnat 1203.

180. Kitto p. 274. Parry (1957) pp. 114ff. is a striking exception.

181. Fornara pp. 64-5.

182. Dion. *Thuc.* 15.

183. See pp. 39-40.

184. See e.g. Pearson (1947) pp. 47-8, Immerwahr (1960) p. 284 and
(1985) p. 447 (calling them '*pathos*-statements'), Grant pp. 83-5, J.H.
Finley (1967) pp. 126-40, Lateiner.

185. Parry (1957) p. 119.

186. See *Iliad* 5.62-3 'disaster-starting [ἀρχεκάκους] ships, which
become a disaster [κακόν] for the Trojans and the man himself', 11.604
'and this was the start of disaster [κακοῦ ... ἀρχή] for him', 22.116
'which was the start of the feud [νείκεος ἀρχή], *Odyssey* 8.81-2 'For then
did the start of suffering [πήματος ἀρχή] roll over the Trojans and
Greeks'; Hdt. 5.97.3 'These ships were the start of disasters [ἀρχή
κακῶν] for the Greeks and barbarians' (a statement criticised by Plutarch
in his essay *On the Malice of Herodotus* 861A), 6.98; Virg. *Aen.* 4.169-70 'ille
dies primus leti primusque malorum/causa fuit', 7.481-2 'quae prima
laborum/causa fuit'. See further Nisbet and Hubbard on Horace, *Odes*
2.13.2.

187. Comparing the imitation of this passage by Sallust (*J.* 44.5),
Gomme (1956) p. 370 remarks that 'in Sallust [but not, by implication, in
Th.!] it marks an artificial excitement of the emotions'. Th. is perhaps
also echoed by Virg. *Aen.* 2.369 'ubique pavor et plurima mortis imago'.

188. Rubincam has demonstrated how Th. can manipulate the
presentation of numerals for rhetorical effect (so too at 7.87.4-6, also

quoted). For the spurious accuracy of numbers see the remarks of M.I. Finley (1985) pp. 28, 43-4.

189. Cf. Aesch. *Pers.* 431-2 'nowhere else in a single day has such a large number of men died' (above p. 27 n. 157).

190. See Griffin. For plague as a popular rhetorical topic at Rome cf. Quint. 2.10.5.

191. See e.g. Grimm pp. 14ff., Eissfeldt p. 281, Ackroyd in Ackroyd and Evans pp. 86-90. On the relationship of early near-eastern and Greek literature see M.L. West (1978) pp. 3-30 (whose statement that 'Greek literature is a Near Eastern literature' cannot be cited often enough, according to Fehling (1975) p. 67 n. 1), and, on the Bible in particular, Gordon (1953) pp. 89-99 and (1962) pp. 229-30.

192. For Theseus cf. Catull. 64.76, Plut. *Thes.* 15.

193. Knox uses Th. to date the play to 425 BC; Müller has argued that it must have been produced before the plague broke out (see especially pp. 32-8). According to O. Taplin, 'the only years we can exclude with confidence as the date for the first performance of *OT* were the years of the plague' (*JHS* 106 (1986) p. 167). Cf also *Hel.* 1327ff. (412 BC).

194. M.L. West (1978) p. 213.

195. Namely, at 1.143-4.

196. References in the remainder of this section are to Book 2 unless otherwise stated.

197. See Katičič p. 195.

198. For the emotional significance of the word 'city' see again Macleod pp. 143-4.

199. 'As has been pointed out by a number of writers, ... it is a feature of fictional as well as historical stories that events should acquire importance from their outcomes. In the early stages of a conventional novel appear references to apparently trivial incidents, though the experienced reader is all too well aware that they will turn out to have significance as the story develops' (Atkinson p. 87). See also below, n. 232.

200. For chapters 18-22 see V.J. Hunter (1973) pp. 11-21.

201. Kitto p. 288. Compare Gomme (1954) p. 144: 'Nobody has yet suggested that the pestilence did not occur just then, or take the form and have the results which he describes; yet the "dramatic" effect, coming as this narrative does immediately after the Funeral Speech, is overwhelming'. See further p. 40, and the remarks of Fénelon quoted by Gossman p. 14; for some other (melo)dramatic coincidences in Th. see Grant pp. 85-7.

202. For the 'particularly powerful echo' of 41.1 see Macleod pp. 151-2, who points out that its effect is doubled when we recall the words of Solon (in Hdt. 1.32.8-9) to which both passages look back: speaking to Croesus, he says that no individual is self-sufficient but the truly blessed man is he who lives with the most advantages and dies happily. The echo of 41.1 at 51.3 is also noted by Gomme (1956) p. 157, Flashar p. 35, Allison p. 15 n. 3, and Connor (1984) p. 67 n. 39, but none of them mentions Hdt.; Allison says that 'verbal similarities between the plague description and the Funeral Oration are not extensive', while Connor compares Xen. *Mem.* 4.7.1.

203. Noted by Stahl p. 80 and Flashar p. 35.

204. Gomme (1956) p. 161 observes that Cornford (whose now famous thesis was that Th.'s history was constructed along the lines of a Greek tragedy) curiously failed to mention the dramatic reversal between the funeral speech and the plague. For further remarks on this reversal see now Flashar pp. 34ff., and for some other comments on the influence of drama on historiography see Fornara pp. 171-2, quoting Herodotus (see also above, pp. 3-4 and n. 22).

205. Parry (1969) pp. 106-18.

206. This technique was imitated and brought to perfection by Tacitus centuries later: see p. 190 below.

207. The alternative version read λιμός ('famine'), and play on the two words was already familiar from Hesiod, *WD* 243, Hdt. 7.172.2 and no doubt elsewhere. Th. repeats the link between war and plague later, at 2.59.1.

208. The passage 3.87.2-4 is quoted above, p. 31.

209. Allison's thesis is that the plague description has significant parallels with Pericles' speech at 1.140-4 which are intended to suggest that he was at least partly to blame for the disaster. See also the remarks of Sontag pp. 44-5.

210. On this see Parry (1957) pp. 171-5.

211. For these characteristics of Pericles and Nicias see e.g. Rawlings pp. 127-35.

212. Some characteristic illustrations of this view are given by Parry (1969) pp. 106ff.

213. Cf. 2.48.3 'having been ill myself and having witnessed personally others suffering' (see further above, p. 26 and n. 147).

214. Cf. 2.48.3 'But I will both say what it was like and display the <symptoms> from which, if it should ever attack again, an observer with foreknowledge should best be able to escape ignorance' (the source of Ranke's famous statement: see above, n. 32).

215. See pp. 2-3, 6-7 above.

216. For which see e.g. Kemmer pp. 77-88, Richardson on *Hom. Hymn Dem.* (5) 22-3; *TLL* 6.3.2875.21ff.

217. For a list of symptoms and many of the diseases which have been canvassed see Littman pp. 274-5. The latest contender is tularaemia (Wylie and Stubbs), but the majority opinion now is that the disease is either long since defunct or else has changed its character quite radically over the centuries (see Holladay and Poole (1979), (1982) and (1984); Longrigg).

218. See above, p. 16 and n. 93.

219. See Woodman (1977) pp. 107-8, 138 (1983) p. 150, with further references. For Th.'s form of words, κρεῖσσον λόγου, see Eur. *Suppl.* 844, *IT* 837.

220. The *praeteritio*, for which cf. Lausberg 2.277. Once again, Th. uses the appropriate verb, since the technical name for this device in Greek is παράλειψις.

221. See Luschnat 1203-4.

222. Cf. Sall. *C.* 3.2 'in primis arduom uidetur res gestas scribere, primum quod facta dictis exaequenda sunt': see Vretska ad loc. (especially his quotation of Isocr. 4.13 χαλεπόν ἐστιν ἴσους τοὺς λόγους τῷ

μεγέθει τῶν ἔργων ἐξευρεῖν) and Avenarius pp. 130ff.

223. For the numerous imitations of Th. see e.g. Gomme (1956) p. 146, and Grimm *passim*. We know from Lucian 15 that an historian of the Parthian Wars inserted into his history a completely fictitious plague modelled entirely on that of Th.

224. On these similarities see Page pp. 97-119; Weidauer. On Th.'s use of medical metaphors elsewhere in his work see e.g. Dover (1970) p. 240.

225. *Bell. Pers.* 2.22-3: see Cameron (1985) pp. 40-3.

226. This point is also made by Mittelstadt p. 148, who asks: 'Is it not possible that Th. took certain poetic liberties in his description of the plague, changing, adapting, selecting, even inventing certain of its symptoms and effects to fit the context?' Though not everyone will agree with Mittelstadt's main thesis, which is that the account of the plague operates as an extended metaphor for the disintegration of Athenian society, his article is well worth reading.

227. See e.g. Munro or Ernout and Robin ad loc.

228. Page p. 109 n. 1.

229. Gomme (1956) pp. 156-7 (my italics).

230. It might be objected that Th.'s contemporary readers, some of whom no doubt caught the plague, would have recognised any 'false symptoms'; but this is to impute modern preconceptions to them, and in any case they were in no position to query the matter since Th. says that the plague affected each person differently (51.1).

231. It is often forgotten that Th. is our *only* evidence for the plague, as for so many other events of the war. It is not mentioned by Aristophanes or in any contemporary medical writing. It is mentioned by Plato (*Symp.* 201d), but many years later. For Sophocles see above, n. 193.

232. In this context it is worth recalling just how similar is Th.'s account to that of Albert Camus in his *novel* entitled *The Plague*. See the excellent discussion of the similarity by Percival; and also above, n. 199.

233. *Thuc.* 18 (where the critic's remarks will be found particularly interesting by those modern scholars who still believe that Th.'s speeches are not largely invention).

234. Dover (1983) p. 57.

235. Gomme (1956) p. 161, a more radical version of his feelings of two years earlier (see above, n. 201).

236. *Ep. Pomp.* 3 (translated Rhys Roberts, with various borrowings from Usher 2.373ff. and adaptations of my own), on which see Scheller pp. 34-5. Dion. repeats his point in *Thuc.* 15 and 41.

237. I think it extremely likely (see pp. 42-3), but it is difficult to prove: sometimes one has to infer a response to Th. from authors who do not actually mention him by name, sometimes he is named by authors whose only interest seems to be in his style. See the survey of *Nachleben* in Schmid and Stählin pp. 207ff. and Luschnat 1266ff., and note also the work of Strebel.

238. See Lloyd, *passim*.

239. Nagy p. 222, refering to Detienne pp. 18-27 (to whom the references to Plut. and Plato are due). Nagy's whole discussion (pp. 222-42) is worth reading.

240. *Lycurg.* 8.2, 14.3, 21.1, 25.2.

241. *Laws* 829c '(The authorities should) compose speeches in commendation or reproof of each other according to the conduct of individuals ... in daily life: those who are deemed to have acquitted themselves particularly well should be honoured, while the failures should be censured' (translated T.J. Saunders).

242. *Poetics* 1448b24ff. 'Poetry soon branched into two channels, according to the temperaments of individual poets. The more serious-minded among them represented noble actions and the doings of noble persons [τὰς καλὰς ἐμιμνοῦντο πράξεις καὶ τὰς τῶν τοιούτων], while the more trivial wrote about the meaner sort of people; thus while the one type wrote hymns and panegyrics, these others began by writing invectives'. See Nagy pp. 253-5. Homer and Archilochus are often linked by ancient writers: while some of these references allude to Arch.'s borrowings from Homer (e.g. [Long.] *Subl.* 13.3), others treat them as founders of a genre (e.g. Cic. *Or.* 4, Hor. *AP* 79, Vell. 1.5.2, Quint. 10.1.46 and 59-60). Since Homer famously praised 'the great deeds of men', while Arch. was renowned for his critical poetry, it would be fascinating to know whether any author (e.g. Heracl. Pont. in his now lost *On Homer and Archilochus*) described them as the founders respectively of praising and critical poetry.

243. See e.g. Lausberg 1.109-10.

244. See Hermog. (quoted on p. 45) and Cic. *Or.* 37 and 66 (discussed on pp. 95-8).

245. See Scheller p. 66, who points to parallels with Isocrates.

246. Cf. also 16.17.8.

247. The expectation naturally reflects facts (cf. e.g. Plb. 1.14.5): much Hellenistic and Roman historiography was blatantly encomiastic (for the former see e.g. Fornara pp. 64-6, for the latter see Woodman (1977) pp. 30ff.). Atkinson remarks that in so far as history is concerned with what people did, not what they failed to do, 'it is to that extent a success story' (35). All this serves to throw into relief Th. and his Roman imitators (on whom see Chapters 3 and 4).

248. See Scheller pp. 48-50, Avenarius pp. 157-63, Fornara p. 108. Criticism of 'the enemy' (on which see further below, n. 250) is of course simply the counterpart of praising one's own side: see Detienne p. 21.

249. See Walbank on Plb. 10.21.8.

250. See e.g. Fornara p. 62 on the inheritance from epic, where the enemy is conventionally treated sympathetically and there is a dearth of villains. Similarly, German press directives of September 1939 warned that 'To present the enemy as cowardly and despicable would only make the achievements of the Wehrmacht less impressive' (Balfour p. 149).

251. Cf. how Homer was consistently represented by his scholiasts as pro-Greek: Richardson pp. 273-4.

252. Cf. especially Plut. *Mor.* 862A (*On the Malice of Herodotus*) on Hdt.'s 'special concern for Athens' and 867C 'some people consider Greece was eulogised [by Hdt.]'. These statements are all the more valuable in that Plut., given the idiosyncratic thesis of his essay, elsewhere argues that Hdt. is pro-barbarian (857A), that at 7.139.5 his praise of Athens is severely qualified (864A), and that he is actually critical of

Athens (871C-D, cf. 872A). The general grounds on which Plut. criticises Hdt. are directly comparable to those mentioned by Dion. in *Ep. Pomp.* 3: thus Hdt. uses severe language rather than moderate, he inserts irrelevant material, he omits creditable material through malice, he regularly prefers the worse of two alternative versions and the worst of various motives through malice (855A-F, 856B). Clearly both Dion. and Plut. are adopting a standard technique.

253. Cic. *Or.* 39 'primisque ab his, ut ait Theophrastus, historia commota est' (the reference presumably being to the *On Historiography*, now lost).

254. See in general Kleingünther. Also Leo pp. 45ff.

255. See in general Focke pp. 339ff. (344-5 on Hdt. and Th.), Fairweather (1984) pp. 329-30.

256. Immerwahr (1960) p. 279. It is of course true that Th. calls his own war ἀξιολογώτατον but Immerwahr again rightly notes that Th. is principally concerned with power rather than splendour (p. 277). See also Breisach pp. 12-13.

257. Cf. e.g. Lucian 8 κολακείαν ~ ἐγκώμιον, 10 ἐπαίνοις καὶ τῇ ἄλλῃ θωπείᾳ, 11 ἔπαινοι ~ κολακείαν.

258. Cf. e.g. Lucian 7 ἐπαινέσαι ~ ψευσαμένῳ 9 ἐγκώμιον ~ τἀληθοῦς ἡμαρτήκασι.

259. See Detienne pp. 21, 24-5, 53ff. (with references to Pindar and Bacchylides).

260. Thuc. 2.35.2 'Eulogies of other men are tolerable only in so far as each hearer thinks that he too has the ability to perform any of the exploits of which he hears; but whatever goes beyond that at once excites envy [φθονοῦντες] and disbelief' (the previous sentence, containing the words διὰ φθόνον, 'through envy', is also relevant); Sall. *C.* 3.2.

261. Hdt. was considered a liar primarily because of his love of (tall) stories, μῦθοι (see Murray p. 205); and μῦθοι are mentioned alongside praise by Lucian, e.g. 8 τὸν μῦθον καὶ τὸ ἐγκώμιον, 10 μύθοις καὶ ἐπαίνοις. Cf. also 59-60 and Joseph. *Contr. Ap.* 1.25.

262. Cf. e.g. Cic. *Fam.* 5.12.4 'si *liberius* (ut consuesti) agendum putabis, multorum in nos perfidiam, insidias, proditionem *notabis*' (the same collocation in Hor. *Sat.* 1.4.5), 12.16.3, Plut. *Mor.* 856D 'skilful and sophisticated flatterers sometimes mingle gentle criticisms [ψόγους ἐλαφρούς] with their otherwise continuous praises, introducing the element of frankness [τὴν παρρησίαν]'. Cf. Avenarius pp. 161-2.

263. Cf. e.g. Plb. 38.4.3-5, Suet. *Claud.* 41.2 'neque libere neque vere', Lucian 61 ἐλεύθερος ... παρρησίας μεστός ... ἀλήθεια ἐπὶ πᾶσι.

264. E.g. Plb. 8.9-11 (see Walbank's introductory n.), Nep. *Alc.* 11, Plut. *Mor.* 862D, *Lys.* 30, Lucian 59.

265. *Ep. Pomp.* 6 (2.394 Usher): see Sacks pp. 71, 73 and Schultze p. 125.

266. Sall. *C.* 3.2 'plerique quae delicta reprehenderis maleuolentia et inuidia dicta putant' (precisely the charge Plb. was rebutting: above, n. 263).

267. See Bramble pp. 190-204 and Dickie.

268. Plb. 8.10.1 πικρία, Dion. *Ep. Pomp.* 6 (2.396 Usher) 'a reputation for malice', Plut. *Mor.* 855A κακοήθεια.

269. For Th. as the best historian see e.g. Dion. *Thuc.* 2; for his concern for truth, ibid. 8. (I am leaving aside for the moment the important question of what exactly is meant by 'truth' here, to which I return at pp.73-40 and 82-3.)

270. Since Dion.'s own purpose is to criticise Th., it is interesting to note that he prefaces his remarks with the standard disclaimer of malice: *Thuc.* 2 'I certainly would not start now to manifest against the foremost of historians a malice [κακοήθειαν] which is not suitable to the character of a free man [ἐλευθέροις] ... If my arguments are truthful [ἀληθεῖς] ...'. Compare also Lucian 61 (above, n. 263).

271. E.g. recently Evans; earlier examples are E. Meyer and F. Jacoby.

272. For his pessimism see Stahl and Pouncey; for his attitude towards Athens see the references in Rhodes p. 36 nn. 1 and 3, especially the article by De Ste Croix (*Historia* 3 (1954) pp. 1-41, though some of his premises are not accepted by Rhodes himself).

273. De Ste Croix p. 23.

274. Immerwahr (1960) p. 275. Cf. also Kazazis pp. 160ff., especially 162.

275. Hermog. *De Ideis* 421.24-422.10 (translated D.A. Russell).

276. Quint. 10.1.73 'densus et breuis et semper instans sibi Thuc., dulcis et candidus et fusus Herod.'

277. *Or.* 39 'sine ullis salebris quasi sedatus amnis fluit' (Hdt.), *De Or.* 2.56 'ita creber est rerum frequentia ut uerborum prope numerum sententiarum numero consequatur: ita porro uerbis est aptus et pressus ut nescias utrum res oratione an uerba sententiis illustretur'.

278. Cf. also 51 'There are few who are capable of understanding the whole of Th., and not even they can understand some of the passages without resorting to a grammatical commentary'.

279. Denniston (1952) pp. 5-6, 20-1.

280. Collingwood p. 29.

281. Cf. Gay p. 5.

282. Gay p. 200.

283. Gay pp. 31-2. Suzanne Curchot, Gibbon's one-time sweetheart, observed that Tacitus was his model (Gay pp. 23-4 and n. 3), and we know from the man himself, who said that 'the style of an author should be the image of his mind', that he experimented long and hard before he hit upon the right style (see *Memoirs of My Life* (ed. B. Radice, 1984) p. 158). For some other examples of 'Tacitism' see Weinbrot Chapter 1 § II.

284. Boyer p. 42.

285. Elton p. 135.

286. Elton pp. 136-7.

2
Theory: Cicero

Introduction: the letter to Lucceius and the *De Oratore*

Though Cicero's friends repeatedly expressed the hope that he
would embark on a major work of history,[1] any such project
remained unwritten by the time of his murder in December 43
BC. Cornelius Nepos, the dedicatee of Catullus' poetry book and
himself a historian, had no doubt that a unique opportunity had
thereby been missed:[2]

> This is the one branch of Latin literature which not only
> fails to match Greece but was left crude and inchoate by the
> death of Cicero. He was the one man who could and should
> have fashioned historical discourse in a worthy rhetorical
> manner [*historiam digna uoce pronuntiare*] ... I am uncertain
> whether the country or historiography lost more by his
> death.

Yet despite Cicero's omission, the great orator was nevertheless
responsible for various statements concerning historiography to
which modern scholars have attached considerable importance.[3]
The two most substantial and famous of these statements both
belong to the year 55 BC.

In the middle of April Cicero wrote a letter to his friend L.
Lucceius, advising him how to approach the work of history on
which he was engaged (*Ad Familiares* 5.12):

> Dear Lucceius,
> I have often tried to raise the following matter with you in
> person, only to be prevented by an embarrassment which is

70

uncharacteristic of my metropolitan temperament. However, now that we're apart, I feel bold enough to broach the subject. After all, a letter can't blush.

You won't believe how much I want you to celebrate my name in your writings — a quite justifiable desire, in my opinion. I know you've often indicated that this was your intention, but please excuse my impatience. You see, I always had high hopes of your particular kind of writing, but it has now exceeded my expectations and taken me by storm: I've a burning desire for my achievements to be entrusted to your monumental works as quickly as possible. It's not just that I can hope for immortality by being remembered by posterity: I also want to enjoy while I'm still alive the authority which only your work can provide — your seal of approval coupled with your literary distinction.

2   It's true that even as I write I am only too well aware of the pressure you're under from the material which you have embarked upon and already arranged. But as I see that you've almost finished your account of the Italian and Civil Wars, and you told me yourself that you've made a start on the remaining period, I don't want to miss the opportunity of asking you to consider this question. Would you prefer to incorporate my story into that remaining period or ... deal with the Catilinarian conspiracy separately from the wars with foreign enemies? As far as my reputation is concerned, I don't see that it makes much difference either way; but I'm frankly impatient and don't want you to wait till you reach the appropriate point in your continuous narrative: I'd much rather you got down to the period of the *cause célèbre* straight away and on its own terms. In addition, if you give your undivided attention to a single theme and a single personality, I can envisage even now the greater scope for rich elaboration [*ornatiora*].

Of course I'm well aware how disgracefully I'm behaving: having first landed you with this considerable responsibility (though you can always plead other engagements and turn me down), I'm now demanding elaborate treatment [*ornes*]. What if you don't think my achievements deserve elaboration

3   [*ornanda*]? Still, once the limits of decency have been passed, one should be well and truly shameless. So I repeat — elaborate [*ornes*] my activities even against your better judgement, and in the process disregard the laws of historiography [*et in eo leges historiae neglegas*]: that prejudice [*gratiam*], which

you discussed quite beautifully in one or other of your prefaces and which, you revealed, could no more influence you than Pleasure could influence Hercules in Xenophon's book, well, please don't suppress it if it nudges you strongly in my favour, but simply let your affection [*amori*] for me take a degree of precedence over the truth [*ueritas*].

If I can persuade you to take on the responsibility, I'm sure you'll find that the material will bring out the best in your fluent artistry. For it seems to me that a modest volume could be compiled if you start with the beginning of the conspiracy and end with my return from exile. On the one hand, you'll be able to capitalise on your knowledge of the civil disturbances by explaining the causes of the revolutionary movement or suggesting remedies for political crises, at the same time criticising whatever in your opinion requires criticism [*uituperanda*] and giving full and reasoned approval [*exponendis rationibus comprobabis*] to whatever you approve of. On the other hand, if you think a more outspoken [*liberius*] treatment is called for, as you often do, you can denounce the disloyalty, plotting and treachery which many people displayed towards me. For my experiences will provide you with plenty of variety [*uarietatem*] when you come to write — variety mixed with the kind of pleasure [*uoluptatis*] which can hold the attention of your readers. For nothing is more calculated to entertain a reader [*delectationem lectoris*] than changes of circumstance and the vicissitudes of fortune [*temporum uarietates fortunaeque uicissitudines*]. I didn't welcome them at the time, of course, but to read about them will be sheer delight [*iucundae*]: it's a pleasure [*delectationem*] to recall past misfortune in the safety of your own home. When people who haven't undergone any troubles of their own look on [*intuentibus*] other people's misfortunes without suffering themselves, they experience pleasure [*iucunda*] even as they take pity on them. After all, which of us does not derive pleasure [*delectat*] as well as a kind of pity from the scene of Epaminondas dying at Mantinea? Remember, he did not order the spear to be removed until he had received a satisfactory answer to his question whether his shield was safe, so that despite the pain of his wound he could die honourably with his mind at rest. Whose attention is not alerted and held [*retinetur*] by reading about Themistocles' exile and death? The monotonous regularity of the *Annales* has as much effect on us as if we were reading through official calendars; but the unpredictable and fluctuating circumstances [*ancipites uariique casus*] surrounding a great figure induce admiration, anticipation, delight, misery, hope and fear [*admirationem, exspectationem, laetitiam, molestiam, spem, timorem*]. And if they have a memorable outcome [*exitu notabili*], the reader feels a warm glow of pleasure [*iucundissima uoluptate*].

6   So I'll be all the more gratified if you do decide to separate the drama (so to speak) of my experiences from the on-going narrative in which you deal with the continuous history of events. You'll find that it has its various 'acts' and numerous examples of dramatic reversal [*multasque mutationes et consiliorum et temporum*].

Though this letter is recognised by scholars as important, it is usually for different reasons from that on which I wish to focus.[4]

It will be seen from section 3 of the letter that Cicero contrasts truth (*ueritas*) with prejudice (*gratia, amor*), from which it appears to follow that Cicero saw the truth in terms of impartiality. As modern readers and critics we have been conditioned, both by a mistaken view of Thucydides and by the conventions of modern historiography, to expect ancient historical writers to be concerned with historical truth in our sense of the term; but if we look closely at what the ancients actually say, instead of what we think they ought to be saying, we shall see that Cicero's view of the truth is by no means peculiar to him.[5] On the contrary, the view is also that of the three major historians of the classical period. Here are Sallust's words at the start of the *Bellum Catilinae* (4.2-3):

> statui res gestas populi Romani carptim ... perscribere, eo magis quod *mihi a spe metu partibus rei publicae animus liber* erat. *igitur* de Catilinae coniuratione *quam uerissume potero* paucis absoluam.

> I decided to write an historical monograph on a Roman theme, especially since I was *unaffected by ambition, fear or partisan politics*. And *for that reason* I will compose my brief account of the Catilinarian conspiracy *as truthfully as possible*.

In the *Histories* Sallust says that during the civil wars partisan politics did not cloud his view of 'the truth' (1.6 'neque me diuersa pars in ciuilibus armis mouit a uero'), words which are later echoed by Livy in his preface (5: see below, p. 131). Later still, Tacitus never even mentions 'truth', which, in the limited sense under discussion, has to be inferred from his coded references to *neque amore ... et sine odio* in the *Histories* (1.1.3)[6] and to *sine ira et studio* in the *Annals* (1.1.3). Finally we should note that even Lucian, whose book on historiography is the only one to have survived from the ancient world and who is always appealed to by scholars as the ultimate authority on 'truth', in fact takes exactly the same view as Cicero and the other historians.[7]

If we can rid ourselves of the mistaken notion that the ancients' view of historical truth was the same as ours, we will be able readily to appreciate why truth and falsehood were seen in terms of prejudice and bias.[8] In both Greek and Roman society, political life was based on a code of honour, with each man pursuing his own τιμή or *gloria*.[9] Now 'envy is characteristic ... of all honour societies, since the man of honour is anxious to promote his own honour at the expense of the honour of others. There is only a limited amount of honour at hand, and one resents and envies the possession of it by other people'.[10] In classical terms, one man's τιμή or *gloria* provoked the φθόνος or *inuidia* of others;[11] and since the historian was responsible for recording and perpetuating men's honour in as elaborate a medium as possible, he found himself in a particularly awkward position. On the one hand he could not risk alienating one group of readers or another by appearing to be either too prejudiced in favour of someone to whom they were opposed, or too biased against someone of whom they approved.[12] This is the risk to which Tacitus testifies in his *Annals*.[13] On the other hand, the historian would not wish to appear invidious on his own part, as both Sallust and Pliny testify.[14] It was therefore quite natural for the historian to disclaim prejudice and bias by means of prefatory statements such as those quoted in the preceding paragraph. Indeed there was all the more reason for such statements if, as I suggested in Chapter 1 (pp. 41-3), ancient historiography itself could be seen in terms of praise and blame.[15]

Thus Cicero's letter to Lucceius is important for illustrating what he meant by 'the truth' in historiography; but it is of course considerably less important than the work which he published seven months later. In November 55 BC he published the *De Oratore*, a treatise on oratory which contains a two-part discussion of historiography (2.51-64). This discussion, consisting of a critique of the early Roman historians (51-61) and an account of how history should be written (62-4), can fairly be described as the most valuable treatment of its subject to have come down to us from ancient Rome.[16] Yet despite the attention which has been paid to it, its key section on the theory of historiography has been consistently and fundamentally misunderstood. It is therefore this section on which I shall be concentrating in the present chapter.

The *De Oratore* is a dialogue, set thirty-six years earlier in 91 BC, between various orators and politicians who were prominent at the time. In the part of Book 2 which concerns us, the conversation is between M. Antonius, who was the most famous orator of his day and is the principal speaker, and L. Licinius Crassus and Q. Lutatius Catulus. After some preliminary paragraphs, which in part recapitulate points made during the previous day's discussion in Book 1, Antonius at length promises to give his view of the whole field of oratory (29).[17] The first stage of his exposition falls into three main parts (30-50, 51-64, 65-73),[18] of which the second is our principal concern; yet historiography itself has already been introduced in the first part, and from the viewpoint of the modern reader it is instructive to see how this introduction is made.

In attempting to describe the province of the orator, Antonius says that nothing at all lies outside his field, provided that it requires elaborate and impressive treatment (34 'neque ulla non propria oratoris est res, quae quidem ornate dici grauiterque debet'). He then lists some examples (35-6): giving advice (*in dando consilio*), arousing (*incitatio*), calming (*moderatio*), prosecution, defence, encouragement (*cohortari*), criticism (*uituperare*), eulogy (*laudare*), accusation (*accusando*), consolation (*consolando*) and historiography (*historia*) — the last of which is climactically described in a series of laudatory phrases: 'the witness of crises, the illumination of reality, the life of memory, the mentor of life, the messenger of antiquity'. That historiography should feature at all in a list of such rhetorical modes strikes the modern reader as very strange, especially since Antonius has earlier stated that rhetoric 'depends upon falsehood' (30 'mendacio nixa');[19] but, like Cornelius Nepos already quoted, Antonius takes it for granted that it is an orator who should write history. The full implications of this assumption become clear in the second part of Antonius' exposition,[20] where historiography is exclusively the subject under discussion.[21]

The deficiencies of the early Roman historians

As I have already said (above, p. 74), Antonius' discussion of historiography falls into two complementary sections, the first of which (51-61) he begins with a question: 'What kind of an orator, how great a speaker, do you think should write history?' ('Qualis oratoris et quanti hominis in dicendo putas esse historiam scribere?'). In the light of the praise heaped on historiography at 36 above, this question clearly invites the answer 'Very great indeed'. Yet Catulus' reply comes in two parts, of which only the first meets our expectations: 'Very great indeed, if you're talking about Greek historiography, but not if you're talking about ours, which doesn't require an orator at all. The sole criterion is not to be a liar'. This reply provides Antonius with the cue for a comparative critique of the early Roman historians and their Greek predecessors.

The critique begins as follows (51-4):

'Atqui, ne nostros contemnas,' inquit Antonius, 'Graeci quoque ipsi sic initio scriptitarunt, ut noster Cato, ut Pictor, ut
52 Piso: erat enim historia nihil aliud nisi annalium confectio, cuius rei memoriaeque publicae retinendae causa ab initio rerum Romanarum usque ad P. Mucium pontificem maximum res omnis singulorum annorum mandabat litteris pontifex maximus referebatque[22] in album et proponebat tabulam domi, potestas ut esset populo cognoscendi, eique
53 etiam nunc annales maximi nominantur. Hanc similitudinem scribendi multi secuti sunt, qui sine ullis ornamentis monumenta solum temporum, hominum, locorum gestarumque rerum reliquerunt; itaque qualis apud Graecos Pherecydes, Hellanicus, Acusilas fuit aliique permulti, talis noster Cato et Pictor et Piso, qui neque tenent, quibus rebus ornetur oratio — modo enim huc ista sunt importata — et, dum intellegatur quid dicant, unam dicendi laudem putant esse brevitatem.
54 Paulum se erexit et addidit maiorem historiae sonum vocis vir optimus, Crassi familiaris, Antipater; ceteri non exornatores rerum, sed tantum modo narratores fuerunt.' 'Est,' inquit Catulus 'ut dicis; sed iste ipse Caelius neque distinxit historiam varietate colorum[23] neque verborum conlocatione et tractu orationis leni et aequabili perpolivit illud opus; sed ut homo neque doctus neque maxime aptus ad dicendum, sicut potuit, dolavit; vicit tamen, ut dicis, superiores.'

But you mustn't be too hard on our historians: after all, in the beginning the Greeks too wrote just like Cato, Pictor and Piso.
52 For historiography was simply an aggregate of the annals. Indeed, it was with this in mind,[24] and also to preserve some kind of public record, that each high priest from the beginning of Roman history down to the pontificate of P. Mucius entrusted all the events of each year to literary form, transposed them onto a whiteboard, and displayed the board at his official residence in the interests of public information. The
53 *Annales Maximi* are still so called even today, and it was this kind of writing which many historians followed: they transmitted, without any elaboration, only plain notices of dates, persons, places and events. So, just as the Greeks had their Pherecydes, Hellanicus, Acusilas etc., we had their equivalents in Cato, Pictor and Piso, who did not possess the subjects required to produce elaborate discourse, which have been imported here only recently. Provided their reports were intel-
54 ligible, they thought brevity was the sole criterion of praise. It's true that Crassus' friend Antipater, an admirable man, gave a better account of himself and employed a more rhetorical form of historiography; but all the others only recorded their subjects without elaborating them.

You're right, of course, said Catulus. But even Crassus' friend Coelius failed to highlight his history with chiaroscuro, nor did he smoothe his work by the arrangement of words or the slow and regular movement of his discourse: rather, he hacked away like the man of limited ability that he was, neither a scholar nor even particularly suited to rhetoric. Still, as you say, he was better than his predecessors.

This passage is of vital importance since it specifies the precise areas to which Antonius will pay attention at 62-4 in his discussion of how historiography should be written. Thus 51-4 and 62-4 are complementary, the former providing the necessary background to the latter (see further below, pp. 88-9).

Here at 51-4 two points require emphasis. First, Antonius twice draws a distinction between the 'hard core', on which historiography is based, and its elaboration, of which the art of historiography consists. At 53 he calls the former *monumenta*, which he subdivides into the four elements of time, person, place and event; the latter he describes as *ornamenta*. Then at 54 he uses the generic term *res* ('subjects') for the former, and *exornatores* for

would-be elaborators. Second, the elaboration which Antonius
has in mind has *nothing to do with style.* Just as the core-elements
(53) are *res* (54), so the items required to produce elaborate
discourse are also *res* (53 'quibus *rebus* ornetur oratio'). In other
words, Antonius is talking about the elaboration of *content by
means of content,* a concept which is puzzling for us but fully
explained in the sections which follow (pp. 83-93). That this is
Antonius' meaning is confirmed by his exchange with Catulus
over Coelius Antipater (54). It is to be inferred from *ceteri non
exornatores rerum* that Coelius himself was an *exornator rerum,* as
Catulus readily grants ('Est ... ut dicis'):[25] where he fell down, in
Catulus' opinion, was style ('neque distinxit ... dolauit'), which is
therefore a different matter from the *exornatio* about which
Antonius has been talking. And indeed Catulus' reservations
about Coelius' style are clearly signalled as an interruption of
Antonius' main argument, since he concludes his little speech by
returning to his initial agreement with what Antonius said ('uicit
tamen, *ut dicis,* superiores').[26]

In the remainder of this section, Antonius first (55-8) provides
a potted history of Greek historiography in order to contrast its
rhetorical nature with the unrhetorical nature of Roman historiography just described in 51-4. Then, after some further
exchanges with Catulus (59) and other discursive remarks (60-1),
Antonius at last says 'But I return to my point', by which he
means the question to which Catulus gave a two-part answer at
51 above (p. 76).

How history should be written

In the second part of his discussion of historiography (62-4)
Antonius gives his own extended answer to the question which he
raised at 51 and which he now begins by repeating in a slightly
different form:[27]

```
     1        2                3      4
62 Videtisne quantum munus sit oratoris historia? haud scio an
   5      (3)           6       (2)                   4
   flumine orationis et uarietate maximum, neque tamen eam
   7      8                               9        10
   reperio usquam separatim instructam rhetorum praeceptis
```

(1)

(‹s›ita sunt enim ante oculos).

┌─ 11 ─┐
nam quis nescit primam esse historiae legem, ne quid falsi

dicere audeat? deinde ne quid ueri non audeat? ne qua

63   suspicio gratiae sit in scribendo, ne qua simultatis? haec

┌─── (11) ───┐
scilicet fundamenta nota sunt omnibus; ipsa autem exae-

12   13   12   14
dificatio posita est in rebus et uerbis. rerum ratio ordinem

┌─── (6) ───┐
temporum desiderat, regionum descriptionem; uult etiam

15   16
— quoniam in rebus magnis memoriaque dignis consilia

(15)   17
primum, deinde acta, postea euentus exspectentur — et de

16   ┌─ 15 ─┐
consiliis significari quid scriptor probet, et in rebus gestis

declarari non solum quid actum aut dictum sit sed etiam

17
quo modo, et cum de euentu dicatur, ut causae explicentur

omnes, uel casus uel sapientiae uel temeritatis, hominum-

┌─ 15 ─┐
que ipsorum non solum res gestae sed etiam, qui fama ac

nomine excellant, de cuiusque uita atque natura.

13   14   (3)
64   uerborum autem ratio et genus orationis fusum atque

(5)
tractum et cum lenitate quadam aequabili profluens, sine

hac iudiciali asperitate et sine sententiarum forensium

aculeis persequendum est.

(2)   1   (8)   10
Harum tot tantarumque rerum uidetisne ulla esse praecepta

9   10
quae in artibus rhetorum reperiantur?

62 Don't you see how great a task history is for an orator? In terms of fluency of discourse and variety it is probably his greatest task, yet I can't find a separate treatment of the subject anywhere in the rules of rhetoric (and they're easily available for inspection).

Everyone of course knows that the first law of historiography is not daring to say anything false, and the second is not refraining from saying anything true: there should be no suggestion of prejudice for, or bias against, when you

63 write. These foundations are of course recognised by everyone, but the actual superstructure consists of content and style. It is in the nature of content, on the one hand, that you require a chronological order of events and topographical descriptions; and also that you need — since in the treatment of important and memorable achievements the reader expects (i) intentions, (ii) the events themselves, and (iii) consequences — in the case of (i) to indicate whether you approve of the intentions, of (ii) to reveal not only what was said or done but also in what manner, and of (iii) to explain all the reasons, whether they be of chance or intelligence or impetuousness, and also to give not only the achievements of any famous protagonist but also his life

64 and character. The nature of style and type of discourse, on the other hand, require amplitude and mobility, with a slow and regular fluency and without any of the roughness and prickliness associated with the law-courts.

These points are both numerous and important, but do you see them covered by any of the rules to be found in books entitled *Art of Rhetoric?*

This passage is impressive because much of it sounds very like what a modern historian would expect to hear. Indeed P.A. Brunt observes: 'Cicero is not expressly advocating a type of historical exposition different from that commonly employed by modern political historians.'[28] Brunt is talking about Cicero's remarks on individuals and their characters, but we may also compare the central section with the following extract from a modern manual on historiography:[29]

The historian must achieve a balance between narrative and analysis [cf. *declarari non solum quid actum aut dictum sit sed etiam quo modo*], between a chronological approach [cf. *ordinem temporum*] and an approach by topic, ... and, as necessary, passages of pure description [cf. *regionum descriptionem*].

The two are indeed very similar, as we see. It is therefore perhaps not surprising that modern commentators, as we shall observe more fully below, interpret Cicero's words as if he were one of themselves.

The foundations of historiography

Of the opening of the above passage P.G. Walsh has written as follows:[30]

> The basic canons of history are ably propounded by Antonius in the *De Oratore*. 'For surely everyone knows', he says, 'that the first law of history is to dare to say nothing false, and again to omit nothing which is true. And in writing there should be no suspicion of either partiality or hatred.'

A.P. Kelley expresses a similar point thus:[31]

> Truthfulness is the essential quality ... Accuracy is the very essence of history. It was laid down as a fundamental law by Antonius in the *De Oratore* that the historian must be, above all else, truthful in recounting the facts ... Cicero had a great interest in historical accuracy.

And again P.A. Brunt, whose contribution to the subject is intended to promote a general thesis different from that of Walsh, has written:[32]

> It was natural for Cicero to emphasise that the historian must be truthful. 'Nam quis nescit primam esse historiae legem ... haec scilicet fundamenta nota sunt omnibus.'

Yet for two reasons these comments entirely misrepresent what Cicero has in fact written.

In the first place it should be clear from the numbered words (above) that the passage is a unified whole and that Cicero returns at the end to the point which he made at the beginning. The passage, in other words, exemplifies ring-composition, and within its outer frame (emphasised by edentation) there is a clearly articulated argument which must be taken as a whole. To extract a sentence or two and say 'this is what Cicero believed', as scholars have done, is to distort Cicero's meaning.[33]

The implication of Antonius' opening question is that his listeners, like the early historians already mentioned at 51-3, do *not* see how great a task history is for an orator.[34] It is precisely for this reason that he proceeds to rectify matters in the course of the present paragraph. *But he does not do so immediately.* Historiography is seen in metaphorical terms as a building consisting of foundations (*fundamenta*) and superstructure (*exaedificatio*), which are expressly contrasted with each other (*scilicet ... autem*). The foundations are disposed of in sentences which begin with the words *nam quis nescit* and end *nota sunt omnibus*, and which, being a further example of ring composition, constitute an interpolation into Antonius' main argument.[35] Since Antonius is concerned only with what is *not* familiar to his listeners, as we have just seen, and since he twice explicitly says that the 'first and second laws of historiography' *are* familiar, as we have also seen,[36] it follows that the foundations are not his principal concern at all. Thus the laws of historiography are subordinate to what is said in the rest of the paragraph, which is exactly the opposite of what scholars have thought.[37] This interpretation is confirmed by its exact correspondence with sections 51-3 above. There the truthfulness of the historian is taken for granted and is therefore a familiar notion, but the rhetorical techniques required for historiography are said to have been imported into Italy only recently: this is given as the reason why they were unfamiliar to the early Roman historians and presumably explains why they are still unfamiliar to Antonius' listeners. Antonius himself, however, is in a privileged position, as his acquaintance with Greek historiography and its techniques, amply demonstrated in the intervening sections (55-9), makes clear.[38]

In the second place it should be clear from the context that by the 'laws of historiography' Cicero does not mean what scholars think he means. Antonius' first pair of rhetorical questions, dealing with *falsum* and *uerum*, are explained by his second pair, which deal with *gratia* and *simultas*.[39] Thus Cicero here sees truth only in terms of impartiality (the historian should not show prejudice for or bias against anyone); and though this interpretation will undoubtedly seem contentious to some readers, Cicero's meaning is confirmed by his letter to Lucceius, written only a few months earlier, in which he wrote: 'Elaborate my activities even against your better judgement, and in the process disregard the laws of historiography [*et in eo leges historiae neglegas*]: that prejudice [*gratiam*], which you discussed ..., well, please don't suppress it if it nudges you strongly in my favour, but simply let your affection [*amori*] for me take a degree of precedence over the truth [*ueritas*]'. Here the wording is virtually identical to that in the *De Oratore*, and the context of the letter makes it plain, as we have already observed, that Cicero resembles the major Roman historians in seeing truth in terms of impartiality (above, pp. 73-4).[40] Thus, contrary to what scholars have generally believed, Cicero in the *De Oratore* does not present truth as the opposite of what we would call fiction.[41]

I hope that in this section I have succeeded in demonstrating, first, that Antonius' remarks on the laws of historiography are relatively unimportant in the context of his argument, and, second, that the truth required by those laws is quite different from what we today might call 'historical truth'.[42] If these conclusions are correct, it follows that we may legitimately concentrate our attention on the superstructure (*exaedificatio*) which is Antonius' principal concern and that we should not be prevented by modern misconceptions from explaining that superstructure in terms of the rules of rhetoric to which Antonius refers at both the beginning and the end of the passage.

The superstructure of historiography: content and style

Antonius explicitly states that the superstructure of historiography consists of *res* and *uerba*, content and style: it is therefore precisely these two items which might naturally have been mentioned in the rhetorical handbooks but which, since they are not mentioned there, Antonius now proceeds to discuss here. This line of argument is confirmed by the very division of the *exaedificatio* into content and style, *res* and *uerba*, since this division is itself one of the most basic in rhetorical theory and practice. As Quintilian says, 'every speech consists of content and style [*rebus et uerbis*]'.[43]

Content. The requirements which Antonius lists under the heading of *rerum ratio* ('nature of content') are introduced by the two verbs *desiderat* ('requires') and *uult* ('needs'), the first of which tells us that a writer of history requires *ordinem temporum* and *regionum descriptionem*. Now according to the usual interpretation of this sentence, Cicero is here referring to accurate dating and scientific topography. Thus Brunt writes:[44]

> With the diversity of eras and fluctuations in calendars in the ancient world, chronological exactitude was not easy to attain or to present clearly, especially if the historian, like Thucydides or Polybius, often had to transfer the reader's attention from one part of the world to another and perhaps to show how transactions in different parts reacted on each other. Elsewhere Cicero goes out of his way to commend Atticus' chronological handbook (*Orator* 120) and evinces a special interest in dating events ... It was a patent truth that, in the absence of maps, military operations, which form a large part of history as Cicero and the ancients in general conceived it, would be unintelligible, at least if they took place in unfamiliar lands, unless the scenes were carefully described. Polybius, who inveighed against fictitious descriptions, also insisted on the need for accurate and relevant topographical explanation.

And Walsh writes that Cicero

> is at pains to distinguish clearly between the functions of history and oratory, showing that history is different both in its material and in its treatment, for chronological order and geographical clarification are essential.[45]

Yet by failing to allow for the contrast between the first and second parts of Antonius' speech these scholars have entirely misrepresented what Antonius is saying.

The contrast between 'haec *scilicet* fundamenta' and 'ipsa *autem* exaedificatio' clearly indicates that the *exaedificatio* or superstructure of historiography is to be explained in terms of the rules of rhetoric to which Antonius refers at the start of the passage (see above, pp. 81 and 83). Now speeches were conventionally divided into six sections, one of which was the *narratio* or 'statement of the case';[46] and if we look at the rules for the *narratio* as expressed by (among others) Cicero himself, we shall see that Antonius has simply transferred their requirements to historiography. Thus Cicero said (*Inu.* 1.29) that 'The *narratio* will be clear if we explain first that which happened first, and keep to the order of events

and times [*temporum ordo*]', repeated at *Rhet. Herenn.* 1.15 'Our
narratio will be clear if we set out first whatever happened first,
and preserve the order of events and times [*temporum ordinem*]'.[47]
Similarly, as Cicero himself again said, the *narratio* required a
demonstration that 'the place was suitable for the events about to
be related' (*Inu.* 1.29):[48] this in its turn might give rise to a digression,[49] which could be 'of various kinds ..., for example, the
praise of ... places or the description of regions [*descriptio
regionum*]'.[50] Thus Antonius is not recommending any sophisticated techniques such as those suggested by the scholars above;
since identical phraseology to his occurs in the other passages I
have quoted, it is clear that he is offering standard rhetorical
advice to the effect that the historian, like the forensic orator,
should not invert the natural order of events and should enliven
his work with topographical digressions.[51]

We have just seen that the two requirements which Antonius
introduced by the verb *desiderat* derive from the requirements of
the *narratio*, and it is important to note that exactly the same is
true of those which he introduces by the verb *uult*. Antonius says
that historiography requires mention of the 'intentions, events
and consequences' associated with any important and memorable issue (*consilia, acta, euentus*), and also the elaboration thereof
(the manner in which things were done or said; the reasons for
things, whether they result from acts of god, a person's innate
qualities or temporary emotions like impetuousness; and a
person's life and character). And again it is Cicero himself who
makes it clear that most of these elements are also those of the
narratio. In *Part. Or.* 31-2 he says:

> Our *narratio* must be clear and convincing [*probabiliter*], but it
> can also be entertaining [*suauitatem*] ... It will be convincing if
> the events correspond to the individuals, times and places
> involved [*personis, temporibus, locis*], and if we set out the reason
> [*causa*] for each event [*facti*] and consequence [*euenti*] ... It will
> be entertaining if it induces surprise [*admirationes*] and
> suspense [*exspectationes*], and if it involves unexpected out-
> comes [*exitus inopinatos*], conflicting emotions [*interpositos motus
> animorum*], dialogues between individuals [*colloquia person-
> arum*], grief, anger, fear [*metus*], delight [*laetitias*] and passion
> [*cupiditates*].

And in *Inu.* 1.29 he says:

The *narratio* will be convincing [*probabilis*] if it appears to contain elements which customarily appear in real life [*in ueritate*]: if the proper qualities of the individuals are maintained, if reasons for their actions [*causae factorum*] are plain, ... and if the subject-matter fits in with the character [*naturam*] of those involved.[52]

When Quintilian deals with the same points, but at greater length, he illustrates Cicero's last statement here by saying that you must make a murderer appear impetuous (*temerarium*) or the opposite, depending upon your point of view.[53] Quintilian also notes that the fourth part of a speech, the *argumentatio*, is really no more than a mirror image of the *narratio*[54] and that on this basis it is legitimate to introduce *argumenta* into the *narratio*.[55] The standard *argumenta*, as Cicero himself tells us, covered the individual concerned and his character (*personis*), the place, time, occasion, manner and conditions of the relevant event (*Inu.* 1.34-8) — a list which makes the similarity to the *narratio* abundantly clear.[56] Thus one could deal with a person's intentions (*consilia*, cf. *Inu.* 1.36)[57] or argue *ab euentu*, i.e. 'from the result of some action, when we enquire what resulted from each activity' (*Inu.* 1.42), a matter to which Cicero devotes more attention elsewhere (*Top.* 67): 'The topics of cause and effect are closely related: just as the cause reveals what results, so the result reveals the cause'.[58] Again, Cicero says that 'one can always introduce the element of chance [*casus*] ... when it can be shown that some supernatural force [*aliqua fortunae uis*] interfered with a man's intentions' (*Inu.* 2.96).[59]

The correspondence between these prescriptions for the *narratio* and those which Antonius introduces by the verb *uult* will, I hope, be obvious enough: the precise items with which orators were trained to deal were also those recommended by him for treatment in historiography. The correspondence is, of course, hardly fortuitous. Like others, Cicero defines the *narratio* as 'an exposition of events that have occurred or are supposed to have occurred' (*rerum gestarum aut ut gestarum expositio*),[60] which accords exactly with the definition of historiography as 'the exposition of events which have occurred' (*historias ... esse ... rerum gestarum ... expositionem*).[61] Given the affinity between the two types of writing, therefore, it is hardly surprising that Lucian should say that 'the body of a work of history [i.e. everything apart from the preface] is simply an extended *narratio*'.[62] Since

Lucian makes this remark immediately after he has been discussing prefaces, his words are extremely suggestive. The preface
was where a historian was expected to profess impartiality,[63]
exactly the topic to which Antonius refers in his opening
sentences about the laws of historiography; the body of the work
was where the historian was expected to deal with the narrative of
events, paying due attention to their antecedents, attendant
circumstances and consequences, exactly as Antonius recommends in his following sentences. Thus the lay-out of Antonius'
historiographical theory corresponds precisely to that of an actual
work of history.

Now it is of the greatest importance to note that each of
Antonius' prescriptions, even the most specific (e.g. the role of
chance, *casus*), falls under the heading of *inuentio*,[64] one of the five
techniques in which rhetoricians were supposed to be expert.[65] As
Quintilian said, 'Every speech consists of content and style [*rebus
et uerbis*]; with reference to content [*in rebus*] we must study
inuentio' (8 pref. 6). It is therefore equally important to realise that
none of Antonius' prescriptions is expected to deal with data
which are necessarily true; on the contrary, *inuentio* is defined by
Cicero himself as 'the devising of matter true or lifelike which will
make a case appear convincing' (*Inu.* 1.9),[66] and what is
convincing is 'that which for the most part happens or which does
not strain credibility or which contains within itself an approximation to either of these, whether it be true or false'.[67] And since
inuentio makes no distinction between the true and the probable,
but accords the same status to the latter as to the former (and
sometimes even more),[68] its prescriptions share no common
ground at all with modern historiography. Antonius and P.A.
Brunt are simply talking a different language.[69]

When Antonius requires that a historian should reveal 'how
something was done or said', his requirement is quite different
from that which a modern narrative historian imposes on himself.
A modern historian would try to satisfy the requirement by
investigating the primary sources and familiarising himself with
the appropriate terrain; naturally some questions would still
remain, which he would try to answer in terms of probability,
with himself in the role of impartial judge.[70] Antonius' historian,
however, would have automatic recourse to the rules of rhetoric
in which he had been trained; he too would deal with matters of
probability, as we have seen, but he would be unlikely to be
responding to any unanswered questions: he would see himself

in the role of advocate and would know in advance, as it were, the case which he would have to make. The reason for this is that his recourse to rhetoric necessarily involved *inuentio*, which, as D.A. Russell has remarked, 'is simply the "discovery" of what requires to be said in a given situation, the implied theory being that this is somehow already "there" though latent'.[71]

Thus when Cicero says that historiography is 'oratorical', we should remember that *orator* is the Latin word for 'advocate'. Cicero is referring to the processes which have just been described and which are different from those in which modern narrative historians are engaged. On the other hand, it is interesting to note that modern economic or sociological historians, if they are concerned with investigating aspects of a society for which there is little or no hard evidence, will often appeal to certain 'models' which are partly based on the evidence of other known societies and are partly theoretical. There is thus a sense in which ancient historiography resembles certain forms of modern historiography, since the ancients had their rhetorical models which were based partly on existing cases in historical and other writing (see above, p. 27) and partly on the theoretical works of authors such as Cicero himself. Yet because the ancients applied their rhetorical models to *narrative* history, and because narrative history is still recognisable and indeed flourishing today, modern scholars tend to assimilate the ancient (and in fact unfamiliar) genre to the modern (and familiar), and thus fail to appreciate how different is the one from the other. It is for this reason that modern scholars, though they may often apply the word 'rhetorical' to classical historiography, do not mean by it what Cicero meant.[72]

How does the theory of *inuentio* work in practice? At 53 above (pp. 76-8) Antonius complained that the early Roman historians did little more than reproduce the techniques and conventions of the annals: they transmitted merely plain notices (*monumenta*) of times, persons, places and events, without any attempt at elaborating them (*sine ullis ornamentis*). What Antonius has in mind, as is made clear by one of the early historians themselves,[73] is presumably the kind of triumphal notice which Livy reproduces in his work (e.g. 36.40.11 'P. Cornelius consul triumphauit de Bois', 'The consul P. Cornelius celebrated a triumph over the Boi'). While such notices correspond fairly closely in general format to the *fasti triumphales* ('triumphal records') which were set up in the late first century BC by Augustus,[74] modern scholars are uncertain about their precise relationship with, and dependence on, any of the earlier categories of record, such as the annals, which are known or thought to have existed.[75] Whatever the truth of this complicated problem might be, it is at least quite likely that these earlier records transmitted the four vital elements which occur in the example from Livy: namely, time (the consulship),[76] person (P. Cornelius), place (the Boi were a Gallic tribe) and event (the triumph presupposes a victory in battle). This was evidently Cicero's view: the annals-like work of the early historians contained precisely the four elements with which Antonius' rhetorical requirements at 62-4 were equipped to deal (see above, pp. 84-6).[77] I shall therefore take the 'Livian' type of triumphal notice as my hypothetical example in what follows.

The qualifications for a triumph were a victory over a foreign enemy and the slaughter of 5,000 of them — qualifications which bring to mind Cicero's definition of historiography as the genre in which 'regions or battles are regularly described' (below, p. 95). Thus a triumphal notice inevitably invited the writer to compose a *descriptio regionis* and a *descriptio pugnae*, both of which were standard issue in rhetorical training.[78] Let us consider the second of these in more detail. A rhetorical theorist in the second century AD writes as follows:

> We describe events if we take into account their antecedents, their attendant circumstances, and their consequences. For example, if we are describing a war, we shall first of all mention the preliminaries such as the generals' speeches, the outlay on both sides, and their fears; next, the attacks, the slaughter, and the dead; finally, the victory trophy, the triumphal songs of the victors, the tears and enslavement of the victims.[79]

Naturally one could always introduce refinements. Perhaps the key battle is envisaged as having taken place at night, in which case a 'mixed description' is called for, since 'night' was also a standard topic of the *descriptio*.[80] Perhaps the victory involved the besieging of a city, in which case there are full instructions in Quintilian 8.3.67-70.[81] Indeed these instructions constitute an example in miniature of precisely the process which I am describing here:

The plain statement 'the city was stormed' no doubt includes

everything which attends such a calamity, but in its similarity
to an official communiqué it has no emotional effect. But if
you make explicit everything which the single word 'stormed'
implies, you will see houses and temples drowned in flames,
hear the crash of falling roofs ... [etc.] Provided it is all lifelike,
we shall achieve the vividness we are after.

The vividness to which Quintilian refers is the familiar technique
of 'expressing a matter in such a way that it seems to be taking
place before our very eyes' — exactly the technique which
Thucydides in my opinion was aiming for and which Cicero
implicitly urged on his friend Lucceius (see above, pp. 25-6 and
72).[82]

There is thus a distinction between a 'singular factual statement about the past', which will normally be one of the 'public
facts' of history (in our case the triumphal notice) and will constitute the hard core,[83] and the *exaedificatio* or superstructure which
required to be built up around it. This distinction may seem
artificial to our way of thinking, but that is simply because our
preconceptions about historiography are so different.[84] In fact the
distinction is exactly that which Thucydides himself voiced about
the speeches in his work, namely that there is a substratum of
truth buried (so to speak) under a superstructure of rhetorical
elaboration (see above, pp. 11-13).[85] The same distinction can be
found elsewhere in Cicero, and in Pliny. At *Brutus* 262 Cicero
describes Caesar's *commentarii* as 'ready material from which
would-be writers of history could select', and the context makes it
clear that any material so selected would then be subject to
rhetorical elaboration. In AD 107 Pliny sent Tacitus an account of
an incident in which he had been personally involved and which
he hoped Tacitus would include in his *Histories*. Pliny ends his
letter, which is clearly inspired by that of Cicero to Lucceius, with
these words (7.33.10): 'This sequence of events, such as it is, you
will be able to make more notable, more distinguished and more
important, though I'm not asking you to go beyond the norm for
an incident of this type: history oughtn't to exceed the truth, and
truth is quite adequate for honourable deeds.' Here Pliny is
drawing a clear distinction between the hard core, with which he
has supplied Tacitus, and the *exaedificatio*, which Tacitus is
expected to provide.[86]

It is alo worth remembering that an analogous distinction lay
at the very heart of Greek and Roman rhetoric. Much rhetorical

training consisted in learning to elaborate *quaestiones* or *causae*, to which the Greek equivalents are θέσεις and ὑποθέσεις.[87] Indeed when Cicero wrote to his brother Quintus in 54 BC, he said this:[88]

> I was delighted to get your letter from Britain. I'd been afraid just thinking of the Ocean and the coastline. That's not to deny the other factors, of course, but they engender hope [*spei*] rather than fear [*timoris*] and I'm exercised by suspense [*exspectatione*] more than by fright [*metu*]. As for yourself, I see that you've got a marvellous topic [ὑπόθεσιν] to write about — those places [*situs*], those strange events and localities [*quas naturas rerum et locorum*], those customs [*mores*] and races [*gentes*], those battles [*pugnas*]! And what a general!

Here Cicero uses precisely the word ὑπόθεσις to describe what I have hitherto been calling the hard core. Its singular form suggests a distinction between Quintus' projected topic and the listed items which will comprise his *exaedificatio* and which, as we may infer from their familiar and conventional nature, he is expected to elaborate according to the rhetorical rules of probability and the rest.

If we now return to our example of the hard core of historiography, namely the triumphal notice, we find that Cicero himself complains that many such notices are simply false. In the course of a discussion of funeral eulogies, by which aristocrats commemorated the achievements of their families for posterity, he says:[89]

> Yet the writing of Roman history has been falsified by these eulogies, since they contain many instances of events which never took place: false triumphs, extra consulships, false genealogies and transfers to the people ...

Livy too makes a similar complaint,[90] yet it may well be asked how these authors can complain that history has been falsified while at the same time they were promoting a method of writing history which depended so heavily on rhetorical *inuentio*. The explanation of the paradox would seem to be that the Romans required the hard core of history to be true and its elaboration to be plausible, and further that they saw no contradiction between these two requirements but rather regarded them as complementary. Thus if a historian had reason to believe that his hard core was false, it seems that he was debarred from using it for the purposes of *exaedificatio*. If, on the other hand, an historian was faced with an awkward but true hard core, he was under an obligation not to omit it:[91] on the contrary, he should employ all his rhetorical skill to put a good interpretation upon it. Such a challenge was indeed the very essence of rhetoric.[92]

To our modern way of thinking it seems very strange to insist that the hard core should be true when the elaboration of that hard core is by definition (in our terms) false. Yet clearly matters did not present themselves this way to the ancients.[93] On the contrary, the concept of a true hard core seems to have been the very thing which distinguished historiography from other types of literature. In 60 BC Cicero sent to Atticus a sketch of his consulship (*commentarium consulatus mei*) in Greek, with the remark that its contents were 'not encomiastic but historical'.[94] Since a *commentarius* was by definition supposed to be a factual account,[95] Cicero's choice of words suggests that he was sending merely a list of hard core elements; but we happen to know from a later letter that the sketch was in fact an elaborate rhetorical composition:[96] Atticus might therefore have been forgiven for wondering in which genre Cicero had been operating — eulogy, where a basis in truth was not required, or historiography, where it was.[97] Cicero's reassurance is designed to forestall Atticus' puzzlement, and also to enhance his own reputation, since an historiographical account, being based in truth, would presumably carry more authority.[98]

This convention raises the whole question of what constitutes a hard core element. Since the hard core is a matter of content, as Antonius said at 54 above (pp. 76-8), and since the *exaedificatio* also involves matters of content, as Antonius makes clear at both 53 and 63, there is no intrinsic means of distinguishing the one from the other.[99] A time-honoured and seemingly fundamental datum of Roman history could be the product of *exaedificatio* and hence false; a neglected and apparently trivial detail could be a core element and hence (but by no means necessarily) true.[100] Given the rhetorical nature of ancient historiography, the relative significance of such data is no guide, since it was the essence of rhetoric to inflate the less significant and deflate the more. It is true that we, with our modern conception of historiography and our research expertise in such areas as archaeology and topography, can on a limited number of occasions isolate the (to us) fictional elements in a particular account.[101] But the ancients themselves, with their different conception of historiography and no criterion of judgement except that of plausibility, had neither the instinct nor the capability to do so.[102] The implications for the modern study of the ancient world are of course momentous, but scholars do not yet seem to have come to terms with them.

Thus the ancients saw a theoretical distinction between the core element and the superstructure of historiography in terms of truth, although in practice the distinction was usually impossible for them to make. If we, with our superior knowledge, were to say to them that a given core element was false, I imagine they would be glad of the information: particularly in the Augustan age, when intellectual life was inspired by the example of Alexandrian scholarship, there was a general desire for increasingly exact knowledge, and historians, like poets, were always on the alert to correct their predecessors.[103] This was simply an aspect of literary *aemulatio*.[104] If, on the other hand, we were to say to an ancient historian that a given example of *exaedificatio* was untrue, he would no doubt reply, with some indignation, 'It *must* have been like that'.[105] To use the language of Antonius at 53, the *monumenta* and *ornamenta* of historiography were both important, but each had its own terms of reference.[106] It is in acknowledgement of this that Livy wrote in his preface: 'New historians always think either that they have some more exact knowledge to impart to the subject matter or that their literary skill will improve on the inferior standards of their predecessors'.[107]

Since Antonius' remarks on truth and falsehood at 62 are to be seen in terms of impartiality and prejudice (above, p. 82), he does not contradict himself when at 63 he requires that content be elaborated by means of *inuentio*.[108] Yet Brunt, quoting Antonius' praise of historiography at 36 (above, p. 75), has argued that since 'history furnished lessons indispensable to the general and statesman', it was necessary that it should also be true: 'as a mendacious witness, it would serve no useful end'.[109] Yet Brunt fails to complete the quotation, which goes on: 'Whose voice but the orator's can entrust her [sc. historiography] to immortality?'. And in the complete sentence, as Wiseman has remarked, the dilemma in which we moderns find ourselves recurs: 'the orator provides a style worthy of the material, but also a technique that cannot help but distort it'.[110] Brunt has simply imputed to the ancients a way of thinking which is prevalent today, a practice which he elsewhere rightly criticises.[111] The ancient evidence is actually different from that which Brunt supposes. Deliberative oratory often aimed to impart moral advice, yet it did not eschew the quintessentially rhetorical technique of *amplificatio* which is at the opposite end of the scale from truth.[112] Indeed Cicero recognised that Xenophon's portrait of Cyrus was beneficial precisely because it was written 'not according to historical truth but as the image of a just ruler'.[113] It has been shown that in practice Livy did not fail to distort 'the truth' in order to enhance the moral aspects of his work;[114] his contemporary Diodorus expressly stated that fictitious myths had moral value, and a similar point was discussed at considerable length by another contemporary, Strabo.[115] Finally Quintilian, in a passage which seems to echo a well known sentence of Cicero's *Brutus*, says that rhetoric is criticised because 'it deals in falsehood and excites the passions. Yet neither of these is disgraceful when the motive is good ... Even philosophers are sometimes permitted to tell lies [*mendacium dicere etiam sapienti aliquando concessum est*], while the orator has no option but to rouse passions if that is the only way he can lead the judge to justice. For judges are not always enlightened: often they need to be deceived in case they make a mistake.'[116] It seems from these examples, therefore, that the moral aspect of Roman historiography should not be used to argue that ancient historiography was not written according to the principles and practice of *inuentio*.

Style. At 64 Antonius at last turns to discuss the nature of historical style (*uerborum ratio*), this being the other element of which the *exaedificatio* of historiography consists (above, pp. 78-80, 83). His statement that the style of historical writing should be ample, mobile and fluent reappears in the work which Cicero published nine years later, the *Orator*, where the same river- or stream-metaphor is used (66): 'the style should be mobile and fluent, without the contortions and bitterness of the law-courts' ('*tracta* quaedam et *fluens* expetitur, non haec contorta et acris oratio'). Earlier in the same work Cicero gave a more detailed account of the style which, by implication, was best suited to historiography (37-8): it demanded a fullness of vocabulary, freer rhythms than forensic oratory, symmetry of sentences, rounded periods, and above all a feeling for balance and corresp.[117] Since in the same work he also describes the style of Herodotus as 'flowing along like a calm stream without any choppiness' ('sine ullis salebris quasi sedatus amnis *fluit*'), whereas that of Thucydides 'is carried headlong in a violent rush' ('incitatior fertur'), it would appear that Herodotus was Cicero's ideal historical stylist.[118] And since Seneca many years later described Cicero's own style as 'moving gradually to its conclusion, landing gently and unhurriedly, and unvaryingly true to its customary rhythm',[119] it is also clear that Cicero was recommending for historiography the very style which he had himself perfected during his long oratorical career.

After his brief remarks on style at 64,[120] Antonius at length returns to the point which he made at the beginning of his speech at 62, the ring composition (see above, p. 81) bringing to an end his discussion of how historiography should be written.[121]

Alternative definitions

Historiography and epideictic

Though Antonius' discussion is recognised by scholars as being of great importance, this assessment is based, as I have tried to argue, on a complete misunderstanding of what Antonius actually says. It is therefore worth asking whether, on this new interpretation, his words are representative of Roman historiography in general.

It is clear, both from the parallels with which I have illustrated his argument (pp. 83-6) and from the articulation of the argument itself,[122] that Antonius sees historiography in terms of *judicial* oratory, of which the *narratio* was an integral part. Yet there were of course two other types of oratory, deliberative and epideictic (or 'display') oratory,[123] and it is well known that Cicero himself elsewhere sees historiography in terms of *epideictic*.[124] At *Orator* 37 he brackets together historiography and panegyrics under the heading of epideictic,[125] and later in the same work (66) he says that 'closest to this type of oratory [i.e. epideictic] is historiography, in which the narrative is elaborate and regions or battles are regularly described [*in qua et narratur ornate et regio saepe aut pugna describitur*]'. Part of the reason for the close relationship between the two types of writing is implicit in the second of these quotations, since epideictic was recognised as a branch of oratory in which elaborate narrative was particularly at home;[126] but part of the reason was also that epideictic was the branch of oratory in which persons, places, cities and buildings were praised or (in the case of persons) blamed,[127] and such material naturally figured prominently also in historiography. Indeed it was argued in the previous chapter that classical historiography falls into two types, based on praise and blame respectively (above, pp. 41-4), and so the connection between historiography and epideictic is established at a fundamental level. Does this association with epideictic therefore invalidate Antonius' view of historiography as analogous to judicial oratory?

At first sight, the answer to this question might appear to be affirmative. We have already seen that the first stage of Antonius' general exposition (30-73) falls into three parts, of which historiography is only one (above, p. 75). In the first of these parts (30-50) his argument is essentially reductive. The rhetorical modes he lists at 35-6 (above, p. 75) almost beg to be divided into deliberative, judicial and epideictic respectively;[128] yet Antonius himself (41) prefers to use an alternative classification consisting of only two types, the so-called 'open-ended' (*infinitum*) and 'specific' (*certum*).[129] By insisting on this classification he is thus able to eliminate a third type (*laudationes* or eulogy, which Crassus had mentioned earlier in the dialogue), on the grounds that it is trivial and does not need rules of its own (43-7).[130] With this dismissal out of the way, Antonius in the third part of his exposition (65-73) attempts to dismiss open-ended topics similarly, on the grounds that they do not constitute a separate branch of rhetoric since their treatment can be subsumed under that of specific topics. By specific topics Antonius in fact means judicial topics,[131] from which it is clear that in the first and third parts of the exposition Antonius is anxious to assert the primacy of judicial oratory.[132] Sandwiched between these two parts is his discussion of historiography, which he sees in terms of judicial oratory. Has he therefore tailored his account of historiography to suit his general position? Or has he supported his general position by appealing to a neutral genre which happens to suit it?

Cicero's remarks on historiography and epideictic, quoted above, no doubt suggest that the first of these alternatives is correct; but the matter is not quite so straightforward: the ancients recognised that the three types of judicial, epideictic and deliberative oratory were in no way mutually exclusive (see e.g. Quint. 3.7.28), and the essential characteristics of one type could surface in either of the other two in a different form. I shall provide three examples of what I mean.

First, Antonius recommends that the historian should 'indicate what he approves of, something which Cicero expanded in the letter to Lucceius (above, p. 72) by recommending that his friend should indicate also what he disapproved of (*uituperanda*). The background of these recommendations is of course the moral aspect of ancient historiography, according to which advice was to be given to readers on how they should conduct their lives;[133] and the kind of oratory which was principally concerned with giving advice was deliberative, which was actually called *hortatiuum genus* by Quintilian (5.10.83). Yet some remarks of Cicero make it clear that advising was also an implicit function of epideictic (*Part. Or.* 69-71): 'There is no type of oratory capable ... of doing more service to the state,[134] nor any in which the speaker is more occupied in recognising virtue and vice ... I will give a brief account of the principles of praising and blaming [*uituperandi*], since they are a valuable guide ... to a moral life [*ad honeste uiuendum*] ... Naturally, everything associated with virtue deserves praise, while everything associated with vice deserves blame [*uituperanda*]'.

Second, Antonius requires that the historian should emphasise the role played by the individual protagonists and their characters. Now we have already noted that a judicial *narratio* might include a digression, for which the traditional topics were 'praise of men or localities' (Quint. 4.3.12 'laus hominum locorumque'). Yet the 'praise of men or localities' would naturally follow the rules for precisely these topics which were laid down in epideictic oratory and which, at least in the case of 'praise of men', Cicero dramatised as follows (*Part. Or.* 72-3):

> Because the whole *raison d'être* of these compositions is the pleasure and entertainment of the listener [*ad uoluptatem auditoris et ad delectationem*] ... we must regularly elaborate our material [*ornamenta rerum*] with surprising or unexpected events [*admirabilia et necopinata*] or ... with what will appear to be occurrences sent by heaven or fate to the person under discussion. For the listener's sense of anticipation [*exspectatio*], the element of surprise [*admiratio*] and unexpected outcomes [*improuisi exitus*] all induce a kind of pleasure [*uoluptatem*].

This passage in its turn is strikingly similar to Cicero's own description of the practice *narrationes* on which young orators trained (*Inu.* 1.27):[135]

In this type of *narratio* the key-note should be liveliness resulting from variety of material [*rerum uarietate*], contrast of characters, seriousness, gentleness, hope [*spe*], fear [*metu*], ... pity
[*misericordia*], reversals of fortune [*fortunae commutatione*],
unexpected disasters [*insperato incommodo*], sudden delight
[*subita laetitia*] and a happy outcome [*iucundo exitu*].

And of course both passages are highly reminiscent of the *historiographical* advice which Cicero gave to Lucceius (above pp. 72-3).[136]

Third, Antonius' tripartite scheme of *consilia — acta — euentus*
presupposes argument and inference, a methodology which we
more normally associate with judicial oratory; yet Quintilian
makes it clear that such a procedure could also be employed in
epideictic oratory too (3.4.8, 5.3, 7.3-6).

There is therefore much less difference between the three types
of oratory than their individual labels might suggest; and Cicero's
own ascription of historiography to epideictic in no way invali-
dates Antonius' subsuming it under judicial oratory. Historiography could be defined equally well in terms of either type;
and we must remember that Lucian, who had no axe to grind,
described a work of history as 'an extended *narratio*' (above, p.
86). I thus conclude that, on this score at least, there is nothing
unrepresentative about Antonius' account of how to write history.

Historiography and poetry

During the last ten years of his life Cicero was at work on the *De
Legibus*, towards the beginning of which there is a well known
passage of dialogue where Atticus tries to persuade Cicero to
write history (1.5):

> potes autem tu profecto satis facere in ea, quippe cum sit opus,
> ut tibi quidem uideri solet, unum hoc oratorium maxime.

> You will of course do justice to the genre, since it's a task
> which is singularly well suited to an orator — or so it has
> always seemed to you at least.

In the light of *De Oratore* 2.62-4 it is of course hardly surprising
that Atticus should impute this view to Cicero himself;[137] but
from the reservation 'tibi *quidem*' ('to you *at least*') it might be

inferred that, more than forty years after Antonius 'spoke' the words which Cicero there attributed to him, most men were still not accustomed to seeing historiography as 'a task which is singularly well suited to an orator'. Such an inference would, however, be mistaken, as a glance at the evidence reveals.

T.P. Wiseman has recently emphasised that there is a massive difference in scale between the history of Cn. Gellius, the early historian who was contemporary with the dramatic date of the *De Oratore*, and those of his predecessors, such as L. Piso and L. Cassius Hemina.[138] Gellius, for example, was treating in his *fifteenth* book an incident which Hemina had treated in his *second*; and historians writing later in the first half of the first century BC wrote at even greater length than Gellius.[139] This difference in scale can only be accounted for by the wholesale employment of rhetorical *inuentio*.[140] It therefore follows not only that Antonius' depreciatory critique of the earlier Roman historians is correct, but also that later historians *did* write history according to the rhetorical principles which he enunciated. Yet, if this is so, how is Atticus' reservation in the *De Legibus* to be explained?

It is, I think, significant that Atticus' remark arises immediately out of a comparison between historiography and poetry.[141] When we recall the close connections between Homer and both Herodotus and Thucydides (above, pp. 1-9, 28-31, 35, 38), it can be inferred that historiography was originally seen in terms of poetry and that there was a continuing debate as to their precise relationship and proximity.[142] Thus Aristotle in the fourth century BC and Polybius in the second each maintained that there were differences between historiography and poetry,[143] while much later Quintilian stated the opposite, that 'historiography is very close to poetry and is rather like a poem in prose'.[144] Yet by Aristotle's time the historian Ephorus had also begun to compare historiography and oratory, something in which he was followed by the historian Timaeus.[145] What impetus was given to this debate by Theophrastus and Praxiphanes, whose works *On Historiography* have both been lost, is impossible to say;[146] but Dionysius in the first century BC was followed by Pliny the younger and Hermogenes in the second century AD in seeing historiography as closely allied to oratory.[147]

There were thus two main alternative ways of defining historiography, and it is hardly surprising that Cicero, the outstanding Roman orator, should prefer the latter definition to the former.

After all, it is clear from numerous passages that he seriously contemplated writing history himself.[148] But since the earlier discussion in the *De Legibus* concerned the relationship between historiography and poetry, *quidem* ('at least') at 1.5 is merely Atticus' acknowledgement that Cicero belongs with those who prefer the alternative definition of historiography as oratory.[149]

Lest it be imagined that there is some essential contradiction between these two definitions, two passages of the *De Oratore*, where *oratory* is seen in terms of *poetry*, show that this is not so.[150] Though we today see poetry, oratory and historiography as three separate genres, the ancients saw them as three different species of the same genus — rhetoric. All three types of activity aimed to elaborate certain data in such a way as to affect or persuade an audience or readership. So when in Cicero's *Brutus* (43) Atticus says that the historians Clitarchus and Stratocles 'were able to elaborate Themistocles' death in a rhetorical and tragic manner [*rhetorice et tragice*]', the two terms represent, not a contradiction, but alternative ways of describing the same phenomenon.[151]

Moreover, the Roman system of education encouraged young men to study and emulate the works of famous orators, historians and poets, with the result that future orators, historians and poets were all reared in the same system.[152] Indeed the sixth-century AD historian Agathias claimed that in his youth he had concentrated exclusively on poetry but that a friend encouraged him to write history by saying that 'there is no great gulf between poetry and historiography: they are close relatives from the same tribe and separated from each other only by metre'.[153] And in exactly the same way Quintilian was able to say that when an orator retires from his profession, he can devote himself to the writing of history.[154] It was thus perhaps the educational system as much as anything which ensured that the debate on the real nature of historiography continued.[155] Aristides in the second century AD maintained that historians 'fall between orators and poets', while four centuries later the biographer of Thucydides, Marcellinus, said that 'some people have ventured to demonstrate that the genre of historiography is not rhetorical but poetic'.[156]

Modern historians from time to time try to argue that their own genre is also poetic: thus Marc Bloch urged, 'Let us guard against stripping our science of its share of poetry'.[157] But the fact that modern historiography is indeed seen principally as a science, as Bloch's words indicate, means that no amount of such exhortation will help to narrow the gap between the ancient genre and its modern namesake. When Bloch talks of poetry, he is referring to the presentation of historiography and he means that works of history should be readable. But when Quintilian or Agathias talk about poetry, they mean the same as those who define historiography in terms of oratory: underlying both definitions is the assumption, which the ancients took for granted, that historiography depends very largely upon rhetorical *inuentio*. It is because Cicero spells this out so systematically in the *De Oratore*, and not for any other reason, that Antonius' words there are so important.[158]

Notes

1. See Kelley pp. 143-54 with references.
2. Fr. 3 (OCT).
3. For a representative sample of the most important during the past thirty years or so see the works of Rambaud, Leeman (1955) pp. 188-91 = (1963) pp. 168-74, Trencsényi-Waldapfel, Walsh (1961) Chapter 2, Kelley, Petzold, Rawson (1972) and Brunt. The arguments of the last named scholar deserve particularly careful treatment, since, despite his wish to appear as a lone voice, his is the most recent and detailed expression of views which are in fact standard amongst modern students of ancient history.
4. It is usually taken as a kind of blue-print for Hellenistic or 'tragic' historiography (on which see below, n. 151). The importance of the letter should not, however, be allowed to obscure its humour, which I have tried to bring out in my translation. Some further points: Cic. describes his embarrassment as *subrusticus* (1), yet he wrote to Lucceius from the country; he professes to forget which of Lucceius' prefaces contained the beautiful discussion of prejudice he is now urging him to discount (3); *modicum uolumen* (4) is false modesty; *enumeratio fastorum* (5) perhaps playfully recalls Plato, *Hipp. Mai.* 285E. In addition, Ullman p. 53 points to various colloquial touches which 'were deliberately introduced to give an air of informality'. On the other hand, Shackleton Bailey (1980) p. 139 says that the letter is written in Cicero's most ornate style, which he naturally (but in my opinion quite wrongly) represents in his Penguin translation.
5. See Herkommer pp. 140-4.
6. For the use of *amor* in particular cf. Cicero's letter to Lucceius.
7. Brunt p. 313 appeals to Lucian 7 as illustrating truth in our modern sense, but it is quite clear that here and elsewhere Lucian is referring to (im)partiality: see e.g. 7 τοῖς ἐπαίνοις, ἐπαινέσαι, 8 ἐπαινέσαι, κολακείαν, τὸ ἐγκώμιον, 9 ἐπαινετέον, τὸ ἐγκώμιον, 10 τῶν ἐπαίνων, ἐπαίνοις, 11 οἱ ἔπαινοι κτλ. The same is true of Polybius: see Herkommer p. 138, who also remarks (pp. 145-6) that Ammianus is the only Roman historian who professes 'truth' in what he (Herkommer)

regards as the 'Thucydidean' sense. It is worth remembering the parody of an historian's preface at Sen. *Apoc.* 1.1 'nihil nec *offensae* nec *gratiae* dabitur: haec ita‹que› *uera*'. [*itaque*, my easy suggestion for an awkward *ita* (on which see P.T. Eden ad loc.), would if correct make the point even clearer: *itaque* is postponed roughly 300 times elsewhere in Sen., though he prefers it in first place, cf. *TLL* 7.2.521.73ff.] Wiseman (1981) p. 387 has rightly seen the limitations of Lucian's words.

8. We should not forget the phenomenon which Veyne p. 222, for example, spotlights when he remarks that 'in the seventeenth century preachers and moralists spoke a great deal about favourites [sc. at court] ... but did not describe the system, for everyone was steeped in it'. Just so in the ancient world they took for granted and referred regularly to a concept of impartiality which, since they had no reason to explain it further, requires a considerable amount of mental adjustment on the part of readers today.

9. For Greek society see e.g. Adkins (1972) pp. 14ff.; for Roman, Earl (1967) and Wiseman (1985) pp. 1-13.

10. Walcot (1973) p. 117, with references in n. 1.

11. See e.g. Walcot (1978), Woodman (1983) pp. 63-4.

12. I say 'too' because all historians are of course biased and pre-judiced to some extent. Realisation of this fact may have been at the back of Cicero's mind when he chose the metaphor of *fundamenta* to designate the laws of historiography (see p. 82): just as foundations (being below ground) are generally invisible, so the laws of historiography (being frequently broken) are also often invisible.

13. *Ann.* 4.33.4. For an extended case-study see Wiseman (1979) pp. 57-139.

14. For Sallust see above, p. 43 and n. 266; for Pliny cf. *Ep.* 5.8.13 'if you praise you're said to have been grudging, if you criticise you're said to have been excessive'.

15. Note that the eighteenth-century theologian Chladenius drew a distinction between 'point of view' (i.e. Dionysius' διάθεσις) and bias as such (see Gossman p. 6).

16. If Cicero is reflecting Hellenistic material which is now lost (see below, nn. 77, 146), this only serves to increase its value.

17. All references are to Book 2 of the *De Oratore* unless otherwise stated.

18. A break after 73 is generally accepted: see e.g. Wilkins p. 221 and O'Mara p. 74 (but the latter's detailed analysis of the dialogue as a whole is most unhelpful: she is concerned almost entirely with its mathematical proportions and ignores the verbal correspondences by which much of the argument is signposted). I have resisted the temptation to provide full analyses of 30-50 and 65-73, despite the complex and at times para-doxical nature of the arguments (see e.g. n. 35 below; also p. 96 and n. 130).

19. His point is (30) that in any kind of rhetorical debate speakers discuss matters of which they are ignorant, and they maintain different opinions on an identical issue (so one of them cannot be true). Hence rhetoric 'depends upon falsehood'.

20. It is a commonplace of classical scholarship that ancient histori-

ography was 'rhetorical' and that its theoretical background can be seen in Antonius' speech (cf. e.g. McDonald (1957) pp. 159-61 and (1968) p. 467); my contention is that, with the distinguished exception of T.P. Wiseman, most scholars have failed to realise the implications of this nomenclature (see above, pp. 87-8). (Some scholars prefer the label 'Isocratean' historiography, on the grounds that it was instigated by the historians Ephorus and Theopompus, who (cf. *De Or.* 2.57) were pupils of Isocrates.)

21. We cannot now know whether or to what extent Antonius' words reflect his own or Cicero's views. For my purposes the question does not really matter, since I am more concerned with the views themselves than with whoever was responsible for them. However, as will become clear (pp. 98-9), I think we can at least infer that Antonius' words reflect the views of Cicero himself. Most scholars would agree with this inference, which explains why I use the names 'Cicero' and 'Antonius' interchangeably.

22. Lambinus' emendation of the MSS's *efferebat.* The latter could still be right: see *OLD* s.v. 7, 8.*

23. Jacobs' correction of the MSS's *locorum*: see below, n. 26.

24. i.e. with historiography in mind. The phrase is obscure, but I take it that *rei* refers back to *historia.*

25. This assessment seems to be confirmed by the surviving fragments: Coelius is likely to have been the first Roman historian to have put fictitious speeches into the mouths of his characters (D'Alton p. 515), and he also described a storm at sea (Badian (1966) p. 16). Cf. frr. 6, 26, 47 (speeches), 40 (storm: doubted by Livy, cf. n. 84 below).

26. Brunt p. 322 gets the argument of 53-4 doubly wrong. First, he says that Antonius censures the early Roman historians 'on the purely literary grounds which are most relevant to his discourse'. It is clear from the rest of his paragraph that by 'literary' Brunt means 'stylistic', although it is clear from Antonius' actual words, as I have demonstrated, that content is being referred to. Second, Brunt says that 'even Coelius who had naively aimed at some verbal effects was defective in "uarietate locorum"', evidently thinking that *loci* refers to a stylistic phenomenon. Yet if *locorum* is what Cicero wrote, the word would refer to general reflections or commonplaces, not style; but in any case it seems certain from the metaphorical use of *distinxit* that Cicero wrote *colorum* (cf. *Rhet. Herenn.* 4.16 'distinctam ... coloribus', *Or.* 65), which here refers to style (see Fantham (1972) p. 170 and n. 31).

27. In the Latin text I use superimposed numbers to indicate verbal repetitions or (when bracketed) correspondences. Note that these numbers, while illustrating the articulation of the argument, obscure certain implications of what is being said. For example, the distinction between '*rerum* [12] ratio' and 'in *rebus* [15] magnis', though valid in differentiating elaboration from hard core, obscures the point I made on p. 78, namely that both are *res.* Again, the sequence *acta — euentus*, in which *acta* is evidently equivalent to 'in *rebus* [15] magnis', suggests that the *euentus* is the elaboration of some hard core; yet in the case of a battle whose *euentus* is a triumph, it is the triumph about which there is likely to be hard core information (see pp. 88-9).

As for my translation, I would like to think it is more accurate than existing versions. That of the Loeb editor, who is followed by Rambaud pp. 13-14 and Kelley p. 45, seems to me simply wrong; that of Fornara pp. 138-9 is a gross distortion (see below, n. 36).

28. Brunt p. 318.

29. Marwick p. 144, cf. Atkinson p. 22 'It is the essence of history ... that it should locate events in space and time'.

30. Walsh (1961) p. 32.

31. Kelley pp. 42, 101. Cf. also Petzold pp. 259-60, Leeman (1955) p. 188 — (1963) p. 171.

32. Brunt p. 313.

33. Brunt p. 312 makes much of the claim that he has interpreted Cicero's key statements 'in their context'.

34. Like most other scholars I accept the vulgate correction ‹s›*ita*. Since this word can only refer to *praeceptis*, it seems that Antonius is drawing a contrast (cf. *tamen*) between *praecepta rhetorum* and *munus oratoris* in terms of familiarity.

35. The interpolation is exactly like that of 54, already noted (p. 78), except that in the present case it also acts as a 'foil' for what follows (cf. *scilicet ... autem*). If this interpretation of the passage is correct, it means that *nam* is not here being used as an explanatory or causal particle but, as often in Cicero, has an elliptical sense (see Pease on *ND* 1.27). Failure to realise this, which seems universal, leads to travesties such as Kelley's, where Antonius is made to say the exact opposite of what he in fact does say: 'Antonius, while affirming that the orator's skill is perhaps called into play more in history than in any other genre, says that this art is not "supplied with any independent directions from the rhetoricians". He suggests that *the reason for this is that* the laws of historical composition are known to all' (87 [my italics, and also note that Kelley mistakenly refers *eam* to *munus*, not to *historia*], cf. also 45). The objection to versions such as this has already been hinted at in n. 34 above. Given the near synonymity of *sita sunt enim ante oculos* and *nam quis nescit ...*, the obvious function of an explanatory *nam* would be to suggest that the latter sentences are an illustration of the former; but this is impossible since truth, which is the subject of the latter sentences, is not a *praeceptum rhetorum*, and it is the *praecepta rhetorum* which is the only familiar element in the former (n. 34).

It follows from the above that Antonius' argument in 62-4 is different from that employed in 44-6 for eulogy, the only other subject which he treats at any length in this part of the dialogue. There the obviousness of eulogistic techniques (45 'quis est qui nesciat quae sint in homine laudanda?') is both given as a reason why the rules for eulogy should not be codified ('neque illa elementa desiderare', cf. 49 'num ... propriis praeceptis instruenda?', 50 'sed ex artificio res istae praecepta non quaerunt') and is also used to introduce a *praeteritio* whereby Antonius proceeds to list (45-6) precisely the rules for eulogy which were in fact codified in e.g. *Rhet. Herenn.* 3.10-15. Despite the element of unintended paradox in this argument, which Catulus naturally seizes upon (47 'Cur igitur dubitas ... facere hoc tertium genus, quoniam est in ratione rerum?'), Antonius nevertheless concludes that eulogy should not be given a rhetorical classification of its own (47-50). At 62-4, on the other hand, Antonius is capitalising on an intentional paradox: namely, that despite the (to himself) obviously rhetorical nature of historiography (62 'haud scio an ... maximum', 63 'ipsa autem exaedificatio ...'), the genre has not been given separate treatment in the rules of rhetoric (62 'neque tamen ... rhetorum praeceptis') and its rhetorical nature has escaped the notice of his interlocutors ('Videtisne ...?'). Thus, despite some similarity of phrasing, there is a different point at issue in each case: at 44-6 the rules for eulogy do not require the codification which they have in fact been given; at 62-4 the rules for historiography have not received the codification which might naturally have been expected. Such variation not only avoids monotony but also fits the view of eulogy as trivial (47 *exigua*) and of historiography as important (36).

36. Fornara p. 138 not only makes Antonius say the exact opposite of this ('Obviously, these foundations are known to everyone, *and also that* its edifice consists of events and speeches'), but prints his mistranslation, which I have italicised, in bold type to indicate its presumed importance. As a result, he too, like Kelley (above, n. 35), completely misinterprets the rest of the passage (p. 139). (It will also be noticed that he renders *uerbis* as 'speeches', a fantasy which the repetition and explanation of the word at 64 ought to have dispelled.)

37. In addition to the quotations already given on p. 81 see, e.g., Piderit and Harnecker ad loc. ('Grundgesetze'), North p. 237 ('the first rule of history' etc.), Herkommer p. 149 (truth is history's 'oberstes Gesetz'), Brunt p. 314 ('truth is the first requirement of history', cf. p. 317). No doubt the derivation of such words as 'fundamental' from *fundamentum* has contributed to the misunderstanding.

38. It is clear from the exchanges of conversation in 59-60 that Antonius' familiarity with Greek historiography is regarded as something unusual; his interlocutors' ignorance of its rhetorical nature and technique is therefore dramatically realistic.

39. That is, there are only two laws of history, expressed by *prima* and *deinde* (for which cf. e.g. *Off.* 1.20, *Rep.* 1.38, *Leg.* 3.19, *Verr.* 5.90).

40. Though the similarity of wording explains what is meant by the *leges historiae*, Cicero is of course contradicting in the letter what he was soon to publish in the *De Oratore*. Scholars have sought to explain (away) the contradiction along four lines (see Herkommer p. 149 n. 3, Kelley pp. 22-32). (1) There is no contradiction since in the letter Cicero is talking about a monograph, the rules for which were different from those for a continuous history. (2) There is no real contradiction since Cicero's words in such theoretical works as the *De Or.* are merely fine-sounding sentiments: his true opinions are revealed in the letter. (3) The letter does indeed contradict *De Or.* but it is a special case deriving from Cicero's particular circumstances and his personal wish to feature in a work of propaganda. (4) The contradiction is only apparent, since Cicero's letter is plainly a joke. — While I do not accept (1), for which (despite Puccioni) there is simply no evidence, or (2), I think there is some truth in (3) and (4). Cicero clearly knew that his request to Lucceius contradicted *De Or.* 2.62, on which he was engaged at the same time; he hoped that his delightful and captivating style (above, n.4) would enable him to get away

with it; if not, he could always pass it off as a joke.

41. So too Wiseman (1981) p. 387. Brunt p. 315 also acknowledges that 'it is bias, however caused, that he [Cicero] sees as the great obstacle to veracity', but he is unaware of the implications of his statement, since he continues: 'He says nothing of the historian's problems in investigating and ascertaining the truth. His silence can easily be explained. He is concerned with history as a literary genre, and therefore with the way it should be written, not with the work preliminary to writing. What his views on this matter were must be a matter for surmise.' Brunt fails to realise that there was no alternative to history 'as a literary genre' in the ancient world; and when he proceeds to surmise Cicero's allegedly scientific historiographical technique from Plin. *Ep.* 5.8.12, he seems to be misusing the letter (see below, n. 137).

42. The second conclusion explains the first: it is because the ancients lacked our concept of 'historical truth' that Antonius was able to dismiss his own limited concept of impartiality which was so often disregarded in practice (above, n. 12).

43. Quint. 8 pref. 6 'orationem porro omnem constare rebus et uerbis: in rebus intuendam inuentionem, in uerbis elocutionem'. The structural similarity of this to our passage of Cicero suggests a standard manner of expression which no doubt derives from some earlier common source. For content and style cf. also Quint. 3.3.1, 5.1; Lausberg 1.99 § 45, 227-8, 279.

44. Brunt p. 318. He rightly says of *regionum descriptionem* that 'at this point "Antonius" is not discussing literary effects at all ... but the content of a history', but mistakenly precedes this remark by saying that the ornamentation of which Cicero approves 'can be restricted to the careful choice of words and rhythms', a topic on which Cicero does not in fact embark until 64 below. It is indeed a feature of scholarship on our passage that writers anxiously slide over the matter of *res* in their haste to reach *uerba*. This is true also of e.g. Leeman (1963) pp. 171-3, and see North p. 237: 'The perfection of history depends on *res* and *uerba*. It was to the second of these elements that most of Cicero's comments were directed' — an observation which simply flies in the face of the evidence of the passage.

45. Walsh (1961) p. 32. See too Leeman (1955) pp. 188-9 = (1963) p. 171.

46. The six sections are: *exordium* (introduction), *narratio* (statement of the case), *diuisio* (division), *argumentatio* or *confirmatio* (proof), *confutatio* (refutation) and *peroratio* (conclusion). See Lausberg 1.238-9.

47. See further Lausberg 1.280 § 317.

48. See also *Rhet. Herenn.* 1.16, Quint. 4.2.36, 52.

49. Cf. Quint. 4.3.12-13; Lausberg 1.293 § 340.

50. Quint. 4.3.12. See Lausberg 2.234-5 § 819.

51. Digressions were a recognised method of entertaining one's audience (Cic. *Inu.* 1.27 'delectationis ... causa', *Brut.* 322, cf. *De Or.* 2.311), and this was particularly true of those dealing with topography (see below, n. 78). For this reason I have suggested by my superimposed number 6 in the Latin text above that *regionum descriptionem* here corresponds to *uarietate* in Antonius' opening remarks (for variety as a source of

delectatio see Lausberg 1.229, 231). It is however possible that *orationis...* *uarietate* refers merely to variety of style (cf. *Rhet. Herenn.* 4.18 'dignitas est quae reddit ornatam orationem uarietate distinguens'), which is of course how Brunt p. 325n. takes it; yet since topographical digressions were themselves an opportunity for a heightened and varied style (cf. Plin. *Ep.* 2.5.5, Quint. 9.2.44, 10.1.33; Lausberg 2.234 § 819), it may be that my suggestion should not be excluded.

52. See further Quint. (n. 48 above); Lausberg 1.287 § 328.

53. Quint. 4.2.52, cf. also 3.7.25.

54. Quint. 4.2.79 'quid inter probationem et narrationem interest, nisi quod narratio est probationis continua propositio, rursus probatio narrationi congruens confirmatio?'

55. Quint. 4.2.54-5. Cf. Atkinson p. 21 on a 'method of presentation recommended and apparently practised' by G.R. Elton, namely 'to weave in the analytical material, thus producing "thickened" narrative'.

56. Compare Cicero's topics for the *argumenta* (*persona, locus, tempus, occasio, modus, facultas*) with Quintilian's for the *narratio* (4.2.55 *persona, causa, locus, tempus, instrumentum, occasio*), to which Quintilian's own *loci argumentorum* are naturally even closer (5.10.23 *persona, causa, tempus, locus, occasio, instrumentum, modus*).

57. Cf. also Quint. 5.10.28-9; Lausberg 1.162, 318, 322.

58. Cf. also Quint. 5.10.86; Lausberg 1.324-5 § 381.

59. Cf. also Quint. 7.4.15; Lausberg 1.178 § 189.

60. *Inu.* 1.27, also at *Rhet. Herenn.* 1.4.

61. Gell. 5.18.6. Cf. Atkinson p. 32 'narrating is basic to history'.

62. Lucian 55.

63. See pp. 73-4.

64. See Lausberg 1.235-367. My remarks in this paragraph are close to those of Wiseman (1981) pp. 388-9.

65. The five techniques are: *inuentio, dispositio* (arrangement), *elocutio* (style), *memoria* (memory) and *pronuntiatio* (delivery). Cf. e.g. Cic. *Inu.* 1.9, *Rhet. Herenn.* 1.3.

66. Cf. also *Rhet. Herenn.* 1.3.

67. *Inu.* 1.46.

68. Cf. *Rhet. Herenn.* 1.16 'si uera res erit, nihilominus haec omnia narrando conseruanda sunt, nam saepe ueritas, nisi haec seruata sint, fidem non potest facere'. Quint. 4.2.34, 56. Wiseman (1981) p. 390 quotes Tac. *Ann.* 11.27 as an example of an episode which was implausible but demonstrably true, 'a paradox with which the historians of the ancient world were ill-equipped to deal'. Herkommer seems to me quite mistaken in saying that 'Das Ziel der "narratio probabilis" ...ist jedoch etwas ganz anderes als das Streben nach historischer "ueritas"' (150 n. 5).

69. Cf. Brunt p. 318, quoted above, pp. 83-4.

70. Wiseman (1979) pp. 47-8 remarks on 'how far the ancient histori-ographical tradition was from the modern concept of the historian as judge, weighing up the evidence'; Atkinson p. 75 enlarges on this by saying that the 'historian is legislator, judge, jury, counsel, witnesses, all in one', but the point remains basically the same. It is true that the historian as 'impartial judge' is mentioned by Lucian 41, but the context is not that

of weighing evidence but the standard one of disavowing malice. Herkommer (p. 140 n. 1) says that Dionysius (*Ep. Pomp.* 6 = 2.394-5 Usher) describes Theopompus as 'der peinlich prüfende Richter', but there the context is the same as that in Lucian, just mentioned (see further above, p. 43).

71. Russell (1967) p. 135, quoted by Wiseman (1981) p. 389. Compare the way in which heroic poetry is composed, as described by Hainsworth (in Foxhall and Davies pp. 115-17).

72. See above, n. 20. A good example is provided by Momigliano (1984) pp. 49-59.

73. Semp. Asell. fr. 2 '[early annalists wrote down] in whose consulship a war started and in whose it finished, and who celebrated a triumph because of it'.

74. See Phillips (1974), esp. pp. 269-70.

75. For the *Annales Maximi* themselves see Frier; for the *fasti* and connected problems see Ridley; for aristocratic epitaphs (*elogia*) and other forms of monument or inscription, both of which were liable to contain the kind of bare information to which Antonius refers, see respectively Earl (1967) pp. 21-3, 27, and Wiseman (1986). There is a good general discussion of these and other possible sources in Wiseman (1979) pp. 12ff.

76. Magistracies were of course a traditional method of dating events.

77. The four elements of time, person, place and event were regarded as the four essential components of historiography by Cicero's contemporary, the obscure Asclepiades of Myrlea (ap. Sext. Emp. *Gramm.* 655.25B), by Sex. Empiricus himself (ib. 657.2B) and by Eustathius (*Geog. Graec. Min.* 2.215.14, though he in fact substitutes genealogy for persons): see Scheller pp. 17-19. The same four elements also constituted standard topics to be elaborated in rhetorical descriptions: see Lausberg 2.225-6; also below, n. 105. All this suggests that the views which Cicero attributes to Antonius had already been given expression considerably earlier — perhaps in the lost works *On Historiography* by Theophrastus and Praxiphanes (see pp. 74-5 and n. 16, p. 99 and n. 146). Professor D.A. Russell has suggested to me that these lost works in their turn may have been a reaction to Aristotle's 'debunking' of historiography in the *Poetics* ('what Alcibiades did or what happened to him'): see above, p. 62 n. 163.

78. For the former see Woodman (1977) p. 107, Brink on Hor. *AP* 16-18 and *Ep.* 2.1.252, Lausberg 2.234-5 § 819; for the latter see Aphthon. 46.21, 47.1, Hermog. 16.17 (quoted), Liban. 8.460-4; Kroll on Cic. *Or.* 66.

79. Hermog. 16.22ff. The sequence antecedents — attendant circumstances — consequences, exactly as Antonius had recommended, is absolutely standard: cf. Theon. 119.14ff., Aphthon. 46.27ff., Nicol. 492.18-19.

80. Hermog. 16.20-2.

81. See further Paul.

82. Quint. 8.3.70. ἐνάργεια was at home in the *narratio*, cf. Quint. 4.2.63-5. Brunt p. 336 says that 'we can well believe that Greek historians, in default of evidence, invented details to make their narratives vivid, thrilling or pathetic: certainly this was the practice of Livy', a statement which seems to contradict one of the principal theses of his essay, since

elsewhere (pp. 311-12) he implies that Livy did *not* adopt the 'rhetorical and sensationalist models' of Hellenistic historiography.

83. The former is Atkinson's phrase (p. 39) to describe statements like 'Caesar was killed on the steps of the Capitol', the latter Kitson Clark's (in McCullagh p. 26) to describe those such as 'the battle of Waterloo was fought on Sunday, 18 June 1815'.

84. For various examples from Greek, Roman and medieval times see e.g. Wiseman (1979) pp. 12-25 and 149, Fleischman pp. 291-5. See also the general remarks of Fornara pp. 134-5, quoted above, p. 49 n. 27.

85. Leeman (1955) p. 188 = (1963) p. 171 attributes to common opinion the (to him) erroneous view of Roman historiography as 'truth being submerged under floods of rhetorical commonplaces', quoting as example G. Boissier, *Tacite* (1903), whom Brunt p. 311 invokes as a supporter!

86. The same distinction is also found in a letter of the emperor Verus to his teacher and historian, Fronto: 'meae res gestae tantae sunt quantae sunt scilicet, quoiquoimodi sunt; tantae autem uidebuntur, quantas tu eas uideri uoles' (2.196 Loeb edn.). It is clear from the examples I have quoted that the whole trend of ancient historiography was towards bigger (and therefore better) narratives: size was equivalent to definitiveness (see Luce (1977) pp. 144-7 and 173-4), and it is noticeable that Livy, for example, even gives versions of events about which he has doubts (thus poisoning at 8.18.1-11 and a sea-storm at 29.27.14-15, both items being stock rhetorical commonplaces). It is mainly for this reason that we rarely find the converse, viz. an historian 'deconstructing' an account to lay bare the hard core, although in practice it would be an almost impossible procedure anyway (for the reasons given on pp. 92-3). The obvious exceptions are rationalisations of myths and *fabulae* (see e.g. Schultze p. 126 and Wiseman (1985a) pp. 196-7, with references), for which the critical criteria are those standard in rhetoric, viz. plausibility and credibility. See also above, p. 49 n. 24 and p. 60 n. 150.

87. See Bonner (1949) pp. 2-11 and (1977) Chapter 18; Fairweather (1981) pp. 104-31. The terms are difficult to reproduce in English, but *quaestiones* refer basically to abstract propositions, *causae* to more concrete topics.

88. *Q. Fr.* 2.16.4, rightly referred to by Norden (1958) in the context of topographical digressions (*Nachträge* 19). Allen p. 158 rightly connects the letter with Cicero's remarks in *Part. Or.* 34 on the standard rhetorical topics of person, place, time, event etc. (though Cic. is there discussing, not the *narratio*, but the *argumentatio*).

89. *Brut.* 62. For some early examples see Wiseman (1986); for an Augustan example see Woodman (1983) pp. 192-6.

90. Liv. 8.40.4-5. It is significant (cf. n. 91 below) that both authors attribute the falsification to *gloria* (see p. 74): Cic. refers to *laus*, Liv. to *fama* (both = 'praise').

91. It will be clear that here I am simply repeating in different words the first and second laws of historiography which Antonius expressed in *De Or.* 2.62. It is therefore perhaps possible to conclude that when Cicero wrote that passage he had in mind the hard core elements of historiography. Indeed this may be another reason why his choice of metaphor

(*fundamenta*, from building) so strongly resembles the metaphor he used at 53 to describe the hard core (*monumenta*, also from building). If this is so, then Cicero's advice to Lucceius that he should ignore the laws of historiography is all the more outrageous (see n. 40). Brunt p. 337 says that 'in asking Lucceius to magnify his own deeds in violation of the "leges historiae" ... [Cicero was not] suggesting that in any other respect his narrative should be untruthful: there is no call for a sensationalism unwarranted by the facts' — a comment which, in so far as I understand it, seems contradicted by everything which Cicero wrote in the letter and which Brunt himself has adequately summarised earlier in his paragraph. For a case in which an historian (Timaeus) evidently did omit some awkward but true hard core material see Plb. 12.15.9-11.

92. See Jerome pp. 370-2, who quotes e.g. Quint. 4.2.66-7, 76-8, 5.13.7-8.

93. I find it particularly interesting that Fornara p. 136 has arrived at the same conclusion ('If you develop the inherent possibilities of a true datum, *ornare* is legitimate; if from a fiction ..., the practice is culpable') by a different route (viz. Cic. *Leg.* 1.1-5, *De Or.* 2.54 [*not* 63] and *Brut.* 43 'mortem rhetorice et tragice ornare potuerunt'). Yet with reference to the last of these passages Fornara comments: 'It is vital to note ... that only the imaginative reenactment is covered by the term *ornare*; the false and contrived nature of the scene is expressed adverbially by *tragice et rhetorice* [*sic*]. *Ornare* in itself is to take a fact and from it to set a scene, developing its latent potentialities. But in a historical work *ornare* subserves the laws of history and is tested by the standard of truth. Otherwise how could Cicero declare that the law of history was truth and yet condemn the Roman writers for the absence of *ornare*?'. It will be clear that with much of this comment I disagree; and his concluding question is one which I hope I have been able to answer in the present chapter.

94. *Att.* 1.19.10 'non ἐγκωμιαστικὰ sunt haec sed ἱστορικὰ quae scribimus'.

95. See Bömer and Eden. An example is the letter of Ser. Sulpicius Galba to Cicero describing the battle of Forum Gallorum in 43 BC (*Fam.* 10.30), which has all the hall-marks of the *commentarius*-style.

96. *Att.* 2.1.1.

97. For epideictic not requiring truth Brunt p. 331 n. 52 quotes Philod. 1.285-7 Sudhaus (his other quotations from Cicero do not seem to me relevant).

98. For some good remarks on this general topic see e.g. Balfour p. 424 ('The skilful propagandist tries to give his argument the appearance of an objective statement' etc.).

99. Cf. Finley (1985) p. 18 'I am unaware of any stigmata that automatically distinguish fiction from fact', Fornara p. 137 'The approach leaves us almost helpless when we attempt to extricate fact from fancy'.

100. I say 'not necessarily' because of course the ancients themselves realised that many hard core elements were false: see p. 91. On the other hand, they no doubt also accepted as true many that they should have considered false, since for them, as for the historians of the middle ages, 'history was what was willingly believed' (Fleischman p. 305, and see also

Ray's excellent account of the phrase *uera lex historiae* in Jerome and Bede).

101. See, for example, the splendid analysis (and demolition) by Horsfall (1982) of Livy's description of the battle of the Caudine Forks; also his more general discussion (1985) of topographical techniques in Latin authors. In referring to topography and archaeology I do not wish to give the impression that I am dismissing or underestimating the value of modern literary analysis (on the contrary, see below, Chapter 4, pp. 176-9). But it is in the nature of the case that literary analysis will not always produce conclusions which modern historians might regard as certain. Some conclusions thus reached will, however, be very likely; and we ought to be far more prepared than we are at present to extrapolate from them.

102. 'The ancients ... would have repudiated any such analytical exercise, for they wrote in the expectation that their histories in fact established the record in a final and conclusive sense' (Fornara p. 137). Luce (1977) p. 161 rightly says that 'antiquarian research could give only limited help to an historian seeking to narrate *res gestae*. Antiquarianism was not history, but the stuff of which digressions were made'. See also Rawson (1985) p. 200 and, on antiquarian research in general, pp. 233ff.

103. Thus Pollio criticised Caesar's *commentarii*, nominally a collection of hard core elements (p. 92) but in fact an elaborately completed work of history (cf. Cic. *Brut.* 262; Eden pp. 75-8): 'parum diligenter parumque integra ueritate compositos putat, cum Caesar pleraque et quae per alios erant gesta temere crediderit et quae per se ... perperam ediderit' (Suet. *Iul.* 56.4).

104. See above, p. 49 and n. 24.

105. Wiseman (1981) p. 389. Very revealing is Ti. Donatus' comment (197.6-9) on *Aen.* 9.80-3: 'He [Virgil] provided the time [*tempus*], place [*locum*], characters [*personas*] and event [*rem*], by means of which he gave his narrative as much credibility [*fidem*] as possible: for it is precisely when we are told when an event took place, and where, and on whose initiative, that it is shown to be true [*uerum*]'. Here the same four key elements of *inuentio* as Cicero mentions (and see also above, p. 108 n. 77) are said to produce credibility, which is expressly stated to be equivalent to truth.

106. If I may literalise the metaphor and introduce a parallel from building, the fourth-century Arch of Constantine (= *monumentum*) was decorated with re-used reliefs and sculptures (= *ornamenta*) from the second century. Whatever the reason(s) for this practice (see Bianchi Bandinelli p. 83), it well illustrates the ancients' unhistorical (in our view) way of thinking. (Interestingly enough, this same parallel had also occurred to Peter (1897) 1.287.) See also above, p. 14 on speeches.

107. *Pref.* 2. Livy's statement, while disproving the allegation of Fornara p. 56 that 'the concept of research finds no place in the Latin prefaces', is not strictly at variance with my remarks on p. 92 since the evidence suggests that such research was always the exception rather than the rule. For *aemulatio* in *exaedificatio* (Livy's *ars scribendi*) see Peter (1897) 2. pp. 190ff.

108. 'When Homer's account of Achilles is accepted as essentially

reliable because he was not writing of him in his lifetime and therefore had no motive for lying, we realise how limited this criterion [of truth] is as an index of historical inaccuracy' (Wiseman (1981) pp. 387-8, referring to Lucian 40).

109. Brunt p. 313. A similar point in Rawson (1985) p. 215.

110. Wiseman (1979) p. 38.

111. Brunt p. 316. See further below, p. 201.

112. Deliberative oratory demanded proof and refutation (*Rhet. Herenn.* 3.8); argument involved *exornatio* (2.28), which in turn employed *amplificatio* (2.46, cf. 47 *fin.*).

113. *Q. Fr.* 1.1.23; cf. Trencsényi-Waldapfel p. 9. Cicero was presumably referring to core elements of the portrait.

114. Walsh (1955), referred to by Herkommer p. 137, who is altogether more realistic than Brunt on this topic.

115. Diod. 1.1.2, Strabo 1.2.8-9.

116. Quint. 2.17.26-8, cf. *Brut.* 42 'concessum est rhetoribus ementiri in historiis' (on which see below, n. 151). Jerome p. 363 remarks that Quintilian 'finds frequent occasion to treat of lying as a fine art', quoting 4.2.89-94, 123-4, 12.1.1-14, 34-5.

117. 'uerborum copia alitur et ... numerus liberiore quadam fruitur licentia. datur etiam uenia concinnitati sententiarum ... certique et circumscripti uerborum ambitus conceduntur, de industriaque non ex insidiis sed aperte et palam elaboratur ut uerba uerbis quasi demensa et paria respondeant, ut crebro conferantur pugnantia comparenturque contraria et ut pariter extrema terminentur eundemque referant in cadendo sonum.'

118. *Or.* 39, and see further above, pp. 45-7. It is usually suggested that the Herodotean style was taken up by Isocrates and his pupils Ephorus and Theopompus and mediated through to the works of Cicero and Dionysius, who also advocates it, by Theophrastus: see e.g. Avenarius pp. 55-9, Leeman (1963) p. 173. Scheller p. 64 seems to argue that the Herodotean style was not that advocated by the Isocrateans; but Ciero and others describe Herodotus, Isocrates and the others in the same terms (cf. *Or.* 39, above, with 207 'in historia placet omnia dici Isocrateo Theopompeoque more illa circumscriptione ambituque'), and it is this which is significant for our purposes. There are full comments on Cicero and the smooth style in Brunt pp. 320-1 and 328-30, who identifies it with the *genus medium* (cf. also Quint. 12.10.60).

119. *Ep.* 114.16 'illa in exitu lenta, qualis Ciceronis est, deuexa et molliter detinens nec aliter quam solet ad morem suum pedemque respondens'. Lucian's comment on the *narratio* that it should progress αὐτῆ ὁμοίως (55) is very like Seneca's remark; but I think it refers to the transitions between topics rather than to style (*contra* Leeman (1963) p. 173).

120. I too have been brief, but I shall return to the subject in the next chapter (pp. 117-20).

121. Since the following sentences in 64 ('cohortationes, consolationes, praecepta, admonita, quae tractanda sunt omnia disertissime sed locum suum in his artibus, quae traditae sunt, habent nullum') echo those which Cicero wrote in 50 ('illa, quae saepe diserte agenda sunt ...

neque habent suum locum ullum in diuisione partium neque certum praeceptorum genus, et agenda sunt non minus diserte quam quae in lite dicuntur, obiurgatio, cohortatio, consolatio') it is clear that Cicero's whole discussion of historiography in 51-64 is included within an outer frame of ring composition. And both passages in their turn look back to 34-6 (quoted on p. 75).

122. The sequence 'uerborum *autem* ratio ... sine *hac iudiciali* asperitate et sine sententiarum *forensium* aculeis' suggests that everything under the heading of *rerum ratio* is to be seen in terms of judicial oratory.

123. See e.g. Lausberg 1.59ff. Together the three make up the *tria genera causarum*, the three types of oratory.

124. This is even implied in *De Or.* 2.35-6 (see below, n. 128).

125. Since he makes only selective reference to *Or.* 37, Brunt p. 330 is able falsely to state that Hermog. 417-25, which he describes as 'a farrago of indiscriminating absurdity', is the only evidence that the ancients made no distinction between historiography and panegyric. Brunt's restriction of *Or.* 66 to 'a stylistic content' (p. 330) is questionable in view of the way the sentence develops ('sed in his tracta quaedam ... oratio'), and his distinction between the two genres on grounds of pleasure (p. 331) is implausible, as he himself is inclined to recognise (cf. pp. 313-14), since historiography also sought to give pleasure (see, e.g., Woodman (1983a) pp. 111-12, Fornara pp. 120-34): see also below, n. 136. As the above evidence on p. 95 clearly shows, there *was* a close affinity between the two genres. Yet there was also a difference (p. 92); but this difference does not of course invalidate the case which I have been making. It was entirely characteristic of the ancients to debate the relationship of one genre to another (see above, pp. 99-100), recognising that no one genre was absolutely identical with another. For an analogous distinction in the middle ages see Fleischman p. 305 (quoted on p. 201).

126. Cf. Cic. *Part. Or.* 71,75, Quint, 3.7.15 and Adamietz ad loc.; Lausberg 1.218.

127. Quint 3.7.6-28.

128. See Wilkins p. 219: 'Cicero keeps in view here the three main genera of eloquence: (1) genus deliberativum, (*a*) in the senate, (*b*) in the contio; (2) g. iudiciale; (3) g. demonstrativum, which includes panegyrics, exhortations, censures, consolations etc. History was added by some, and Cicero inclines to agree with them'.

129. For these see e.g. Lausberg 1.118-22.

130. See further above, n. 35. Despite the present elimination of eulogy, O'Mara pp. 151-2 rightly notes that the structure of Antonius' discussion 'affirms the threefold division' (see above, n. 128) and that he does in fact acknowledge its generic nature later at 341-9, where he repeats at more length the rules which he professed to deny at 45-6. This is just a further example of the paradoxicality which characterises Antonius' arguments in the dialogue.

131. Cf. 42-3 'certum autem ... quae in foro atque in ciuium causis disceptationibusque uersantur. ea mihi uidentur aut in lite oranda ...', 70-1; Fantham (1979) p. 443, though she is of course wrong to add that 'history is distinguished from oratory'.

132. There is a similar emphasis on judicial oratory at Cic. *Inu.* 2.13-

154 (only 155-76 on deliberative, and 176-7 on epideictic). This emphasis on judicial oratory has a 'primitivist' aspect to it, since it alone was the subject of the earliest rhetorical handbooks (see Hinks).

133. Leeman (1963) p. 172 recognises this, but chooses to repeat his earlier statement of (1955) p. 189 that this is the only subjective element in the whole of Antonius' discussion!

134. Compare esp. Semp. Asell. fr. 2, Sall. *J.* 4.4.

135. Repeated almost verbatim in *Rhet. Herenn.* 1.13; and see also Ullman p. 33.

136. These similarities seem to disprove Brunt's statement (p. 330) that 'we are not to infer that he [Cicero] conceived true histories as such epideictic displays [as *Inu.* 1.27]'.

137. Atticus' statement (particularly *maxime*) is naturally an embarrassment to Brunt. On the one hand he suggests that 'perhaps "maxime" should not be taken too seriously: strictly it implies that history is more oratorical than oratory itself' (p.325 n. 30a); alternatively he suggests that *maxime* distinguishes historiography from law and philosophy because these 'were recognised as hard disciplines only to be mastered by prolonged application', whereas 'the collation and investigation of historical evidence, though time-consuming, required no technical preparation' (p. 327). Yet this seems inconsistent with his earlier contention that ancient historians undertook 'extensive enquiries, involving the examination of eye-witnesses, consultation of documents and travel to distant scenes' (p. 315), a contention for which he offers no real evidence. The drawback of contemporary historiography at Plin. *Ep.* 5.8.12 is *not* that it required personal research but that it was dangerous ('graues offensae, leuis gratia', omitted by Brunt); and when he says that 'others claimed to have done what Pliny assumes to be normal', his reference to Walbank (1972) pp. 82-3 demonstrates only that such claims are to be regarded with the greatest scepticism.

138. Wiseman (1979) pp. 9-12.

139. Wiseman (1979) p. 11; Woodman (1975) p. 286.

140. Wiseman (1979) pp. 21-6.

141. The comparison concludes with the following exchange between Cicero and his brother Quintus (1.5): Q. 'I understand that in your opinion different laws obtain in historiography and poetry'. M. 'Yes. In history most things have their basis in *ueritas*, whereas in poetry they have it in pleasure, although in both Herodotus, the father of history, and Theopompus there are countless *fabulae*.' Cicero's reply here has naturally been used by those scholars who wish to assert that his views on historiography are similar to our own (e.g. Brunt pp. 313-14, Fornara p. 128 n. 5, Kelley pp. 105-6); yet I am certain that they are misinterpreting the word *ueritas* here. The context, and in particular the reference to *fabulae*, suggests that *ueritas* = 'real life', as it does at *Inu.* 1.29 (quoted on p. 85), *De Or.* 2.34, 36 (p. 75), 94 (see below); other examples in *OLD* s.v. 2a. That is: *ueritas* embraces the *uerisimile* and is contrasted with *fabula*, as at *Inu.* 1.27 'fabula est in qua nec uerae nec ueri similes res continentur', *Rhet. Herenn.* 1.13, and see further my interpretation of Thuc. 1.22.4 on pp. 23-4 above. Cicero is drawing a comparison between 'credible' texts on the one hand, a category into which historiography normally falls, and

the far-fetched Roman stories of §§ 3-4 on the other, with which the *fabulae* of Herodotus and Theopompus have everything in common.

The text of Cicero's reply to Quintus is also problematical. Above I have translated my own version: *Quippe, cum in illa ad ueritatem <pleraque>, Quinte, referantur, in hoc ad delectationem <pleraque>*, the assumption being that *pleraque* was mistakenly omitted from the first colon, where it is needed, and added on at the end. Others prefer versions which include *omnia* or *cuncta* in the first colon. It is immaterial to my interpretation whether *pleraque* or *omnia/cuncta* is read; but I think it is more realistic if Cicero is made to say *pleraque*, since it was well known that histories almost inevitably contained *some* 'fables', and on this view the word *innumerabiles* will have some point.

As for the meaning of *De Or.* 2.94 (reference above), it too is problematic (Fantham (1978) p. 9 and n. 27, (1979) p. 445). My own view is that 'tamen *omnes* sunt in *eodem* ueritatis imitandae genere uersati' corresponds to the preceding colon 'etsi *inter se pares non* fuerunt' in the same way 'uoluntate autem *similes* sunt' corresponds to 'multique alii naturis *differunt*' earlier in the paragraph: i.e. *eodem* is not intended to suggest any similarity between historiography and oratory in terms of imitating real life (though the similarity obviously exists, as I have tried to demonstrate in the present chapter).

142. See e.g. Peter (1897) 2.203-4, Norden (1958) pp. 91-3, Avenarius pp. 16-22, Wiseman (1979) pp. 143-53.

143. Arist. *Poetics* 1451b1ff. (on which see above, p. 62 n. 163), Plb. 2.56.11.

144. Quint. 10.1.31.

145. See Plb. 12.28.8-28a.2 (the comparison is with epideictic).

146. Norden (1958) p. 84 suggests that Cic. *Or.* 66 (above, p. 95) derives from Theophrastus, which is no doubt quite likely (see above, n. 77). The existence of these works does not of course necessarily disprove Antonius' repeated statements that there were no separate instructions for historiography in *rhetorical* handbooks: see Walbank (1957) pp. 418-19 and (1972) p. 36 n. 20 (*contra* Fornara pp. 137-9 and n. 59, who has however completely misinterpreted Cicero's remarks: see above, n. 36).

147. Dion. *Thuc.* 9 refers to histories as ῥητορικαὶ ὑποθέσεις, an extremely interesting combination of words (see pp. 90-1), though he elsewhere (*Ep. Pomp.* 3 = 2.384 Usher) refers to the works of Herodotus and Thucydides as ποιήσεις! Pliny (*Ep.* 5.8.9) says that 'historiography and oratory have, of course, much in common'; Hermog. *De Ideis* 417.28-418.1 says that 'historians should be set alongside panegyrists, as is in fact the case, I think: their aims are amplification and entertainment' etc.

148. See above, n. 1.

149. The only passage which casts doubt on this, so far as I am aware, is *Brut.* 286: 'Demochares ... et orationes scripsit aliquot et earum rerum historiam quae erant Athenis ipsius aetate gestae *non tam historico quam oratorio genere* perscripsit' (not really capitalised on by Brunt p. 321 and n. 20). Fantham (1979) p. 447 explains the contrast, to which she is in general sympathetic (above, n. 131), by suggesting that the reference is to style rather than content. But I doubt this. There is a passage of Diodorus, roughly contemporary with the *Brutus*, in which the historian

complains that some other historians put too many (and too long) speeches into their histories, thus almost turning them into works of pure oratory (20.1.1-3). Since Cicero tells us that Demochares wrote speeches as well as histories, I suspect that his contrast between *historico* and *oratorio* may be intended to make a similar point to that of Diodorus.

150. 1.70 'The poet is a very close relative of the orator', 3.27 'poets have the closest relationship with orators'; further examples in Kroll on *Or.* 66.

151. Modern scholars (cf. McDonald (1968) pp. 467-8) tend to see a distinction between what they call 'rhetorical' historiography (above, n. 20) and so-called 'tragic' historiography, such as that outlined in the letter to Lucceius (see e.g. Ullman and Walbank (1960)). But for two reasons I believe this distinction to be mistaken: (a) scholars have not realised what is meant when they describe Antonius' words as rhetorical (see above, pp. 87-8); (b) Cicero's account of historiography in the letter (above, p. 73) is strikingly similar to that of rhetorical *narrationes* in *Inu.* 1.27 (above, p. 97) and *Part. Or.* 31-2 (above, p. 85).

Brut. 42-3 is also the notorious occasion on which Atticus is made to say: 'concessum est rhetoribus ementiri in historiis, ut aliquid dicere possint argutius'. I agree with those who believe this is a reference to historical *exempla* in oratory, not to historiography itself: so Walbank (1955) p. 13 n. 58, Wiseman (1979) p. 32, Brunt pp. 331-2, Fornara p. 136 n. 57.

152. See Bonner (1977) Chapters 16-19.

153. Agath. pref. 7-13 (the quotation from 12), quoted by Norden (1958) p. 92. See Cameron (1970) pp. 58-9, who (n. 5) compares Menand. Protect. fr. 1 Μουσῶν ἐραστὴς ποιημάτων τε καὶ ἱστορίας ἐπαΐων and contrasts Procop. 1.1.4, where a strong distinction is made between oratory, poetry and historiography.

154. Quint. 12.11.4. Cf. Theon 70, who says that training in rhetoric is required by an historian.

155. Cf. e.g. Quint. 3.8.49 on *prosopopoeia* (impersonation): it 'is of the greatest use to future *poets* and *historians*, while for *orators* of course it is absolutely essential' (Adamietz ad loc. compares Theon 60.22, where a similar point is made). See in general Jerome p. 360, whose quotations (n. 1) include Quint. 2.17.26-7, 39, 5.12.22, 9.2.81.

156. Arist. *Or.* 49, Marc. *Vita Thuc.* 41.

157. Bloch p. 8. See further e.g. Marwick p. 14.

158. The statement by the second-century AD Rufus of Perinthus (399) to the effect that historiography is a branch of rhetoric is described by Brunt p. 332 as an 'isolated' piece of evidence which 'would never have been accepted in principle by any historian' and which 'Cicero would certainly have never countenanced'. In view of the evidence accumulated in the present chapter I find this description beyond belief; yet it well illustrates the gulf which exists between historical and literary interpretations of ancient historiography in modern times.

3

Style and Attitude:
Sallust and Livy

Sallust

Cicero's 'Nature of Style'

Shortly after Cicero's murder in 43 BC, Sallust began his career as a historian by publishing the *Bellum Catilinae*, a monograph on the Catilinarian conspiracy of 63 BC.[1] He followed this with the *Bellum Iugurthinum*, a monograph on the Jugurthine War of 118-105 BC, and finally with the *Histories*, a full-length account of the years 78 to perhaps 40 BC.[2] In these works Sallust amply fulfilled the requirements for 'nature of content' (*rerum ratio*) which Cicero had put into the mouth of Antonius in the *De Oratore* some fifteen or so years earlier (above, pp. 78-80, 83-6). Cicero had asked for topographical descriptions: Sallust gives a description of Africa in *BJ* and of the Black Sea in *H.*[3] Cicero had required that the historian should reveal in what manner things were said: Sallust puts speeches into the mouths of the various personages in all three works.[4] Cicero had asked for biographical and character sketches of any famous protagonists: Sallust obliges in each monograph, while he introduces the convention of the obituary notice in *H.*[5] Yet if Sallust thus followed Cicero as far as the nature of his content was concerned, he signally failed to do so in the other major area which Cicero had emphasised: the 'nature of style' (*uerborum ratio*).

It will be remembered that Cicero, through Antonius, had said that the nature of style requires 'amplitude and mobility, with a slow and regular fluency' (above, pp. 78-80). The importance of this requirement is borne out not only by its being repeated in Cicero's other theoretical writing (above, p. 94) but also by its having been put into practice by the great orator himself. Though Cicero of course did not write the great work of history for which his friends hoped, there is in his *oeuvre* a passage which 'seems to fulfil the demands of historical writing'.[6] It is his account of the last political act of L. Licinius Crassus in 91 BC (*De Oratore* 3.2-3).

Ut enim Romam rediit extremo ludorum scaenicorum die, vehementer commotus oratione ea, quae ferebatur habita esse in contione a Philippo, quem dixisse constabat videndum sibi esse aliud consilium; illo senatu se rem publicam gerere non posse, mane Idibus Septembribus et ille et senatus frequens vocatu Drusi in curiam venit; ibi cum Drusus multa de Philippo questus esset, rettulit ad senatum de illo ipso, quod in eum ordinem consul tam graviter in contione esset invectus. Hic, ut saepe inter homines sapientissimos constare vidi, quamquam hoc Crasso, cum aliquid accuratius dixisset, semper fere contigisset, ut numquam dixisse melius putaretur, tamen omnium consensu sic esse tum iudicatum ceteros a Crasso semper omnis, illo autem die etiam ipsum a se superatum. Deploravit enim casum atque orbitatem senatus, cuius ordinis a consule, qui quasi parens bonus aut tutor fidelis esse deberet, tamquam ab aliquo nefario praedone diriperetur patrimonium dignitatis.

Returning to Rome on the last day of the drama festival, he was greatly disturbed by the speech which Philippus was said to have delivered in the assembly and in which it was agreed that he had said 'he would have to find another policy since he could not govern in conjunction with that senate'. On the morning of 13 September, Crassus and the senate crowded into the curia at Drusus' request; there Drusus, after lodging numerous complaints against Philippus, put a motion in front of the senate about the key issue, namely that the consul had subjected the senate to fierce criticism in the assembly. Then — and this is something on which I have noticed general agreement among those qualified to judge — although it almost always happened that when Crassus delivered a prepared speech he was reckoned never to have spoken better, it was nevertheless universally accepted that, while Crassus habitually outshone everyone else, on that day he outshone

even himself. For he deplored the plight and destitution of a
senate whose traditional dignity was being snatched away by
the consul, as if he were some criminal or vandal rather than
the good parent and loyal guardian that he ought to be.

A long periodic sentence sets the scene: an *ut*-clause, followed by
a participial phrase (*commotus*) upon which depends a relative
clause (*quae*); a second relative clause (*quem*) depends upon the
first and contains indirect speech ('*uidendum* . . .'); finally the main
verb, in a phrase employing one of Cicero's favourite clausulae (*in
cūriām uēnit*).[7] Next, a shorter sentence in which a *cum*-clause
gives the chronological order of events, followed by the main verb
(*rettulit*), which is further explained by *quod* . . . *ēssēt inuēctūs* (same
clausula as before). The third sentence is longer again and is
remarkable for its symmetry and balance: *ut* . . . *uidi* ~ *omnium
consensu, quamquam* ~ *tamen, cum* ~ *semper* ~ *numquam, ceteros a
Crasso semper omnes* ~ *illo autem die etiam ipsum a sē sūpērātūm* (a
hexameter ending, one of those freer rhythms which Cicero
himself said were more normally to be associated with historical
writing than with forensic oratory: see above, p. 94).[8] The final
sentence illustrates very well Cicero's liking for fullness of
vocabulary: *casum atque orbitatem, parens bonus aut tutor fidelis, quasi
. . . tamquam*. Again the concluding rhythm (*dīgnītātīs*) is a
favourite of his.[9]

Shortly after this passage, Cicero gives a brief account of
Crassus' death (6), whereupon the style becomes even more
elevated (7-8):

O fallacem hominum spem fragilemque fortunam et inanis
nostras contentiones, quae medio in spatio saepe franguntur et
corruunt aut ante in ipso cursu obruuntur, quam portum
conspicere potuerunt! Nam quam diu Crassi fuit ambitionis
labore vita districta, tam diu privatis magis officiis et ingeni
laude floruit quam fructu amplitudinis aut rei publicae
dignitate; qui autem annus ei primus ab honorum per-
functione aditum omnium concessu ad summam auctoritatem
dabat, is eius omnem spem atque omnia vitae consilia morte
pervertit. Fuit hoc luctuosum suis, acerbum patriae, grave
bonis omnibus; sed ei tamen rem publicam casus secuti sunt,
ut mihi non erepta L. Crasso a dis immortalibus vita, sed
donata mors esse videatur. Non vidit flagrantem bello Italiam,
non ardentem invidia senatum, non sceleris nefarii principes

civitatis reos, non luctum filiae, non exsilium generi, non acerbissimam C. Mari fugam, non illam post reditum eius caedem omnium crudelissimam, non denique in omni genere deformatam eam civitatem, in qua ipse florentissima multum omnibus praestitisset.

How false is man's hope, how fragile fate, and how futile our struggles, which often crash and break up in mid-course, or else are overwhelmed *en route* before the harbour is in sight! For while Crassus was preoccupied with effort and ambition, his personal responsibilities and intellectual reputation enjoyed even more success than his public and political achievement; but his first year out of office, which by general consent brought him unparalleled influence, overthrew by death all his life's hopes and plans. It was a grievous blow to his friends, bitter for his country, and serious for every right-minded citizen; yet such disasters were in store for the state that it seemed to me that the gods had not snatched away Crassus' life but generously granted him his death. He saw neither Italy ablaze with war, nor the senate burning with hatred, nor leading politicians convicted of treason, nor his daughter's grief, nor his son-in-law's exile, nor Marius' most bitter flight, nor that most cruel of all massacres that followed his return, nor finally did he see the complete desecration of the state in which, while at its peak, he stood head and shoulders above the rest.

Three virtual synonyms (*fallacem ... contentiones*) are balanced by a further three (*franguntur ... obruuntur*); *quam diu ...* by *tam diu*, *fructu amplitudinis* by *rei publicae dignitate, qui annus ei ... dabat* by *is eius ... peruertit.* A tricolon (*fuit hoc ... bonis omnibus*) precedes the final corresponsion (*ut mihi non erepta ... mors ēssĕ uĭdēātūr*),[10] which introduces a conclusion of mounting crescendo framed around anaphora of *non*.

The reaction of Sallust

Passages such as those above only served to reinforce the requirements for historical style which Cicero laid down in the *De Oratore* itself and elsewhere. Yet when contemporary readers opened the first page of Sallust's first historical work, they read the following:

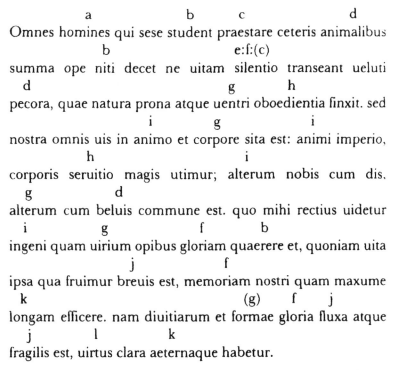

```
              a              b    c              d
Omnes homines qui sese student praestare ceteris animalibus
                b                   e:f:(c)
summa ope niti decet ne uitam silentio transeant ueluti
   d                        g      h
pecora, quae natura prona atque uentri oboedientia finxit. sed
                    i         g           i
nostra omnis uis in animo et corpore sita est: animi imperio,
            h                    i
corporis seruitio magis utimur; alterum nobis cum dis,
   g          d
alterum cum beluis commune est. quo mihi rectius uidetur
   i         g         f        b
ingeni quam uirium opibus gloriam quaerere et, quoniam uita
                    j              f
ipsa qua fruimur breuis est, memoriam nostri quam maxume
   k                          (g)    f    j
longam efficere. nam diuitiarum et formae gloria fluxa atque
   j      l        k
fragilis est, uirtus clara aeternaque habetur.
```

All men who endeavour to surpass other animals ought to strive their utmost not to pass their lives in silence like sheep, which by nature gaze downwards and obey their bellies. *Our* capabilities are mental as well as physical, and *we* use the superiority of the mind to govern the inferior body: the former we share with the gods, the latter with beasts. Therefore it seems to me preferable to seek a reputation with the resources of the intellect rather than with those of the body; and, because our actual life is short, we should ensure that our posthumous reputation lasts as long as possible: a reputation for wealth is transient and for beauty fragile, but virtue[11] is a shining possession that lasts indefinitely.

The superimposed letters indicate corresponsions, which, since they are dialectical and not merely ornamental, contribute both to the rigour of the argument and to the density of the passage. In its tautness and almost obsessive logic it is quite different from the 'amplitude, mobility and fluency' recommended for historiography by Cicero.

It is true that in the penultimate clause the duplication of the adjectives *fluxa* and *fragilis* appears at first sight to exemplify

Ciceronian fullness; yet closer inspection shows that this is not the case: each adjective refers to different types of loss (slow ~ sudden), while the former is perhaps more appropriate to *diuitiarum* and the latter to *formae*.[12] Why then, it may be asked, are the two nouns *diuitiarum* and *formae* themselves there? The latter is chosen because it relates to *corpus*, which has already been mentioned several times (hence it has the same letter as *corpus* but in brackets). The former does not refer back but prepares us for the moral arguments about decadence which Sallust will put forward in later chapters. This technique, of putting an idea into the reader's mind only to return to it later, occurs frequently in the preface and constitutes one of the subtleties of Sallust's style.[13] Thus *uentri oboedientia* at 1.1 is resumed at 2.8 *dediti uentri*; *natura* at 1.1 is resumed at 2.9; and *fortuna* at 8.1 is resumed at 10.1. A particularly good example is *silentio* at 1.1. Since it was proverbial that speech distinguishes man from animals, it is likely that *silentio* is to be understood actively, meaning 'without speaking': the word thus prepares us for one of the main themes of the preface which emerges fully only later at 3.1-2, namely that the products of the brain (i.e. speaking and writing) are as worthwhile as those of the body. Yet most commentators have understood *silentio* passively, meaning 'without being spoken about', i.e. without a reputation:[14] the word in this sense is a perfect preparation for *gloriam quaerere* just below, which is the second of the preface's main themes and which otherwise occurs with almost intolerable suddenness. Since there are thus excellent arguments in favour of each interpretation of *silentio*, it would appear that the word is ambiguous:[15] hence it has two superimposed letters, 'e' anticipating 3.1-2 and 'f' anticipating the sequence *gloriam — memoriam — gloria* immediately below; and since in either sense the word denotes a quality by which men are distinguished from animals, it also requires the letter 'c' to link it with *praestare* just above. It would be difficult to imagine writing of a more condensed nature.

It could of course be argued that a preface of its very nature is untypical of an historian's narrative style; yet prefaces also have a programmatic function, and contemporary readers of the above extract will have noticed the un-Ciceronian rhythms of Sallust's clausulae,[16] the succession of short sentences, and the archaising form *maxume*. Each of these features is characteristic of his work as a whole, and indeed a case can be made that the narrative is even more idiosyncratic in style than the preface. Let us consider, for example, the famous sketch of Sempronia in chapter 25, whose decadence typified the followers of Catiline:

> sed in iis erat Sempronia, quae multa saepe uirilis audaciae facinora conmiserat. haec mulier genere atque forma, praeterea uiro liberis satis fortunata fuit; litteris Graecis Latinis docta, psallere saltare elegantius quam necesse est probae, multa alia quae instrumenta luxuriae sunt. sed ei cariora semper omnia quam decus atque pudicitia fuit: pecuniae an famae minus parceret, haud facile discerneres; lubido sic adcensa ut saepius peteret uiros quam peteretur. sed ea saepe antehac fidem prodiderat, creditum abiurauerat, caedis conscia fuerat; luxuria atque inopia praeceps abierat. uerum ingenium eius haud absurdum: posse uersus facere, iocum mouere, sermone uti uel modesto uel molli uel procaci; prorsus multae facetiae multus lepos inerat.

Among them was Sempronia, whose frequent and daring crimes rivalled those of any man. This woman was blessed with a nice family, appearance, husband and children; well versed in Greek and Latin literature, she could play the guitar and dance with rather more panache than you would expect in a lady; and there were numerous other things which aided and abetted her extravagance. Respectability and modesty were the least of her concerns: you could hardly tell which she squandered more, her money or her reputation: her sex-drive was so strong that she more often pursued men than was pursued by them. Many times in the past she had betrayed a confidence, forsworn credit, and been a party to murder; through extravagance and bankruptcy she had quickly joined the dregs of society. Yet she was no fool: she could write poetry, tell a joke, and her conversation ranged from the wholesome through the risqué to the bawdy. She possessed a great deal of wit and charm.

Though the clausulae here happen to show only a modest deviation from Ciceronian practice,[17] it will be clear that Sallust's over-all style is radically different from the smooth and balanced writing which Cicero recommended.

The second sentence illustrates Sallust's abruptness and variation: two pairs of ablatives depend on *fortunata* and are linked awkwardly by *praeterea*; the first pair is joined by *atque*, the second employs asyndeton. There are three cola in the third sentence, the construction of which is deliberately obscure. Either *docta* is a main verb (with *est* omitted) and governs, in addition to *litteris*, the infinitives *psallere* and *saltare* (asyndeton again) and *multa alia* (which would thus be internal accusative);[18] or *docta* is a participle and governs only *litteris*, the infinitives are historic, and a main verb has to be supplied with *multa alia* (which would thus be nominative).[19] The next sentence comprises three main verbs, each with a different subject: we might expect the first verb to be plural after *omnia* and *decus atque pudicitia*, but it is singular by virtue of its position next to *pudicitia*; next, *utrum* is omitted after *haud facile discerneres*; and *est* is omitted after the third verb *adcensa*. The penultimate sentence is an exercise in calculated inelegance: it begins *sed ea saepe* as its predecessor, which also includes the word *saepius*, had begun *sed ei*; each of its four main verbs is placed last in its clause and ends *-erat*. These are the distinctive features of an archaising style,[20] and the sketch finally concludes with yet another asyndeton (*multae facetiae multus lepos*).[21]

Thus Sir Ronald Syme was quite right to say that Sallust is 'out to destroy balance and harmony' and 'is hostile to the smooth and the redundant'.[22] Yet these were precisely the qualities which Cicero had required for the nature of style (*uerborum ratio*) in the *De Oratore*, a requirement which he had underlined by himself putting it into practice later in the same work (above, pp. 117-20). Why then did Sallust, who follows Cicero so closely in the matter of content, choose to deviate from him so radically on the question of style? This question has two principal answers, one negative and the other positive.

Decline and Dissent

It is clear from the letter which he wrote to Lucceius in 55 BC that Cicero regarded his suppression of the Catilinarian conspiracy as the most successful achievement of his already successful career (see above, pp. 70-3). His recent triumphal return from a brief exile in 58/7 only served to emphasise his own estimation of the heroic stature and popular acclaim which his victory over Catiline had brought him; and in Lucceius' history he saw the opportunity for his own *uirtus* and *gloria* to be immortalised. Cicero was thus urging upon his friend the kind of encomiastic historiography which was expected of ancient historians and

which can be traced back through Lucceius' Roman predecessors to the Greek tradition (see above, pp. 41-2).[23] It is true that
a very few second-century historians, perhaps as a result of the
Gracchan upheaval, had adopted the attitude that Rome was on
the decline;[24] but the majority had naturally taken the view that
the history of Rome was a success story.[25] This was certainly the
view of Cicero himself. His friends assumed that if he were ever to
write history, he too would adopt an encomiastic attitude by
celebrating the Roman state and by praising those, like Pompey,
whom he considered to be its heroes.[26]

Sallust saw those same events from an entirely different perspective. When he wrote the *Bellum Catilinae*, almost fifteen years
had passed since the production of the *De Oratore* and the letter to
Lucceius. Civil war had broken out in 49 BC and showed no signs
of abating; as a result of the war, first Pompey and then Caesar
and Cicero himself had been killed. As for Sallust, he had been
expelled from the senate in 50 (perhaps on a trumped up charge);
and though he was re-admitted, he was later charged with extor-
tion after his governorship of Africa and forced to leave political
life.[27] Thus his personal circumstances and the general political
situation were both equally grim, and, disillusioned with the
society which he saw as having rejected him, he resorted to the
medium of history to obtain his revenge. Capitalising on the
turmoil in contemporary politics, he, like the small cluster of
second-century historians noted above, chose as his theme the
decline of Rome. In chapters 10-13 of the preface he traces the
progressive degeneration of Rome after the fall of Carthage in 146
BC and then at 14.1 introduces the Catilinarian conspiracy as its
climax.[28] Sallust thus used history to express his dissent from the
direction in which society was moving, and he chose the Catilinarian conspiracy as his subject because he regarded it as sympto-
matic of that movement. 'He attacks his own times and criticises
their failings', as a later reader, the historian Granius Licinianus,
remarked.[29]

It is therefore clear that Sallust's attitude to his subject (his
διάθεσις, to use the technical term of Dionysius: above p. 41) was
quite different from that which Cicero urged upon Lucceius. It is
almost as if Sallust had read Cicero's letter and, in the standard
rhetorical manner, treated the same subject with a different *color*,
thus giving it a different 'complexion', 'angle' or 'slant'.[30] The difference naturally extends to the man whom Cicero had regarded
as the principal character in the affair: himself. Whereas Cicero

had seen his own role as that of an heroic saviour of a constitution which was worth saving, Sallust consistently treats him with the studied ambiguity of one whose disillusionment embraces society at large.

Now it is well known that the Romans in general had a highly developed sense of stylistic propriety: the style which was appropriate to one genre or type of writing was unlikely to be equally appropriate for another.[31] A good example of this is Tacitus' *Dialogus* which, being a dialogue on oratory, is written in an appropriately neo-Ciceronian style which is quite different from that used by Tacitus in his historical works.[32] Given this sensitivity to style, and given also that Sallust's attitude to his subject was so different from that recommended by Cicero to Lucceius, it is hardly surprising if Sallust found himself with a very good reason for avoiding the style which Cicero had required for historiography in general. The fact that Cicero's ideal historical stylist was Herodotus (above, p. 94), with whom encomiastic historiography was so closely associated (above, p. 42), no doubt served only to confirm Sallust in his view. And since the style required by Cicero for historiography was also that for which he himself had become famous (above, p. 94), it must not be forgotten that the ancients, like us (see pp. 46-7), believed that style reflects the life and personality of the writer.[33] Cicero himself, for example, had said that the style of the orator Q. Aelius Tubero was as rough and uncouth as the man, and that the elder Cato's life and style were a fair reflection of each other.[34] To Sallust it must therefore have seemed that Cicero's own style — characterised by balance, amplitude and correspondion — did indeed reflect a complacency and conservatism which were utterly at odds with the attitude adopted in the *Bellum Catilinae*.

These considerations explain why Sallust chose not to follow Cicero's recommendations on the nature of style;[35] but they do not explain his positive choice of a style which, as we have seen from representative excerpts (pp. 121-4), combines abruptness, variation, brevity and archaising.[36] The fact is that these precise features were also thought to characterise the style of Thucydides.[37] When the younger Seneca, for example, described Sallust's style with reference to 'sentences which stop short and phrases which end before you expect, and brevity to the point of obscurity',[38] he was repeating almost exactly the description which Dionysius had given of Thucydides' style roughly three quarters of a century earlier (see above, p. 45).[39] This evidence, coupled with Sallust's well known addiction to Thucydides' phraseology,[40] leaves little doubt that he intended his work to be a pervasive and comprehensive imitation of that of Thucydides.[41] And it was as a 'second Thucydides' that he was seen by Seneca's father, by Velleius, and by Quintilian.[42]

It will be remembered that Dionysius described not only Thucydides' style but also his attitude (διάθεσις) to his subject matter, saying that it was 'severe and harsh' (above, p. 41). Now although Dionysius was writing about twenty years after Sallust wrote the *Bellum Catilinae* and it cannot be proved beyond doubt that others had held a similar view of Thucydides before him, nevertheless the likelihood is that Dionysius was not the first to see Thucydides in this way (above, pp. 41-3). Indeed, since Sallust both imitates Thucydides' style and also adopts towards his own subject matter an attitude which is 'severe and harsh', it seems fairly clear that the Dionysian view of Thucydides was current at least in Sallust's day. Sallust, in other words, imitated Thucydides' style 'to produce an equivalence of manner and atmosphere';[43] but there was of course an even closer affinity between the two writers. Sallust had been forced out of Roman political life in the 40s in much the same way as Thucydides had been exiled from Athens in 424, the event which, in Dionysius' opinion, was responsible for souring his attitude towards the Athenians. By the simple method of imitating his style, Sallust was thus able to present himself as the Roman reincarnation of the great Greek historian.[44]

By preferring the style of Thucydides to that required by Cicero, Sallust therefore underlined his attitude to his subject and at the same time reflected the dissenting qualities of his own personality. Another dissenter was his younger contemporary Asinius Pollio, who nurtured a hatred for the republic's most eloquent supporter until long after Cicero's death,[45] and then, having successively supported Caesar and Antony during their periods of glory, lived through much of Augustus' long reign as self-appointed custodian of the republican conscience.[46] Pollio's critical spirit is unlikely to have deserted him in the history which he wrote of the years 60 BC onwards,[47] since that period saw the effective destruction of the republic and the ground prepared for the dictatorship of Augustus. This is a matter on which we cannot be certain, since his work has survived only in the merest fragments; but it is perhaps significant that he too, like Sallust, seems to have adopted a Thucydidean style. Seneca described

Pollio's style as 'choppy and jerky and leaving off when you least expect it' (*Ep.* 100.7 'compositio ... salebrosa et exsiliens et ubi minime exspectes relictura'):[48] 'choppiness' was the word Cicero used to describe the antithesis of his ideal Herodotean style (above, p. 94), while 'leaving off when you least expect it' echoes Seneca's own description of Sallust (above, p. 126), which in turn echoes Dionysius' description of Thucydides himself (above, p. 45). It would therefore appear that Pollio followed Sallust in his rejection of Ciceronian ideals and his imitation of the Thucydidean style.[49] If our inferences about Pollio's politics are correct, it seems that his work confirms the link between attitude and style which Sallust had done so much to establish.[50]

Livy

After Sallust and Pollio, Rome's next major historian was Livy, whose monumental work in 142 volumes covered Roman history from the founding of the city down to 9 BC. It is generally believed that Livy began writing in the 20s BC and that the preface in particular can be dated after 28 BC (below, pp. 132-3). This being so, scholars have naturally speculated about Livy's response to the momentous political developments which were taking place during that decade: namely, Augustus' establishment of himself as *princeps*. Indeed for the past fifty years, as P.G. Walsh has observed, 'the dominant preoccupation of scholars writing on Livy has been the relationship between the historian and the emperor Augustus'.[51] Walsh himself, after surveying the available evidence on the question, has concluded that 'Livy does not consciously lend his services as historian to the consolidation of the Augustan régime'.[52] Others have gone even further, and posited that Livy was actually out of sympathy with the emperor and his aims.[53] If these conclusions are correct, they suggest that Livy has entirely disregarded the link between attitude and style which had been established by Sallust and confirmed by Pollio. For it is well known that Livy's style was compared by Quintilian with that of Herodotus and contrasted with that of Sallust.[54]

Preface

Everyone accepts that the preface constitutes one of the crucial pieces of evidence in any debate concerning Livy's relationship with the emperor Augustus. I therefore propose to examine it again to see whether it does indeed produce the conclusions which scholars have usually drawn. The key passages, for our purposes, are as follows:

Facturusne operae pretium sim si a primordio urbis res populi Romani perscripserim nec satis scio nec, si sciam, dicere
2 ausim, quippe qui cum ueterem tum uolgatam esse rem uideam, dum noui semper scriptores aut in rebus certius aliquid allaturos se aut scribendi arte rudem uetustatem
3 superaturos credunt. Vtcumque erit, iuuabit tamen rerum gestarum memoriae principis terrarum populi pro uirili parte et ipsum consuluisse; et si in tanta scriptorum turba mea fama in obscuro sit, nobilitate ac magnitudine eorum me qui
4 nomini officient meo consoler. Res est praeterea et immensi operis, ut quae supra septingentesimum annum repetatur et quae ab exiguis profecta initiis eo creuerit ut iam magnitudine laboret sua; et legentium plerisque haud dubito quin primae origines proximaque originibus minus praebitura uoluptatis sint, festinantibus ad haec noua quibus iam pridem praeua-
5 lentis populi uires se ipsae conficiunt: ego contra hoc quoque laboris praemium petam, ut me a conspectu malorum quae nostra tot per annos uidit aetas, tantisper certe dum prisca illa tota mente[55] repeto, auertam, omnis expers curae quae scribentis animum, etsi non flectere a uero, sollicitum tamen efficere posset ...

9 ... ad illa mihi pro se quisque acriter intendat animum, quae uita, qui mores fuerint, per quos uiros quibusque artibus domi militiaeque et partum et auctum imperium sit; labante deinde paulatim disciplina uelut dissidentes primo mores sequatur animo, deinde ut magis magisque lapsi sint, tum ire coeperint praecipites, donec ad haec tempora quibus nec uitia
10 nostra nec remedia pati possumus peruentum est. Hoc illud est praecipue in cognitione rerum salubre ac frugiferum, omnis te exempli documenta in inlustri posita monumento intueri; inde tibi tuaeque rei publicae quod imitere capias, inde foedum inceptu foedum exitu quod uites ...

Whether it will be worthwhile to give a full account of Roman history from the founding of the city, I do not know; and if I
2 did know, I would not venture to say so. In the first place, the subject is traditional and popular, and new historians always

think either that they have some more exact knowledge to impart to the subject matter or that their literary skill will improve on the inferior standards of their predecessors.[56]

3 Whether or not my suspicion will prove to be justified, I shall nevertheless take pleasure in doing my personal best to entrust to posterity the achievements of the leading nation on earth. If it should transpire that in such a large group of historians my own reputation remains obscure, I should console myself with the thought of their nobility and distinction.

4 Second, the subject involves immeasurable labour in that it is to be traced back more than seven hundred years and from an unprepossessing start has grown consistently until it has now reached the point where it is labouring under its own size. I am confident that the majority of my readers, in their haste to reach the present period when the forces of a long-standing super-power are bent on self-destruction, will derive less pleasure from the origins of Rome and the immediately

5 succeeding period. But I personally regard it as a bonus, at least while the archaic age has my undivided attention, to avert my gaze from the misfortunes which for so many years our own age has witnessed. Then too I shall be free of all those considerations which, even if they failed to divert him from the truth, could still put pressure on a historian ...

9 ... My concern is that each reader should note carefully the kind of life and morality, the kind of individuals and qualities which delivered us an empire at home and abroad and then expanded it. He should then trace how, as discipline began gradually to slip, morality showed its first cracks, next became increasingly unstable, and then began to collapse until the present time was reached when we can sustain neither our

10 disorders nor their remedies. This in fact is an area where familiarity with history can be particularly salutary and beneficial, since it provides, in a clear and permanent setting, object-lessons in every kind of behaviour. You can select both what to emulate, if it benefits yourself and the state, and what to avoid, if it is loathsome from start to finish.

Here Livy, like Sallust and his second-century predecessors (above, p. 125), clearly sees Roman history in terms of decline. Indeed it is clear from the verbal parallels that he invites us to see his work in the context of Sallust's *Histories*, where decline had been a dominant theme: 1 *a primordio urbis res populi Romani perscripserim* ~ *H.* 1.8 *a principio urbis* and 1.1 *res populi Romani . . . composui*; 3 *in tanta scriptorum turba* ~ *H.* 1.3 *nos in tanta doctissimorum copia*; 5 *non flectere a uero* ~ *H.* 1.6 *neque . . . mouit a uero*; 9 *domi militiaeque* ~ *H.* 1.1 *militiae et domi*; 9 *paulatim . . . mores . . . praecipites . . . pati* ~ *H.* 1.16 *mores . . . paulatim . . . praecipitati . . . pati.* From these parallels the reader is intended to infer that Livy is writing history in the tradition of Sallust; and the fact that he has omitted to mention *ambitio*, to which Sallust in his analysis of decline had attached considerable significance,[57] will signal to the learned reader that his is an alternative and therefore improved version compared with that of his distinguished predecessor. Such rivalry (*aemulatio*) was of course normal practice in ancient historiography from the earliest times.[58]

Now the decline of civilisation was a theme which also went back to the earliest days of Greek literature and which gave rise to a large number of theories such as the Golden Age and Cyclic History.[59] Numerous authors were attracted by the view that societies contain within themselves the seeds of their own degeneration and ultimate destruction. This was certainly the view of Polybius (6.57.1-7),[60] and evidently that of Livy too. In section 4 of the preface he says that Rome 'now . . . is labouring under its own size' (*iam magnitudine laboret sua*), and he refers to 'the present period when [its] forces . . . are bent on self-destruction' (*haec noua quibus . . . uires se ipsae conficiunt*). These forms of expression find a striking analogy in the opening couplet of Horace's sixteenth epode, written in 39/38 BC:[61]

> Altera iam teritur bellis ciuilibus aetas,
>   suis et ipsa Roma uiribus ruit.

> Another generation now is being worn away by civil war,
>   and Rome itself is collapsing under its own strength.

Horace is referring to the renewed violence of the civil war which manifested itself at the time, and his image of a self-destroying Rome became almost a conventional code for describing civil war: Propertius 3.13.60 *frangitur ipsa suis Roma superba bonis* ('hybristic Rome itself is being broken on it own successes'), Manilius 1.912 *imperiumque suis conflixit uiribus ipsum* ('the empire itself in conflict through its own strength'), Seneca, *Const. Sap.* 2.2 *uitia ciuitatis degenerantis et pessum sua mole sidentis* ('the disorders of a state degenerating and sinking to destruction under its own weight'), Lucan 1.71-2 *nimioque graues sub pondere lapsus/ nec se Roma ferens* ('severe collapsings under too much weight, and Rome failing to sustain itself'), Petronius 120.84-5 *ipsa suas uires odit Romana iuuentus/ et quas struxit opes, male sustinet* ('Rome's young men actually hate their own strength and hardly sustain the resources which they have accumulated': in the poem on the civil war). In the light of this evidence it is difficult not to believe that Livy is using the same code for the same purposes.[62] Either he borrowed it directly from Horace, or, in view of the similarities which exist between the epode and the works of Sallust, both he and Horace derived it from a passage of Sallust now lost (presumably the preface to the *Histories*).[63]

It is clear, both from the passages quoted above and from Livy's own use of the motif elsewhere, that the cause of Rome's self-destruction varied from author to author. Some attribute it to hybris, some to the immorality which accompanies the acquisition of an empire, some to power struggles within the state, some to what might loosely be called the 'dinosaur syndrome'.[64] In section 4 of the preface Livy does not specify which of these, if any, he has in mind; but his very use of the motif itself suggests that by *iam* ('now') and *haec noua* ('the present period') he means the time of the civil wars. This seems to be confirmed by his imitator Florus, who uses the same motif for the same purposes (1.47.6): 'eo *magnitudinis* crescere ut *uiribus suis conficeretur*' ('growing to such a size that it was destroyed by its own strength').[65] And since Livy refers to the present time on two other occasions in the preface, at 5 *quae [mala] nostra tot per annos uidit aetas* and 9 *haec tempora quibus nec uitia nostra nec remedia pati possumus*, it would seem perverse not to maintain that these passages too refer to the civil wars.[66] It therefore follows that Livy wrote his preface while the civil wars were still in progress: that is, before the future emperor Augustus defeated Antony at Actium in 31 BC.

The above argument no doubt seems relatively uncontroversial, and indeed most scholars are content to explain sections 4-5 of the preface in terms of the civil wars. But this has not been the case with section 9.[67] Since the beginning of this century it has been generally held that the clause *quibus nec uitia nostra nec remedia pati possumus* ('when we can sustain neither our disorders nor their remedies') is a critical allusion to the degeneration of public and private morality which Augustus allegedly tried to remedy through legislation which he attempted to introduce in 28 BC but was compelled to withdraw in the face of fierce opposition.[68] If this view is correct, it follows that Livy's preface must post-date 28 BC.[69] Yet there is no firm evidence to support this view, which is merely a hypothesis based on the seeming appropriateness of the words *uitia* and *remedia* to the circumstances in which Augustus' legislation is said to have been introduced and withdrawn. And, to make matters still more interesting, it has recently been argued by Badian that the legislation of 28 BC never existed in the first place.[70] Can Livy's expression therefore be interpreted differently?

It was common in ancient times to use illness metaphors to describe the state:[71] Sallust, for example, had done so,[72] and Livy himself does so at 3.20.8: 'non ita ciuitatem aegram esse ut consuetis remediis sisti possit' ('the state was not ill in such a way that it could be checked by conventional remedies'). *remedia* in section 9 of the preface clearly indicates that Livy is using the same metaphor here; and *uitia*, a word regularly used in the context of illness,[73] is an integral part of the metaphor. Again, the Greeks and Romans, like us, often used the metaphorical expression 'the cure is worse than the disease': Livy himself does so at 34.49.3 'intermori uehementioribus, quam quae *pati posset*, *remediis ciuitatem* sinere' ('allowing the state to die from remedies too powerful for it to be able to sustain'). Other Latin examples of the expression include the following: Seneca, *Contr.* 6.7.2 *quaedam remedia peiora ipsis periculis sunt*, Seneca, *Ben.* 5.16.3 *patriam durioribus remediis quam pericula erant sanauit* (of Sulla), *Medea* 433-4 *remedia . . ./periculis peiora*, [Quintilian] *Decl.* 377.8 (p. 274W) *malis . . . ipsis tristiora remedia*, Tacitus, *Annals* 3.28.1 *consul . . . grauior remediis quam delicta erant corrigendis moribus*.[74] Given this metaphorical complex of ideas, it would be entirely natural if Livy used the word *uitia* to describe the civil wars which were raging at the time when he wrote the preface. But what of the word *remedia*?

Livy's contemporaries recognised that, whoever won the civil war, the result would be some form of autocracy.[75] It is therefore interesting to note that on two other occasions when Livy uses the same metaphor of *remedium*, the context is that of the constitutional dictatorship of the republic. The first passage is 3.20.8, part of which has already been quoted above: 'non ita ciuitatem aegram esse ut consuetis remediis sisti possit: dictatore opus esse rei publicae'; the second is 22.8.5, which has been preceded by a whole series of illness words: 'itaque ad remedium iam diu neque desideratum nec adhibitum, dictatorem dicendum, ciuitas confugit' ('so the state sought refuge in a remedy which for a long time had been neither needed nor called for: appointing a dictator'). These passages suggest that Livy might well have had the same idea in mind in the preface.[76] That the state cannot sustain the *uitia* of civil war is self-evident; but the conclusion of the war means the powers of an unconstitutional dictatorship, *remedia* to which the Romans were traditionally averse and which Livy therefore thought were also incapable of being sustained. Tacitus uses precisely the same metaphor towards the beginning of the *Annals*, and it may be that he too understood Livy's preface in this way: 1.9.4 'non aliud discordantis patriae remedium fuisse quam <ut> ab uno regeretur.' ('there had been no other remedy for the country divided against itself than being ruled by one man').[77] Whether or not this is so, there can be no doubt that this interpretation of section 9 accords perfectly with the suggestion made above (pp. 131-2) that the preface was written while the civil wars were still in progress.[78]

This conclusion, if true, seems to me to be of considerable significance. The preface has been accepted as one of the crucial pieces of evidence in the debate concerning Livy's relationship with the emperor Augustus (above, p. 128): when dated after 28 BC it has been thought to reveal disenchantment with the emperor and his policies (above, p. 132).[79] But if it is right to date the preface before the end of the civil war in 31 BC, Livy in section 9 is merely expressing a natural distaste both for the war itself and for the prospect of dictatorship which alone would end the war. On this interpretation the preface fails to provide us with any evidence at all for Livy's relationship with Augustus once the latter became *princeps*, a topic which we have yet to consider. First, however, we must ask how this new dating of the preface fits in with the early books of Livy's history.

The early books

It is generally accepted nowadays that Livy wrote in five- or ten-book units,[80] and there are signs that the first decade of books was composed at a relatively early date. At 7.40.2 Livy writes 'they were not yet brave for shedding blood in civil war nor indeed did they have experience of any but foreign wars', and at 9.19.15 'May the civil wars remain silent', closely followed by 'provided that our love of the peace which we are now enjoying and our concern for civil concord remain for ever' (17).[81] The latter passage, as T.J. Luce has rightly remarked, 'suggests that the civil wars were recent and that Augustus' rule was still quite new. The later the passage is dated, the more peculiar the passionate vehemence becomes: unflattering to the government and to the emperor, impolitic for the writer.'[82] As for the former passage, 'the same considerations apply': even if it does not prove that the civil wars were still in progress when Livy wrote it,[83] it at least shows that they were not long over and that their memory was still fresh in his mind. And since both these passages are from the second pentad, it follows that the first pentad was written even earlier — no doubt, in view of our dating of the preface, before the civil wars ended.[84]

There are, however, two pieces of evidence which seem to conflict with this conclusion. At 1.19.2-3 Livy refers to Octavian as 'Augustus', a name which he was given in 27 BC, and he mentions the closing of the temple of Janus in 29 BC. It follows that this passage was written between 27 and 25 BC, since in the latter year there was a second closure of the temple which Livy does not mention.[85] Again, at 4.20.5-11 Livy reveals that Augustus provided him with an apparently ancient inscription concerning the *spolia opima* ('prize spoils'): the circumstances suggest that Augustus' intervention took place not earlier than 29 BC; and since the name 'Augustus' is used here too, it is probable that this passage also was written later than 27 BC.[86] Both these passages would constitute insurmountable obstacles to an early dating of the first pentad were it not that T.J. Luce, in a brilliant article, has shown (conclusively, to my mind) that both of them were inserted into the main narrative at a later date.[87] The inevitable conclusion has been expressed, albeit cautiously, by Luce himself: 'If it can be shown that the passages concerning Augustus in Books One and Four ... are later additions, the composition of the first pentad must be pushed back, possibly before the Battle of Actium.'[88] It is of course true, as Luce admits, that 'hypotheses of second editions are generally distasteful, for they smack of the drastic and desperate';[89] but Livy's procedure is easily paralleled (Ovid's *Amores* come immediately to mind).[90] And since Luce himself was concerned neither with Livy's preface nor with arguing the case for pre-Actian composition, it seems reasonable to regard his article as complementing and supporting the argument I put forward in the preceding section.

The Augustan historian

Although we know that Livy eventually wrote 142 volumes of history, a stray sentence of his, preserved by the elder Pliny, suggests that his original intention had been to write rather fewer: 'he had acquired enough fame and could have stopped writing, but his restless temperament thrived on the work'.[91] This sentence, which derives from a lost preface and seems to allude pointedly to the erstwhile diffidence he had expressed in the preface to Book 1 (pref. 3 'If it should transpire that ... my own reputation remains obscure'), indicates that at some point Livy decided to extend his original plan. But what was that plan, and of what did the extension consist?

Book 121, according to its summary, 'is said to have been published after the death of Augustus',[92] a statement which scholars have generally taken to refer to Books 121-42 as a whole.[93] It has therefore been inferred that Livy's original intention had been to write Books 1-120, that Books 121-42 are the extension, and that the stray sentence preserved by Pliny derives from the lost preface to Book 121 in which Livy explained his decision to continue writing.[94] Unfortunately, there is no way of proving this attractive hypothesis; but some radical change after Book 120 seems likely since Livy's practice of working in five-book units, which he sustains consistently up to this book, breaks down in Books 121-42.[95]

If the hypothesis is correct, it means that the final episode in Livy's original plan was the murder of Cicero in December 43 BC, the event with which Book 120 is closed and which Livy dignified by a laudatory obituary notice for the dead orator and statesman.[96] Since Cicero had come almost to symbolise the republic, this was a most appropriate finale for an historian who had set out, in the dark days of the civil wars, to trace the decline of Rome.[97] Taking his cue expressly from the *Histories* of Sallust (above, p. 131), Livy aimed to modernise and surpass the achievement of his great predecessor. It is in this sense, on the basis of his original plan, that he can justly be called 'the last of the republican writers'.[98]

Yet since Livy at some point decided to add Books 121-42, covering the years from 42 to 9 BC (i.e. mid-way through Augustus' reign), we must ask why he did so and what effect these extra books would have had on his work as a whole.

When Livy conceived the idea of a great history, his sympathies lay with the earlier and glorious periods of Rome's history, which emphasised by contrast the later periods of progressive decline. So much is clear from the preface and elsewhere.[99] But since it is also clear from the preface (sections 9-10) that he intended his work to have exemplary value and to be useful, it follows that he did not believe the decline to be irreversible.[100] In other words, one of the purposes of the early books was to place before his readers examples of behaviour which might encourage a return to the old ways and away from the troubles of the present time. Thus many of the early books, as is well known, have a moral theme (such as *moderatio* in Book 3 and *pietas* in Book 5).[101] Within each book a hero(ine) will represent a moral virtue: thus Lucretia in 1.57-9 stands for *pudicitia*,[102] and Camillus in 5.51-4 utters 'an appeal for peace, for the defence of civilisation …, for concord and, above all, for the preservation of Rome'.[103] Many of the books applaud Rome's foreign conquests, which Livy describes in loving detail;[104] but at the same time his own abiding concern is for domestic peace.[105]

It will be obvious from this evidence that Livy's moral and social aims coincided with those of Augustus once he became *princeps*. By defeating Antony at Actium he brought peace to Rome and Italy after twenty years of civil war,[106] while at the same time he spent much of his reign projecting an image of himself as the conqueror of foreign peoples.[107] *pietas* featured on the golden shield which the senate presented to Augustus in 27 BC;[108] and when Augustus introduced legislation concerning adultery and marriage in 18 BC, he read to the senate the speech which Q. Metellus had delivered on a similar occasion in 130 BC and which Livy dealt with in Book 59.[109]

Now if Livy began to write his history as early as I have argued, he cannot have had Augustus in mind when he wrote his early books. He was simply putting forward a series of ideals with which Augustus later came to identify himself. Though the coincidence might look too good to be true at first sight, this is not the case: it has long been recognised that as *princeps* Augustus claimed many of the virtues of the ideal ruler (*rector rei publicae*) which were to be found in Cicero's philosophical writings on government and no doubt elsewhere too.[110] Such writings would also be a natural source for anyone, like Livy, who attempted to write history with a highly developed moral slant. And it is recognised, even by scholars who accept the traditional (later) dating of Livy's work, that the historian is unlikely to have been influenced by Augustus in the early books. Thus R.M. Ogilvie says of Camillus' speech, mentioned above, that 'only in so far as Augustus shared the same aims can the speech be said to be Augustan in outlook or in sympathy'.[111]

This evidence, coupled with Livy's known decision to extend his history into Augustus' reign, suggests that the historian came to see Augustus as the realisation or personification of the ambitions which he personally entertained for the Roman state. We must remember that the careers of the two men, historian and ruler, overlapped and lasted for almost half a century. When he began his work in the midst of civil war, Livy had little option but to choose as his theme the decline of Rome. Hence his preface strikes a note familiar from Horace's poetry of the same period. But as Livy proceeded with each successive volume, he had ample opportunity to reflect that the nadir was now past and that with the principate of Augustus the good old days were being restored. This is a trend familiar from the later poetry of Horace. And just as Horace became progressively closer to the régime until in 17 BC he was asked to write the *Carmen Saeculare*, so Livy was drawn closer to Augustus through acting as mentor to the young Claudius when the future emperor branched out into historiography himself.[112] It is highly unlikely that Augustus would have sanctioned Livy in this role if he had had any doubts about his loyalty. Because Livy's working life spanned both the civil wars and the Augustan principate, the question whether or not he was an 'Augustan historian' is too static to be meaningful. Nothing was more natural than that he, like the poets, should abandon the grim view of history which he had formed in the 30s and should come to sympathise with the principate and support the emperor in his writing.

The ancient views of historical change were able easily to accommodate the change in Livy's own outlook. As we have already noted (above, p. 131), theories of historical decline could be expressed in cyclic form: this meant that, no matter how severe the decline had been, there was always the possibility that history would come round full circle and return to its previous high point.[113] The classic example of this is Florus, who saw Roman history in biological terms.[114] The years 43 BC-AD 9, at which his work stops, are the period of maturity, to be followed by that of old age; but with the advent of the emperor Trajan, under whose principate (AD 98-117) Florus seems to have lived, 'the old age of the empire regains its strength as if its youth were restored to it' (pref. 5-8). Florus' great contemporary, Tacitus, adopted a similar line on Trajan's reign;[115] and a century earlier Livy's younger contemporary, the elder Seneca, probably adopted an analogous view, seeing the civil wars as the nadir and Augustus' reign as the period of renewal.[116]

It is likely that this was also the procedure of Livy himself. On his original plan, the latest years of his narrative were intended to be those of the civil wars, providing an unhappy comparison with Rome's glorious past.[117] On his revised plan, however, he was able to represent Augustus' victory over Antony at Actium in 31 BC, which he described in Book 133, as the turning-point in Rome's fortunes.[118] In the remaining books (134-42), which dealt with the years up to 9 BC, Livy seems to have concentrated on wars against foreign peoples;[119] and since many of his earlier books had dealt with the acquisition of Rome's empire, he was thus able to suggest that history had come full circle and that the Augustan age was challenging the past in glory. Thus, as Luce has rightly remarked, 'Livy's account of his own times was at once the climax and crowning achievement of the *Ab Urbe Condita*'.[120] Indeed, the wars of Tiberius and Drusus in 12-9 BC, with which Livy concludes his work, were (in Syme's words) 'the high epoch of the Augustan conquests', and the year 9 BC itself, to which Livy devotes his final volume, was 'the ideal date' on which to close.[121] This circular movement of the narrative was in exact accord with one of the dominant concerns of Augustus himself, namely that his principate should be seen as an era of glorious restoration.[122]

Thus Livy's decision to add Books 121-42 was caused, in my opinion, by his realisation that Augustus' principate was of benefit to the Roman state. And that decision radically affected the perspective of his whole work: its latest volumes no longer provided a contrast with the past, as would have been the case on his original plan, but an analogy. Against this background let us now reconsider the question of Livy's style, which was raised but not discussed above (p. 128).

When Livy composed his account of Rome's early years, for which he had such enthusiasm, he employed a style which is the historical counterpart of Cicero's oratory: he sought and achieved the 'amplitude, mobility and fluency' which Cicero himself had required for the nature of style (*uerborum ratio*) in the *De Oratore* (above p. 94). Thus, for example, the speech which Livy puts into the mouth of Camillus at the end of Book 5 is 'consciously Ciceronian'.[123] But whether this style was sustained throughout the remainder of the work must remain doubtful. We have already seen that Livy originally conceived of Roman history in Sallustian terms of decline (above, p. 130), and it seems to me quite likely that in his account of the civil wars, which he began in the now lost Book 109, he consciously adapted his style to make it more like Sallust's.[124] In this way he would have been able to capitalise on the link between style and attitude which Sallust had promoted. Equally, however, it seems inconceivable that Livy would have kept up such imitation once he reached the reign of Augustus in the additional books. Here he will have returned to the style in which he had already narrated the glorious years of Rome's expansion in the early books, thus reinforcing the similarity between the two periods (p. 139). This would certainly explain why Quintilian, who was able to judge the history on the basis of all the books, likened Livy's style to that of Herodotus and contrasted it with that of Sallust. For even if Livy imitated Sallust for the relatively brief period when that style was appropriate, his work as a whole, on the revised plan, will have created the impression on readers that its over-all slant was encomiastic of Roman history and that it was written in the style which Cicero had prescribed.

Influence of Sallust and Livy

Sallust and Livy established themselves as the outstanding historians of the late republic and early empire, the Roman equivalents of Thucydides and Herodotus. Their respective achievements constituted a challenge to subsequent historians, but which of them was considered the more suitable for rivalry and imitation? Sir Ronald Syme has characteristically suggested alternative answers to this question. Writing in 1964 he maintained both that Sallust 'heralds the empire' and that the possibility of 'anyone among the annalistic predecessors of Cornelius Tacitus [being] a strong Sallustian ... may be doubted'.[125] It is very difficult to decide which of these answers is correct, since very little of the work of the first-century AD historians has survived. But there is perhaps just enough evidence to clarify the picture.[126]

L. Arruntius, a contemporary of Pollio and Livy, was elevated to the consulship of 22 BC, which effectively means that he was recognised as a supporter of the emperor's.[127] He wrote a monograph on the Punic Wars of which nothing has survived except for a handful of short quotations in the younger Seneca, who regarded him as an example of literary imitation gone mad: 'mannerisms which were rare in Sallust occur frequently and almost non-stop in him'.[128] Since the Romans were victorious in the Punic Wars, and since Arruntius presumably adopted an encomiastic attitude towards the victory in his work, his Sallustianism is at first sight surprising: it seems to breach the relationship between attitude and style which Sallust himself had helped to establish. Yet it emerges from the rest of Seneca's comment that Arruntius' precise vice was not the comprehensive iconoclasm of Sallust but an overdeveloped taste for archaising language; and this was no doubt only to be expected in a work which dealt with events of the third century BC.[129]

Velleius Paterculus, praetor in AD 15, published a universal history in summary form in AD 30.[130] It is one of the very few first-century histories to have survived. Velleius regularly resorts to Sallustian phraseology for its immediate effect,[131] but there is no attempt to reproduce Sallust's abrupt and contorted style; on the contrary, Velleius' work is characterised by the balance, corresponsion and amplitude which Cicero had recommended.[132] This is particularly obvious in those passages where he is concerned with Cicero himself,[133] but as a 'neutral' example let us consider the account of events in Illyricum in AD 7 (112.3-5):

3   Ita placebat barbaris numerus suus, ita fiducia uirium ut. ubicumque Caesar esset, nihil in se reponerent. pars exercitus eorum, proposita ipsi duci et ad arbitrium utilitatemque nostram macerata perductaque ad exitiabilem famem, neque instantem sustinere neque cum facientibus copiam pugnandi derigentibusque aciem ausa congredi, occupato monte
4   Claudio munitione se defendit. at ea pars quae obuiam se effuderat exercitui quem A. Caecina et Siluanus Plautius consulares ex transmarinis adducebant prouinciis, circumfusa quinque legionibus nostris auxiliaribusque et equitatui regio (quippe magnam Thracum manum iunctus praedictis ducibus Rhoemetalces, Thraciae rex, in adiutorium eius belli secum trahebat) paene exitiabilem omnibus cladem intulit.
5   fusa regiorum equestris acies, fugatae alae, conuersae cohortes sunt; apud signa quoque legionum trepidatum. sed Romani uirtus militis plus eo tempore uindicauit gloriae quam ducibus reliquit, qui multum a more imperatoris sui discrepantes ante

in hostem inciderunt, quam per exploratores, ubi hostis esset, cognoscerent.

Although the barbarians had a large force and confidence in numbers, they placed no reliance on themselves if Tiberius was in the vicinity. The part of their army that was exposed to the leader himself, having been mauled at will (and to our advantage) and reduced to murderous starvation, had the courage neither to withstand his attacks nor oppose him when he offered open battle or formed his battle-line; instead they dug themselves into a defensive position on Mt Claudius. But the part which had swarmed out to meet the army which the ex-consuls A. Caecina and Plautius Silvanus were bringing up from the overseas provinces, having surrounded five of our legions together with the auxiliaries and the king's cavalry battalion (for Rhoemetalces the king of Thrace had joined up with the generals just mentioned and had brought with him a large company of Thracians to help the war effort), inflicted on all of them an almost fatal defeat. The king's cavalry line was routed, the wings were put to flight, the cohorts were turned in their tracks; there was even panic amongst the legionary standards. But in that crisis the courage of the Roman soldier won more glory for himself than he left over for his leaders, who, in trying to fall on the enemy before their intelligence could discover exactly where the enemy was, could not have behaved more differently from their commander-in-chief.

The first sentence gives us the theme of the episode, namely the enemy's paradoxical situation; it is expressed by two balanced main clauses (*ita . . . ita*), in each of which the subject is followed by a modifier: in the second case *fiducia uirium* imitates a favourite phrase of Livy.[134] The next two sentences together illustrate the opening paradox. The subject of the first is *pars*, which is qualified first by three positive participial phrases (*proposita . . . et . . . macerata perductaque*: one chiasmus superimposed on another) and second by a participial phrase divided into two negative parts (*neque . . . sustinere neque . . . ausa congredi*: word-order basically parallel). In the midst of this plethora of phrases the expression *ad utilitatem* is a favourite of Cicero's.[135] The subject of the second and even longer sentence is also *pars*, which is qualified first by a relative clause (*quae . . .*: further subordination follows with *quem . . .*) and second by a participle (*circumfusa . . .*: further subordination again follows with *quippe . . .*). The disaster with which the

142

second sentence ends is described briefly in the third, in which there are four different main verbs and subjects (the last impersonal). The extract ends with a contrast which is familiar from the pages of Livy (*miles ~ duces*).[136]

By no stretch of the imagination can this exercise in balance and amplitude of expression be ascribed to the stylistic tradition of Sallust; on the contrary, it is clearly written in a style which is a development of that of Livy. This is just what we should expect, since Velleius broadly follows Livy's interpretation of Roman history: he sees progressive decline up to the civil wars, but Actium represents a turning-point after which the reign of Tiberius is an improvement even on that of Augustus.[137] A similarly encomiastic attitude towards Tiberius' reign is thought to have been adopted by Aufidius Bassus in his now lost history;[138] the scope both of this work and of his narrative of the German wars is uncertain, although the flavour of the latter no doubt resembled comparable sections of Velleius' narrative, such as that extracted above. Of the man himself we know virtually nothing, although conjecture has it that 'his health and brand of philosophy are consonant with the quiet existence of a literary man, in the succession of Livy'.[139] Bassus' name is linked with that of another lost historian, Servilius Nonianus, by both Tacitus and Quintilian. Tacitus contrasts the two of them with the old-fashioned writers Sisenna and Varro,[140] while Quintilian says that Servilius is 'less condensed than historiography normally demands' (10.1.102 'minus pressus quam historiae auctoritas postulat'). Quintilian's remark reveals, as Syme has rightly noted, that Servilius was 'certainly not' a Sallustian writer;[141] and the fact that his name is twice linked with that of Bassus suggests that the latter also was no Sallustian. If this is so, then Bassus will have maintained the link between style and attitude which we have observed in his predecessors. Whether the same can be said of Servilius is uncertain, since virtually nothing is known of his historical output; but his elevation to the consulship in AD 35 and to the proconsulship of Africa in about AD 47 indicates that he was hardly regarded as an opposition figure.[142]

In the last decade of the first century AD the younger Pliny replied to a friend who had been trying to encourage him to write history. Pliny's letter, which is written in conscious imitation of Cicero's letter to Lucceius (above, pp. 70-3), discusses various aspects of historiography including the appropriate style (*Ep.* 5.8.9-11):

Habet quidem oratio et historia multa communia, sed plura
diuersa in his ipsis, quae communia uidentur. Narrat illa
narrat haec, sed aliter: huic pleraque humilia et sordida et ex
medio petita, illi omnia recondita splendida excelsa conu-
eniunt; hanc saepius ossa musculi nerui, illam tori quidam et
quasi iubae decent; haec uel maxime ui amaritudine instantia,
illa tractu et suauitate atque etiam dulcedine placet; postremo
alia uerba alius sonus alia constructio.

Of course historiography and oratory have much in common;
but there are considerable differences in precisely those areas
which appear to be common ground. They both employ
narrative, but of different kinds.[143] Oratory is generally characterised by a low, lack-lustre and indifferent style, but historiography by one which is choice, gleaming and elevated; bare
bones, muscles and sinews normally suit the former, but all
kinds of external embroidery the latter; the former entertains
by its power, pungency and pressure, the latter by being
mobile, sweet and gentle; finally, they differ from each other in
vocabulary, tone and structure.

As Perret has remarked, 'it is well seen that Pliny's notion of the
ideal style is above all that of Livy'.[144] The word *tractus* in
particular (which I have translated as 'mobile') reminds us of
Cicero's ideal historical style (above, p. 94), while its opposite
instantia ('pressure') is the characteristic which Quintilian singled
out in Thucydides (above, p. 45). Pliny, like his hero Cicero,
never got round to writing the history which his friend urged; but
it is clear that, had he done so, he would have chosen the style
required by Cicero and employed by Livy. It is also fair to
assume, from what we know of Pliny's politics, that any history of
his would have been encomiastic of Rome.

Encomium was certainly the attitude adopted by Florus in his
summary history, written 'to contribute something in recognition
of the leading nation by displaying all its greatness' (pref. 3 'non
... nihil ad admirationem *principis populi* conlaturus si ... uniuer-
sam magnitudinem eius ostendero'), phraseology which intentionally echoes that of Livy's preface (3: above, p. 129).[145] A
typical extract deals with Augustus' successful campaign in Spain
in 25 BC (2.33.54-60):

Astures per id tempus ingenti agmine a montibus niueis

descenderant. Nec temere sumptus, ut barbaris, impes; sed positis castris apud Asturam flumen trifariam diuiso agmine tria simul Romanorum adgredi parant castra. Fuissetque anceps et cruentum et utinam mutua clade certamen cum tam fortibus, tam subito, tam cum consilio uenientibus, nisi Brigaecini prodidissent, a quibus praemonitus Carisius cum exercitu aduenit. Pro uictoria fuit oppressisse consilia, sic tamen quoque non incruento certamine. Reliquias fusi exercitus ualidissima ciuitas Lancia excepit, ubi cum locis adeo certatum est, ut, cum in captam urbem faces poscerentur, aegre dux impetrauerit ueniam, ut uictoriae Romanae stans potius esset quam incensa monumentum.

Hic finis Augusto bellicorum certaminum fuit, idem rebellandi finis Hispaniae. Certa mox fides et aeterna pax, cum ipsorum ingenio in pacis artes promptiore, tum consilio Caesaris, qui fiduciam montium timens in quos se recipiebant, castra sua, quia in plano erant, habitare et incolere iussit: ibi gentis esse consilium, illud obseruari caput.

At this moment the Asturians came down *en masse* from the snow-covered mountains. As you would expect with barbarians, they had mounted their attack cunningly: having pitched camp by the River Astura, they divided their force into three and prepared to advance on the three Roman camps simultaneously. The clash with such courageous adversaries, approaching at speed and according to plan, would have been dangerous and savage but at least (I would hope) no less damaging to their side than to ours; as it was, however, the Brigaecini betrayed them by giving advance warning to Carisius, who arrived with his army. Just stifling the enemy's plan was as good as a victory, but even so there was a savage clash. The fortress town of Lancia took in the remains of the routed army, and the place posed so many difficulties for the troops that when it was finally captured and they were demanding to set it on fire, the general was scarcely able to save it in order that there should be a lasting memorial to Rome's victory rather than mere ashes.

This constituted the end of Augustus' campaigns, and also of the Spanish rebellion. Their subsequent loyalty was assured, and they remained at peace: after all, their natural instincts were for the pursuits of peace, and Augustus, dreading the security of the mountains into which they customarily retreated, judiciously ordered them to occupy and settle in his own former camp since it was in the plain: there they should have their seat of government and capital.

Despite some short sentences, the general impression here is one of Livian complexity. The sentence constructed round *fuissetque ... nisi ...*, itself a favourite device of Livy,[146] has three words or phrases qualifying *certamen* and forming a tricolon crescendo, and these are balanced by a further three elements employing triple anaphora of *tam*. The sentence describing the town of Lancia consists mainly of a subordinate *ubi*-clause which is further subordinated by *adeo ... ut ...*, which in turn is subordinated first by *cum* and then by a second *ut* (note the contrast *stans ~ incensa*). The final sentence begins with an illustration of verbal amplitude (two nouns of similar meaning, each with its own adjective), and is subsequently divided by *cum ... tum ...*: the former employs complex alliteration, the latter is subordinated by one causal and two relative clauses, one of them again exhibiting verbal amplitude (*habitare et incolere*). This is certainly not the style of Sallust.[147]

By preferring the Thucydidean style to the Herodotean recommended by Cicero, Sallust himself had reinforced the critical attitude which he adopted towards his theme of the declining republic. Initially attracted to the same theme of decline, Livy generally came to adopt an optimistic view of Roman history which he reinforced by writing in the style that Cicero had recommended. In the sensitive political atmosphere of the first century AD, when historians and their works were equally at risk,[148] it is hardly surprising that writers chose to follow Livy rather than Sallust. Of the six writers whom we have considered in this section, only Arruntius was a thoroughgoing imitator of Sallust; yet he was writing fifty years earlier than any of the others, and in any case his theme of the Punic Wars provided ample justification for the Sallustian archaising by which he was known. Of the remaining five writers, four clearly avoided any comprehensive imitation of Sallust in their works, while Pliny expressly advocated the style of Livy. Thus, if these five writers are at all representative of the historiographical tradition at Rome in the century which followed the death of Livy,[149] it cannot be said that Sallust 'heralds the empire' (see above, p. 140).[150] It is Livy himself who has that distinction,[151] and it is Sallust, not Livy, who is 'the last of the republican writers' (see above, p. 136).

146

Notes

1. Vretska (1.23) says that in view of the comparison between *BC* 4.3 *de Catilinae coniuratione . . . paucis absoluam* and *BJ* 5.1 *bellum scripturus sum quod populus Romanus cum Iugurtha . . . gessit*, the title of the work should be *De Catilinae Coniuratione*, which is not in any MS (so too Horsfall (1981) p. 107). The MSS offer various titles like *Bellum Catilinae*, which I prefer since war was the standard subject of classical historiography and Sallust sees the conspiracy in terms of a war (e.g. 16.4, 17.6, 21.1, 26.5, 31.2, 32.1-2). The work, whatever its title, is thought to have been written before the end of the decade but its precise date is uncertain (cf. Syme (1964) pp. 127-9).

2. On the scope of this work, see Syme (1964) pp. 190-2 with n. 54.

3. *BJ* 17-19, *H*. 3.61-80. See R.F. Thomas pp. 2-5.

4. The most famous example is the pair of speeches, put into the mouths of Caesar and Cato respectively, in *BC* 51-2. In general see Miller (1975).

5. For character sketches cf. e.g. *BC* 5.1-8, 25 (above, pp. 123-4), 53.6-54.6, *BJ* 6-7.1, 95.2-4. We owe our information on Sallust's obituary notices to Sen. *Suas.* 6.21, who implies that they were in imitation of Thucydides. In fact, no example is to be found in Sallust's extant work, so we must assume that they occurred in the large portions of the *Histories* which are now lost.

6. Rawson (1972) p. 43.

7. The frequency of this clausula in Cicero's speeches is 16.2% and in Sall. *BC* and *BJ* 3.4%. In these and the following statistics I have used the tables in De Groot for Cicero and those in Aili for Sallust and Livy: Aili is of course more up-to-date and perhaps also more convenient, but his Ciceronian statistics are based on only two speeches whereas those of De Groot are comprehensive. I hope this practice will result in a reasonably balanced picture.

8. The frequency of the so-called 'heroic clausula' is 1.9% in Cic., 10.9% in Sall. and 8% in Livy.

9. A frequency of 25.3% in Cic. and 6.7% in Sall.

10. This famous clausula, the subject of ironical amusement in Tac. *D*. 23.1 and Quint. 10.2.18, in fact has a frequency of no more than 4.7% in Cicero's speeches over-all, according to De Groot. However, on Aili's statistics of *Sull.* and *Mur.* from 63 BC, the figure leaps up to 10% (see pp. 60-2, 136). The figure for Sall. is 0.5%.

11. i.e. a product of the mind (cf. Earl (1961) p. 8).

12. So too Vretska ad loc.

13. The technique is also common in Lucretius and has been called 'suspension of thought': see Williams (1968) pp. 720-1 and Wiseman (1974) pp. 33-4. In general, see Williams (1980) Chapter 4.

14. This is the only interpretation mentioned by McGushin ad loc.

15. For further arguments in favour of this conclusion, which is also that of Vretska ad loc., see Woodman (1973) p. 310.

16. Of the principal clausulae, the first (*oboedi/ēntiā finxit*) and last (*aet/ērnāqu(e) hābētur*) are the heroic (above, n. 8); the second (*belu/īs commūn(e) ēst*) is the dispondee, which is 6.4% in Cic. and 27.5% in Sall.;

the third (*lŏng(am) ĕffĭcĕrĕ*) is 1.8% in Cic. and 10.5% in Sall. The comparative figures for Thucydides are 7.9%, 18.2% and 5% respectively (Aili pp. 73-4). On this evidence Sallust is clearly closer to Thuc. than to Cic. (see p. 124). Of the two subsidiary clausulae, *cor/pŏrĕ sĭt(a) ĕst* is 2.3% in Cic., 3.3% in Sall. and 8.5% in Thuc., and *sĕruĭtĭ/ō mǎgĭs ǔtĭmǔr* is 1.2% in Cic., 3% in Sall. and 2.1% in Thuc. (see Aili p. 74 and De Groot p. 105).

17. *quǎm pĕtĕrētǔr* is the 'heroic' and *hǎud ǎbsǔrdǔm* the dispondee (see above, nn. 8 and 16). For *lĕp/ōs ĭnĕrǎt, pudĭcĭt/ĭǎ fŭĭt* and *conscĭ/ǎ fŭĕrǎt* see n. 16; *for/tūnǎtǎ fŭĭt* is 1.8% in Cic., 10.5% in Sall., and 5% in Thuc. (Aili pp. 74, 136-7). *cōnmīsĕrǎt* (also *dĭscĕrnĕrēs*) and *lǔxǔrĭāe sǔnt* (also *mol/lĭ uĕl prŏcācī*) are both Ciceronian.

18. So Vretska ad loc.

19. So McGushin ad loc.

20. See Eden pp. 78-89. For repeated pronouns in particular, 'one of the characteristic peculiarities of the narrative style in early Latin', see also Laughton pp. 38-9. There is a full study of Sallust's archaising vocabulary, with some striking statistics, in Lebek pp. 291ff.

21. This is the reading of P; other MSS read *multusque*. McGushin ad loc. rightly notes that *-que* is more likely to have been added than omitted. The clausulae cannot help decide (cf. Aili p. 137, nos. 1-2).

22. Syme (1964) p. 265, whose whole chapter on 'History and Style' (pp. 240-73) should be consulted. Sallust's conscious rejection of Ciceronianism is analogous to what has been called 'the rhetoric of anti-rhetoric' (Valesio pp. 41-60). See also n. 35 below.

23. For the early Roman historians see Badian (1966).

24. Livy's account (39.6.7) of the year 187/6 BC is thought by some to derive from an anonymous contemporary annalist who emphasised the theme of decline (see Earl (1961) pp. 42-5), though Lintott has argued that the theme might well be an invention of the propaganda of the Gracchan period which has been retrojected to 187/6. Cf. also L. Calpurnius Piso (cos. 133 BC), frr. 34 and 38.

25. I say 'naturally' because the ancients tended to see history in terms of warfare and during this period Rome had conducted a whole series of successful foreign campaigns which resulted in the foundation of their empire.

26. Cf. e.g. Cic. *Leg.* 1.5 (Atticus to Cicero) 'mihi uideris ... patriae debere hoc munus ut ea ... per te eundem sit ornata', 1.8 (Atticus to Q. Cicero) 'Cn. Pompei laudes inlustrabit'. Rawson (1972) p. 36 observes that the survey of Roman history given in *Rep.* 2 functions as a *laudatio* of Rome, though it is described as *historia* (cf. 2.33).

27. For an account of his political career see Syme (1964) pp. 29-42.

28. 14.1 'in *tanta tam*que corrupta ciuitate Catilina ... omnium flagitiorum atque facinorum circum se tamquam stipatorum cateruas habebat'. Cf. Earl (1961) p. 86: 'In its immediate context it [sc. the preface] puts Catiline in his setting as a child of his age, the typical product of the process of degeneration which began with the destruction of Carthage'. Degeneration reappears in the *Bell. Iug.* (e.g. 41-2) and forms the *Leitmotiv* of the *Histories* (cf. 1.11, 12, 16, all from the preface).

29. 36 (p. 59 Camozzi) 'et tempora reprehendit sua et delicta carpit'

(second century AD).

30. For rhetorical *colores* and their use see Bonner (1949) pp. 55-6 and Fairweather (1981) p. 390 (index). For their relevance to historiography see Wiseman (1979) pp. 7-8, 199 (index). Whether Sallust had in fact read Cicero's letter to Lucceius is uncertain. Cicero had intended to publish some letters during his lifetime, but Shackleton Bailey (1965) 1.59ff., while admitting that the Lucceius letter may have been one of these, argues that a general publication did not take place until mid-way through Nero's reign. However, certain letters were undoubtedly known long before then (see e.g. Woodman (1983) on Vell. 62.3), and I think that the Lucceius letter was probably known to Livy in the 30s (see below, n. 55).

31. See e.g. (briefly) D'Alton pp. 423-6. In the *Orator* Cicero had proposed that each of the three functions of the orator was associated with one of the three types of style: see Douglas (1955).

32. For this reason the *Dialogus* used often to be thought spurious.

33. The most well known expression of this belief is Sen. *Epist.* 114.1 'talis hominibus fuit oratio qualis uita'; other examples in Bramble pp. 23-5.

34. *Brut.* 117 'Q. Aelius Tubero ... ut uita sic oratione durus incultus horridus', *Rep.* 2.1 'orationi uita admodum congruens'.

35. For a similar stylistic reaction in the sixteenth and seventeenth centuries, see Croll, part 1 'The anti-Ciceronian movement: "Attic" and baroque prose syle'. For Tacitus, and also Gibbon, see below, p. 168; and for 'anti-rhetoric' in general, above, n. 22.

36. These were also the features which the ancient readers of Sallust singled out: for abruptness cf. Quint. 4.2.45 'abruptum sermonis genus', for variation see Seneca, quoted in the text; for brevity cf. Quint. 4.2.45 'illa Sallustiana ... breuitas' (also 8.3.82), 10.1.101 'immortalem Sallustii uelocitatem'; for archaising cf. the accusation of Pollio that Sallust had employed a scholar to make a collection of old-fashioned words for him to use (Suet. *Gramm.* 10; cf. Lebek pp. 316ff.). There is a large selection of *testimonia* on Sallust in the Teubner edition by A. Kurfess, pp. xxii-xxxi.

37. See e.g. Dion. *Thuc.* 24, 51 and 53, with Pritchett's notes.

38. *Epist.* 114.17 'amputatae sententiae et uerba ante exspectatum cadentia et obscura breuitas', cf. Quint. 8.3.82.

39. When commenting on a Roman writer, ancient scholars often borrowed some of their critical material from existing commentaries on whichever Greek writer was thought to be the Roman's 'model': see Fraenkel (1964) 2.383-8.

40. For a study, see Scanlon.

41. The process of imitation will not have been difficult for a writer who had had the usual rhetorical education, an important part of which was the detailed study and imitation of the great masters of earlier literature, including Thucydides: see e.g. [Long.] *Subl.* 13.2-14; Bonner (1977) pp. 273-5.

42. Sen. *Contr.* 9.1.13 discusses Sallust as if he were a second Thuc.; Vell. 36.2 'aemulumque Thucydidis Sallustium', Quint. 10.1.101 'nec opponere Thucydidi Sallustium uerear'. Sallust's clausulae will have helped the association between the two authors (see above, n. 16, and the

detailed study of Aili pp. 71-5).

43. Syme (1964) p. 56 (the whole paragraph is relevant). Earlier, Syme (1958) p. 135 had suggested that Sallust imitated Thucydides' style because it 'seemed to convey a serious guarantee of incorruptible veracity'; but see above, pp. 45-7 and below, 205-6.

44. For the notion that a Roman author will try to present himself and his whole life in terms of a Greek predecessor, in a kind of metempsychosis, see Macleod pp. 245-6 on Horace. Perhaps the most famous example is Ennius' claim to be Homer.

45. Pollio's objections to Cicero seem to have been both personal and stylistic (cf. Sen. *Suas.* 6.14 'infestissimus famae Ciceronis permansit', 24, Quint. 12.1.22; also Tac. *D.* 25.6). Ancient references to Pollio very often concern his criticism of others: of Caesar (see above, p. 111 n. 103), of Sallust (above, n. 36), of Livy (Quint. 1.5.56, 8.1.3), of Labienus (Quint. 9.3.13 etc.), and of numerous others (see e.g. Fairweather (1981) p. 286). See also Sen. *Contr.* 4 *praef.* 3.

46. For this view of Pollio's career see Syme (1939) p. 291 and (1958) p. 136; Clark Chapter 3. For a different view see Bosworth, some of whose arguments have however been countered by Woodman (1983) pp. 233-4. It is presumably significant that when the Greek historian Timagenes fell out of favour with Augustus, it was to Pollio's house that he went to stay (Sen. *Ira* 3.23.5).

47. The date at which Pollio's *Histories* stopped is uncertain. For the various possibilities see Nisbet and Hubbard on Hor. *Odes* 2.1 (intro. n., p. 8), who themselves favour 42 BC. I incline to think that he continued into the 30s.

48. Since Seneca continues by contrasting Pollio with Cicero, his comment seems in fact to be directed at the former's oratory rather than his *Histories*. This is also true of the other references we have to Pollio's style (usefully collected by Malcovati, *ORF*[3] pp. 516-18), and whether they are applicable also to his *Histories* must strictly remain a matter of conjecture. The only substantial fragment of the *Hist.* which we have is the obituary notice for Cicero preserved by Sen. *Suas.* 6.24. According to Clark p. 74, this passage 'has all the characteristics ascribed to Pollio by literary critics; a tense, nervous style (bleak, to those who disliked it), lacking the smoothness and fullness of Cicero, and somewhat disconcerting in cadence and word-order'; but she unfortunately fails to illustrate her comment with reference to the text, which is in fact a good deal more complicated than she allows. It is true that there are signs of Pollio's characteristic *asperitas*, such as the repetition of words (especially of the pronoun *is*, on which see above, n. 20, and André p. 111), numerous hyperbata (André pp. 110 and 111 with nn. 1-3; Leeman (1963) p. 189), and a future participle used in an abl. abs. (an innovation for which Sallust seems to have paved the way, cf. Quint. 9.3.12-13). Yet the clausulae (on which see André 111-12, De Groot 108) in part follow Ciceronian practice, there are at least four allusions to Cicero's own works, and several examples of Ciceronian amplitude of expression. The explanation for these features no doubt lies in the Ciceronian context (*imitatio cum aemulatione*), but more important for our purposes is the strong implication by Seneca (*Suas.* 6.25) that the passage is *un*character-

istic of Pollio's usual style in his history (cf. Lebek pp. 143ff., especially 145). From this we may reasonably infer that the style of his *Hist.* did indeed resemble that of his oratory, and hence that comments on his oratory may fairly be taken as applicable also to his historiography. (Note, finally, that three letters of Pollio have been preserved in Cic. *Fam.* 10.31-3.)

49. 'Thucydides' influence on Pollio is more easily assumed than proved', says Syme (1964) p. 55 n. 62 (see now Lebek pp. 136-9), but this is to disregard the parallel comments of Dionysius on Thuc. and of Seneca on Pollio. According to Clark p. 74, 'it may even be misleading ... to locate him [Pollio] on a line drawn from Sallust to Tacitus', but this is to disregard Seneca's parallel comments on Sallust and Pollio. Lebek p. 139 uses Quint. 10.2.17 ('qui praecisis conclusionibus obscuri Sallustium atque Thucydidem superant, tristes ac ieiuni Pollionem aemulantur') to separate Pollio from Sallust and Thuc., but it is surely equally important to note that all three authors are juxtaposed. Leeman (1955) pp. 183-208 postulated three different 'phases de l'atticisme' at Rome, of which two are relevant to this discussion: 'un atticisme "primitiviste", qui prend exemple sur Thucydide' and which is represented by Pollio, and 'un atticisme "moderniste" ... qui prend également exemple sur Thucydide' and which is represented by Sallust (pp. 201-2). Hence Leeman is able to dissociate Pollio from the 'thucydidisme moderniste de Salluste' (p. 200). But this hypothesis seems to me too schematic and fanciful. For example, though Pollio criticised Sallust for archaising (above, n. 36), Suetonius strongly implies that Pollio was liable to fall into the same trap himself (*Gramm.* 10), and Pollio's style did indeed seem archaic in comparison with Cicero (Quint. 10.1.113 'a nitore et iucunditate Ciceronis ita longe abest ut uideri possit saeculo prior').

50. This is the opposite conclusion from that of Millar (1981) p. 146: 'His [Pollio's] truculence was a matter of style and personality, and did not extend to any significant independence from the new régime, to which he accommodated himself just as did so many others.'

51. Walsh (1974) p. 5.

52. Walsh (1974) p. 6.

53. E.g. recently Marino. For a survey of other recent opinions see Phillips (1982) pp. 1034-6.

54. For the comparison with Herodotus, in whom 'omnia ... leniter fluunt' (9.4.18) and who is 'dulcis et candidus et fusus' (10.1.73), cf. 10.1.101 'nec indignetur sibi Herodotus aequari T. Liuium, cum in narrando mirae iucunditatis clarissimique candoris ...'; the contrast with Sallust is made both here and at 10.1.32.

55. Ogilvie (1965) p. 26 defends *tota*, which has been queried, with reference to Cic. *Clu.* 190, *Phil.* 10.23; I think the context makes it at least as likely that Livy has in mind the letter to Lucceius (*Fam.* 5.12.2 *mens ... tota*).

56. By 'new historians' I think Livy has in mind those who in the future will attempt to outdo his work and perhaps make his efforts seem redundant. (This in fact turned out not to be the case: see p. 136.)

57. See Ogilvie (1965) pp. 23-5.

58. See above, p. 49 n. 24.

59. There is an enormous bibliography on these theories: see e.g. Guthrie (1957) 63-79, De Romilly (1977), M.L. West (1978) pp. 172-7, Trompf (all with further references).

60. See Walbank on 6.10.3 and 57.3.

61. For the date see Nisbet (1984) pp. 2-3. The parallel with Livy was noted by Porphyrio ad loc.

62. This is taken for granted by Dutoit p. 370, Jal (1963) p. 253 and Häussler p. 273, to whom the various quotations are due. Weissenborn and Müller (1885) pp. 58, 77 and Syme (1959) p. 37 ▬ (1979) 1.411 assume that *haec noua* (4) refers to the civil wars but do not mention the language of the *quibus*-clause. For other coded ways of referring to the civil wars see Jal (1963), especially pp. 66-9.

63. So too Nisbet (1984) p. 5. Häussler notes (p. 273) that the germ of the expression *suis uiribus ruere* is in Sallust's earlier *Bell. Cat.* 51.42 'uirtus atque sapientia maior illis fuit qui ex paruis opibus tantum imperium fecere, quam in nobis qui ea bene parta uix retinemus'.

64. For hybris cf. Prop. quoted (*superba*) and in general De Romilly (1977) pp. 59-60; for immorality cf. the references in n. 24 above and also Liv. 7.25.9 'adeo in quae laboramus sola creuimus, diuitias luxuri- amque', and Petron. quoted; for internal power struggles cf. Plb. quoted; for the 'dinosaur syndrome', whereby a society simply gets too big for its own good, cf. Liv. 7.29.2 'quanta rerum moles! quotiens in extrema periculorum uentum, ut in hanc magnitudinem quae uix sustinetur erigi imperium posset!' It will be clear that these various causes are not mutually exclusive of one another.

65. Florus goes on to blame *nimia felicitas*, which caused the civil wars.

66. The fact that 5 contains an allusion to Sall. *H.* 1.6 (see p. 131), which in turn contains a reference to the civil wars ('neque me diuersa pars *in ciuilibus armis* mouit a uero'), may be regarded as confirmation. As for 9, Weissenborn and Müller (1885) p. 58 and 80 rightly saw no distinc- tion between that section and the rest of the preface; but they of course wrote before H. Dessau (see below, n. 68).

67. In a paper which Walsh (1974) p. 5 has aptly described as 'characteristically ambivalent', Syme (1959) says that Livy's words in section 9 'might apply to a time before the War of Actium. Or a time subsequent. Or even both' (42 ▬ (1979) 1.416); 'his remarks would fit the aftermath of Actium ... but they do not (it can be claimed) produce a date subsequent to the settlement of 28 and 27 BC' (43 ▬ 417); 'the tone and sentiments of the *Preface* might even have been in harmony with the contemporary situation, had it been composed as late as 23 BC' (49 ▬ 424); 'the tone of the *Preface* [can be said to encourage] an early date' (50 ▬ 425). In n. 70 ▬ 416 n. 5 Syme acknowledges that he owes the pre- Actian possibility to M. Hammond, though it will be seen from the above quotations that he does not favour it himself. The preface is dated by Bayet (1947) p. xx to the re-edition of Books 1-5 which he hypothesises in 27-25 BC. See also below, n. 88.

68. This theory was first suggested by H. Dessau in 1903 and has been taken up by Bayet (1947) p. xx, G. Williams, *JRS* 52 (1962) pp. 28ff. (a most influential article) and Ogilvie (1965) p. 28 amongst others, but not by Syme (1959) pp. 42-3 ▬ (1979) 1.416-17 or Walsh (1961) p. 11.

Luce (1965) p. 239 and n. 86 rejected it but Luce (1977) p. 291 and n. 141 accepted it.

69. Syme (1959) pp. 37 and 42-3 = (1979) 1.411 and pp. 416-17 dates it to 27 BC without the help of Dessau's theory.

70. Badian (1985).

71. For some Greek and Latin examples see Fantham (1972) pp. 14ff.

72. See Skard pp. 145-6.

73. See *OLD* s.v. 2*b*. It is mistaken to say that *uitia* interprets a political crisis 'in terms of morality' (Syme (1959) p. 42 = (1979) 1.416-17).

74. Cf. also Aesch. fr. 695 Mette (cf. also *Ag.* 199-200), Soph. *Aj.* 362-3, fr. 77P, 589P.4, Eur. fr. 292, Hdt. 3.53.4, Thuc. 5.65.2, Plato, *Protag.* 340E, Plut. *Mor.* 504B, 523E, *Mar.* 6.3, Virg. *G.* 3.510-11 (the context is one of disease), Virg. *Aen.* 12.46, Publil. Syr. 238.

75. Cf. Nep. *Att.* 20.4 'cum se uterque [sc. Octavian and Antony] principem non solum urbis Romae sed orbis terrarum esse cuperet'.

76. Metaphors from health were exploited extensively throughout the civil war period with reference to one or other of the great protagonists. Thus *salus* appeared on the coins of 49 BC, evidently in expectations of a Caesarian victory (*RRC* 1.461 no. 442), and again on the coins of Sex. Pompeius in 45/44 BC (*RRC* 1.486 no. 477). In 46 Cicero wrote of Caesar: 'tua salute contineri suam et ex unius tua uita pendere omnium' (*Marc.* 22, the metaphorical nature of which is guaranteed by 24: 'quae quidem tibi nunc omnia belli uulnera sananda sunt, quibus praeter te mederi nemo potest'), and after the wars were over Valgius Rufus opened a medical treatise, addressed to Augustus, with a prayer 'ut omnibus humanis illius potissimum principis semper mederetur maiestas' (Plin. *NH* 25.4). See in general Weinstock (1971) pp. 166-71, 217-20; also Woodman (1983) p. 84.

77. This parallel is mentioned by Syme (1959) pp. 42-3 = (1979) 1.417 as a way of supporting the interpretation of Livy's preface which I am discussing but which he himself rejects. According to Clark p. 12, 'it is most unlikely that the *remedium* Livy had in mind was government by one man'. She interprets the word as meaning 'self-reformation'.

78. This interpretation is not the only one possible. It was a common-place of Roman thought that external war, or the threat of it (*metus hostilis*), was an effective way of preventing the moral degeneration (*otium, luxuria* etc.) which was thought to be caused by the acquisition of an empire. This view is particularly associated with Sallust (see Earl (1961) pp. 41ff.), and in section 9 of the preface Livy has followed Sallust in saying that Rome has suffered from a calamitous decline in morals (see above, p. 130). Yet instead of being engaged in a foreign war, which might have been expected to halt this decline, Rome instead is currently preoccupied with *civil* war, which is an even worse fate. It is this contrast between the terrible reality of the present civil war and the glorious prospect of preferable foreign wars which lies behind many of Horace's poems, and we have already seen one parallel between Horace and Livy (above, p. 131). It therefore seems to me very possible that by *uitia* Livy means the moral degeneration to which he has just referred, and that by *remedia* he means the war which, by a bitter twist of fate, cannot hope to

cure it. Yet despite the attractiveness of this possibility I have not preferred it to that given in the main text because, as Luce (1977) p. 271 n. 86 points out, the theory of *metus hostilis* (though regular in Livy) is not actually mentioned in the preface. It is of course the case that on either interpretation Livy is expressing himself metaphorically, and it may be that he did so precisely because he wished his statement to be capable of more than one interpretation. Although this might appear an unsatisfactory suggestion from a literary critical point of view, such ambiguity is of course to be expected in literature which is produced under the pressures of civil war (the fourth *Eclogue* springs immediately to mind).

79. This is true even if one does not accept Dessau's theory: see e.g. Walsh (1974) p. 6 'The Preface is markedly pessimistic about the immediate prospect of moral resurgence at Rome', referring to sections 5 and 9. See also Gabba (1983) p. 17.

80. So Stadter (1972), Walsh (1974) pp. 8-9, Luce (1977) pp. 3ff. Fifteen-book units have been proposed by G. Wille, *Der Aufbau des liv. Geschichtswerks* (1973) and T. Crosby, *LCM* 3 (1978) pp. 113-19.

81. 7.40.2 'nondum erant tam fortes ad sanguinem ciuilem nec praeter externa nouerant bella', 9.19.15 'ciuilia bella sileant ... [17] modo sit perpetuus huius qua uiuimus pacis amor et ciuilis cura concordiae'. See also below, n. 83.

82. Luce (1965) p. 231.

83. However, taken together with the two other passages of Book 7 already quoted (above, n. 64), it does strongly suggest that the civil wars were still in progress when Livy wrote it. If so, they were of course over by the time he got to Book 9 (above, n. 81).

84. Clark believes that most if not all of the first pentad was written after Actium (p. 4) and that the preface was written 'last of all' (p. 12).

85. See Ogilvie (1965) ad loc.

86. See Ogilvie (1965) ad loc. and Luce (1965) p. 232.

87. Luce (1965) pp. 211-18. That 1.19.2-3 might be a later addition seems first to have been suggested by Weissenborn and Müller (1885) p. 10; the case of 4.20.5-11 was suggested by W. Soltau in 1894. Bayet (1947) pp. xvii-xxi suggested numerous later additions throughout Books 1-5: see also next n. I ought to emphasise that Luce himself does not argue the pre-Actian case: see next n.

88. Luce (1965) p. 210, adding that 'A sizeable body of literature, predicated on the assumption that the composition of the first pentad is "Augustan", whether in tone, attitudes, themes, or allusions, would thus be called into question' (p. 211). Luce concludes that Livy, born in 64 BC (p. 231), would 'have been in his *late* thirties when he began the first of his 142 books' (my italics); 'he must have begun composition about the time of the battle of Actium (possibly earlier)' and 'the first pentad was complete by 27 BC' (p. 238). Bayet (1947) argues that the publication of Books 1-5 was 'antérieure aux années 31-29 [which I do not understand], suivie d'une réédition ... entre 27 et 25' (p. xviii); 'la Préface se date donc bien du moment de la réédition des livres I-V' (p. xx). According to Syme (1959), 'No unequivocal evidence demands the completion of Books I-V as early as the period 31-29 BC. Their publication in 27-25 BC, however, remains a reasonable assumption' (p. 49 = (1979) 1.424); 'Livy began his

work about the time of the War of Actium — or, rather, shortly after it' (p. 50 — 425).

89. Luce (1965) p. 210.

90. On which see Cameron (1968). Strictly speaking, the passage in Book 4 need only have been a later addition; but my thesis requires that there was a second edition of Book 1 — otherwise Livy would surely have altered the pessimistic sentiments of the preface at the same time as he inserted chapter 19.2-3, and the only reason he did not alter the preface is that it was already too well known to be altered. These were regular hazards in the ancient world, given the nature of their book production (see Luce (1965) pp. 233-8; Kenney in *CHCL* 2.10-11, 19), and Luce (1965) has noted that 'since Book Two has its own preface, it is probable that Book One was published separately' (p. 210 n. 2). Bayet (1947) has argued the converse thesis, that Book 1 was indeed published first and separately (pp. xvii-xviii) but that the preface was added later with the second edition (above, n. 88); yet Bayet's arguments for Book 1 are not really convincing (see e.g. Syme (1959) pp. 47-9 — (1979) 1.421-5).

91. Plin. *NH* pref. 16 'iam sibi satis gloriae quaesitum et potuisse se desinere, ni animus inquies pasceretur opere', adding that the statement derives from the beginning of a volume.

92. *per.* 121 'qui editus post excessum Augusti dicitur'.

93. So Syme (1959) pp. 38-9 and 71 (— (1979) 1.411-12 and 448), pointing out (as does Clark p. 26) that there is nothing in the contents of Book 121 to make it a special case for being withheld on its own; Luce (1965) p. 231 n. 61, (1977) pp. 5 n. 5, 8 n. 17, Walsh (1974) p. 9. Similarly, a statement by Pliny that Ennius 'added' Book 16 of the *Annals* is usually taken by scholars to refer to Books 16-18 (*NH* 7.101).

94. So Stadter (1972) pp. 299-300, accepted by Walsh (1974) pp. 8-9 and Luce (1977) p. 8 n. 17, who notes that as early as H. Nissen in 1872 it was suggested that the statement in Pliny is from the preface to Book 121. Stadter mentions Ennius' *Annals* as another work which its author later extended by adding books (see last n.); Polybius and Ammianus also come to mind. There is certainly nothing exceptional in the practice.

95. So Stadter (1972) p. 300, Luce (1977) p. 24 n. 50. It may also be relevant that Servius (on *Aen.* 1.373) distinguishes between Livy's past and contemporary history ('Liuius ex annalibus et historia constat').

96. The notice is preserved by Sen. *Suas.* 6.22.

97. The potential popularity of the topic is well attested by Sen. *Suas.* 6 and 7, and the quotations there from the works of various historians. Stadter (1972) p. 299 also mentions the appropriateness of Cicero's death but, since he does not envisage an early date for Livy's inception, also sees significance in the emergence of Octavian, whose consulship was mentioned in Book 119: 'The *Ab urbe condita* would range from Romulus to the new Romulus'.

98. Syme (1964) p. 289, cf. (1959) p. 75 — (1979) 1.452. See also above, p. 146.

99. Pref. 4-5, 9-10, and the references given below in n. 117.

100. So too Luce (1977) pp. 279, 289ff., though he does not mention pref. 10. See also below, n. 111.

101. See Ogilvie (1965) pp. 390 and 626.

102. See Ogilvie (1965) pp. 18, 218ff.

103. Ogilvie (1965) p. 743.

104. See especially the programmatic statements in the preface: 7 'ea belli gloria est populo Romano ut cum suum conditorisque sui parentem Martem potissimum ferat, tam et hoc gentes humanae patiantur aequo animo quam imperium patiuntur', 9 'ad illa mihi pro se quisque intendat animum ... per quos uiros quibusque artibus domi militiaeque et partum et auctum imperium sit'.

105. See Ogilvie (1965) p. 2.

106. See Weinstock (1960) pp. 47-50.

107. See Woodman (1977) pp. 38-9, Seager (1980) p. 117. It was conventional in the Augustan age to see *pax* in terms of the military power which made peace possible: cf. Weinstock (1960) pp. 45-6, 49-50.

108. *Res Gestae* 34.2.

109. Cf. Liv. *per.* 59, Suet. *Aug.* 89.2.

110. See the balanced discussion of Douglas (1968) p. 32, with further references.

111. Ogilvie (1965) p. 743, cf. Syme (1959) p. 48 — (1979) 1.422-3. See especially Luce (1965) pp. 238-40: 'The first pentad ... can scarcely be termed "Augustan" either in inspiration or in execution; it was written in the years before the title was given to Octavian and before most of his policies and programs had been enacted. In truth, all the passages in which scholars have ventured to discern allusions to the emperor and his reign are tenuous at best; some interpretations are fanciful in the extreme. Many are as suited to the period before c. 30 BC as after ... It is true that in many significant ways Livy's views in the first pentad coincide with Augustus' program of religious, social, and moral reform. Yet many of these reforms came years after the first pentad had appeared, whatever theory of dating be invoked ... Instead of searching for Augustan allusions in Livian history, it might be more profitable to investigate to what extent Augustan policy was influenced by the Livian concept of the Roman past' (cf. also (1977) pp. 291-2). If this last suggestion were to be taken up, it might be found that Livy's ambition (above, p. 137) was realised more successfully than he could ever have hoped. For a survey of other opinion see Phillips (1982) pp. 1033-4.

112. Cf. Suet. *Claud.* 41.1. There are, however, two familiar pieces of evidence which appear to contradict this view of Livy. (a) According to the speech of self-defence which Tacitus put into the mouth of the prosecuted historian Cremutius Cordus (*A.* 4.34.3), 'Livy praised Pompey so much that Augustus called him a Pompeian [*Pompeianus*], but it did not interfere with their friendship'. From this statement some scholars have inferred that Livy was known to Augustus for his republican (i.e. anti-Augustan) sympathies. According to Clark p. 15, 'Perhaps (despite Tacitus) Augustus meant not that Livy praised Pompey, but that he sympathised with the efforts of the "Pompeian" senate to support the tyrannicides and resist the Caesarian cause, as represented by Antony and Octavian himself.' I do not think either of these views is correct, and Clark's seems anyway contradicted by what she says herself about Livy's later narrative (below, n. 118). My own view is in fact the converse of hers. It was common for men in the early empire to glorify Pompey, the

soldier-citizen whose death was a tragedy, but to criticise the *Pompeiani* who under his banner resisted first Caesar and then Octavian (cf. Grenade (1950)). I have little doubt that Livy too praised Pompey in the appropriate books of his history (perhaps especially in an obituary notice), as a result of which Augustus punningly called him 'Pompeianus' — i.e. jokingly suggesting that Livy sympathised with his followers rather than admired the man himself. Jokes and *bons mots* of this kind were a standard element in ancient biographies of great men such as Augustus. (b) According to Sen. *NQ* 5.18.4, Livy debated whether Julius Caesar's birth was a good thing or not. Yet Virgil seems to have entertained comparable doubts (see Austin on *Aen.* 1.286ff.), and one could hardly accuse him of being anti-Augustan. See in general the remarks of Syme (1979) 1.214.

113. See e.g. Walbank (1972) pp. 130ff.

114. His expression and application of the theory are not, however, without difficulty: see the discussion of Jal (1967) 1 pp. lxix sqq.

115. See *H.* 1.1.4, *Agr.* 3.1.

116. See Sussman pp. 148-9.

117. Quoting 3.20.5, 4.6.11-12, 7.2.13, 25.3-9, 10.9.3-6 and 26.22.15, Luce (1977) p. 245 and n. 31 has said that when Livy compares the behaviour of the ancients with that of contemporaries, 'in every instance the latter come off badly'. But this remark needs to be seen in the context of his earlier observation that most of Livy's pessimistic references to his own time 'are confined to the first decade; thereafter they become rare ... Sentiments such as that at 26.22 are infrequent' (1965, p. 231 and n. 60). And neither 26.22.15 nor the famous passage at 43.13.1-2 is really comparable in tone with the remarks made in the preface.

118. 'From the point where Octavian makes his appearance (Per. 116) the Periochae suggest that Livy treated him quite well' (Luce (1977) p. 15 n 33 [p. 16]). Clark is even more positive: 'When, with book 117, the narrative reaches Octavian's arrival in Italy, the value-judgements are explicitly in his favour'; Books 117-19 are 'a thoroughly Augustan account'; 'it seems impossible that Livy gave Antony anything of a case'; 'Livy, then, produced, independently of any pressure by Augustus, an account of the events both before and after Actium which gave essentially Augustus' idealised view' (pp. 15 and 27).

119. See Walsh (1961a) p. 34.

120. Luce (1977) p. 154, adding 'everything we know about the writing of history in antiquity shows that this must have been so'.

121. Syme (1959) p. 70 = (1979) 1.447, adding that 'to advertise the achievement, the *pomerium* of the city of Rome was extended in 8 BC.'

122. *Res Gestae* 8.5; Syme (1939) pp. 440ff.

123. Ogilvie (1965) p. 743.

124. The ideal orator was expected to be able to vary his style appropriately within a single work, and to be a master of all the styles (Cic. *Or.* 100, 110).

125. Respectively (1964) p. 289 (cf. (1958) p. 202 and elsewhere) and (1964a) p. 418.

126. For other accounts of Roman historiography between Livy and Tacitus see e.g. Bardon 2 pp. 91-102, 161-73, 203-12, Syme (1958) pp.

132-56, Klingner, Leeman (1963) and Wilkes.

127. Though he had Pompeian connections (Syme (1939) p. 425), Arruntius also commanded for Octavian at Actium (Vell. 85.2).

128. *Epist.* 114.18 'quae apud Sallustium rara fuerunt, apud hunc crebra sunt et paene continua'.

129. Livy's practice is parallel: Ogilvie (1965) p. 19 and Adams (1974).

130. See Woodman (1975) pp. 272-87.

131. See Woodman (1968) and (1983) p. 65.

132. See E.G. Sihler, *TAPA* 25 (1894) pp. xlv-xlix, E.A. De Stefani, *SIFC* 18 (1910) pp. 19-31, P. Freitag, *Stilistische Beiträge zu Vell. Pat.: Pleonasmus und Parenthese* (diss. Vienna, 1942), Woodman, *Latomus* 25 (1966) pp. 564-6; Woodman (1977) and (1983) index 1 s.vv. 'Cicero', 'pleonasm'. Velleius is also 'a Ciceronian in his choice of clausulae' (Aili p. 126, with statistics).

133. See Woodman (1983) pp. 65 and 144ff.

134. Liv. 1.30.4, 6.23.2, 42.54.5, 62.12 (*TLL* 6.1.699.50-2).

135. Cic. *Verr.* 1.119, 3.21, *Sest.* 91.

136. See Woodman (1977) p. 169, adding Liv. 3.61.2 and Ogilvie (1965) p. 510.

137. See Woodman (1983) pp. 218ff., 250ff., (1977) pp. 234ff.

138. See Syme (1958) pp. 274-6, 288-9, 697-700. The principal surviving fragment of his work concerns Cicero's death (Sen. *Suas.* 6.23).

139. Syme (1958) p. 276.

140. *D.* 23.2. Though the judgement is anachronistic from the point of view of literary history, it no doubt implies that neither Bassus nor Servilius was an archaiser.

141. Syme (1964a) p. 418, cf. (1964) p. 291 n. 79.

142. Klingner, however, attaches considerable importance to Servilius' Stoic connections (p. 200). For a thorough study see Syme (1964a); also Wilkes pp. 197-9.

143. I assume that in the following sequence of contrasts *illa* refers to *historia* and *haec* to *oratio*: so too Sherwin–White ad loc. and Gamberini pp. 58-81.

144. Perret p. 95.

145. For the encomiastic nature of Florus' work see Jal (1967) 1.xxxix sqq.

146. See Walsh (1961) pp. 201-2, Chausserie-Laprée pp. 636-8.

147. Analysis of Florus' clausulae shows marked affinity with the practice of Cicero (see Jal (1967) 1.lvii-lxix).

148. Under Augustus the historian Timagenes suffered *renuntiatio amicitiae* (see above, n. 46), while T. Labienus had his books burned in AD 12 (Sen. *Contr.* 10 pref. 5-8, Dio 56.27.1). Under Tiberius the historian Cremutius Cordus (above, n. 112) also had his books burned and was himself compelled to commit suicide (AD 25). From this period onwards, as Bonner (1949) p. 43 n. 5 remarks, men incurred severe penalties for using declamatory themes on tyrants as a method of promoting political criticism (cf. Dio 59.20.6, 67.12.5).

149. I have omitted to consider Curtius Rufus, whose history probably belongs to the early years of Claudius' reign: though large portions of it are extant, its subject matter (Alexander the Great) is hardly

relevant to this discussion. (Curtius is, however, usually regarded as a Livian.) I have also omitted some other historians whose works are largely lost and about whom too little is known. Thus the Augustan historian Pompeius Trogus, knowledge of whose work depends mostly on its epitome by Justin, has been considered as a Sallustian (M. Rambaud, *REL* 26 (1948) pp. 171ff.) and as an opposition writer (J.W. Swain, *CP* 35 (1940) pp. 16-18), though the latter is denied by Clark Chapter 7. Leeman (1963) pp. 256-7 has argued that Fabius Rusticus (? d. AD 108) was not a Sallustian, though he concludes by saying that he was: since Tacitus (*Agr.* 10.3) compares him with Livy, the former is presumably more likely to be correct.

150. Syme's judgement was also that of Leeman (1955) and (1963) p. 243.

151. So too Perret pp. 94-7 and Ogilvie (1967) p. 24.

4

History and Alternative Histories: Tacitus

Tacitus' reputation as the greatest Roman historian rests chiefly on the *Annals* and *Histories*, which together produced a total of thirty volumes and, when complete,[1] began with the death of Augustus in August AD 14 and ended eighty-two years later with the death of Domitian in September 96. The scale of treatment, which is ample, and the annalistic format, which is rigorously sustained throughout, alike served to remind his readers that Tacitus was writing history in the grand and time-honoured manner.

Preface to the *Histories*

Although the *Histories* deal with the last third of Tacitus' chosen period, they were in fact written before the *Annals*.[2] We have already seen sufficient evidence in the cases of Thucydides, Sallust and Livy that historiographical prefaces were replete with 'signals' from which readers might infer what line a historian was intending to take. The preface to the *Histories* falls into three clearly defined sections: (a) Scope and impartiality (Chapter 1), (b) content (2-4.1), (c) retrospective survey of June-December AD 68 (4.2-11.3). What would a contemporary reader have inferred from it? The text of the first two of these sections is as follows:

1   Initium mihi operis Servius Galba iterum Titus Vinius
       consules erunt. nam post conditam urbem octingentos et
       viginti prioris aevi annos multi auctores rettulerunt, dum
       res populi Romani memorabantur, pari eloquentia ac liber-
       tate: postquam bellatum apud Actium atque omnem

potentiam ad unum conferri pacis interfuit, magna illa ingenia cessere; simul veritas pluribus modis infracta, primum inscitia rei publicae ut alienae, mox libidine adsentandi aut rursus odio adversus dominantes: ita neutris

2 cura posteritatis inter <in>fensos vel obnoxios. sed ambitionem scriptoris facile averseris, obtrectatio et livor pronis auribus accipiuntur; quippe adulationi foedum crimen servitutis, malignitati falsa species libertatis inest.

3 mihi Galba Otho Vitellius nec beneficio nec iniuria cogniti. dignitatem nostram a Vespasiano inchoatam, a Tito auctam, a Domitiano longius provectam non abnuerim: sed incorruptam fidem professis neque amore quisquam et

4 sine odio dicendus est. quod si vita suppeditet, principatum divi Nervae et imperium Traiani, uberiorem securioremque materiam, senectuti seposui, rara temporum felicitate, ubi sentire quae velis et quae sentias dicere licet.

2 Opus adgredior opimum[3] casibus, atrox proeliis, discors seditionibus, ipsa etiam pace saevom. quattuor principes ferro interempti; trina bella civilia, plura externa ac plerumque permixta; prosperae in Oriente, adversae in Occidente res: turbatum Illyricum, Galliae nutantes, perdomita Britannia et statim missa, coortae in nos Sarmatarum ac Sueborum gentes, nobilitatus cladibus mutuis Dacus, mota

2 prope etiam Parthorum arma falsi Neronis ludibrio. iam vero Italia novis cladibus vel post longam saeculorum seriem repetitis adflicta: haustae aut obrutae urbes, fecundissima Campaniae ora; et urbs incendiis vastata, consumptis antiquissimis delubris, ipso Capitolio civium manibus incenso. pollutae caerimoniae, magna adulteria;

3 plenum exiliis mare, infecti caedibus scopuli. atrocius in urbe saevitum: nobilitas, opes, omissi gestique honores pro crimine, et ob virtutes certissimum exitium. nec minus praemia delatorum invisa quam scelera, cum alii sacerdotia et consulatus ut spolia adepti, procurationes alii et interiorem potentiam, agerent verterent cuncta odio et terrore. corrupti in dominos servi, in patronos liberti; et quibus deerat inimicus, per amicos oppressi.

3 Non tamen adeo virtutum sterile saeculum, ut non et bona exempla prodiderit. comitatae profugos liberos matres, secutae maritos in exilia coniuges; propinqui audentes, constantes generi, contumax etiam adversus tormenta servorum fides; supremae clarorum virorum

necessitates, ipsa necessitas fortiter tolerata et laudatis anti-
2 quorum mortibus pares exitus. praeter multiplices rerum
humanarum casus caelo terraque prodigia et fulminum
monitus et futurorum praesagia, laeta tristia, ambigua
manifesta; nec enim umquam atrocioribus populi Romani
cladibus magisve iustis indiciis adprobatum est non esse
curae deis securitatem nostram, esse ultionem.
4   Ceterum antequam destinata componam, repetendum
videtur, qualis status urbis, quae mens exercituum, quis
habitus provinciarum, quid in toto terrarum orbe validum,
quid aegrum fuerit, ut non modo casus eventusque rerum,
qui plerumque fortuiti sunt, sed ratio etiam causaeque
noscantur.

1   My chosen starting point will be the consulships of Servius
Galba and (for the second time) Titus Vinius, since many
historians have recorded the preceding period of 820 years
from the foundation of the city. For as long as the achievements of the Roman people were their subject, their record
combined eloquence with free speech in equal proportions;
but after the Battle of Actium, when peace depended upon
establishing an autocracy, there were no more literary
giants. Truth was shattered at exactly the same time — first
through blameless ignorance of a governmental system
which treated its subjects like aliens, later through a lust for
sycophancy or alternatively disgust towards the autocrats
themselves. In either case, opponents and victims
2 abandoned all concern for posterity between them. Yet
readers are automatically resistant to blatant canvassing on
the part of an historian, whereas they will readily lend their
ears to denigration and spite: adulation is open to the loathsome accusation of servitude, but malice gives a false
3 impression of free speech. For myself I had no personal
contact with Galba, Otho or Vitellius for either good or ill.
That my political career was started by Vespasian,
enhanced by Titus and carried further by Domitian, I have
no wish to deny; but no one should be treated with either
affection or disgust once a writer has stated that his reli-
4 ability is beyond corruption. If I live long enough, I have
reserved for my later years the more fertile and less haz-
ardous material provided by the reigns of the Deified Nerva
and Trajan, a period of rare delight, when you can think
what you want and say what you think.

2   The work on which I am now embarking is rich in crises, terrible with battles, riven with rebellion, and savage even when at peace. Four emperors perished by the sword. There were three civil wars, still more against foreigners, and often conflicts which combined elements of both. Success in the East was balanced by failure in the West. The Balkans were in turmoil, the Gallic provinces wavered in their allegiance, and Britain was left to fend for itself no sooner than its conquest had been completed. The Sarmatian and Suebian peoples rose upon us, the Dacian distinguished himself in desperate battles won and lost, and thanks to the activities of a charlatan masquerading as Nero, even Parthia was on the brink of declaring war.

2   Finally, Italy itself fell victim to disasters which were quite unprecedented or had not occurred for many centuries. Whole towns were burnt down or buried throughout the richest part of the coast of Campania, and Rome suffered severely from fires that destroyed its most venerable temples, the very Capitol being set alight by Roman hands. Things holy were desecrated, there was adultery in high places. The Mediterranean swarmed with exiles and its

3   rocky islets ran with blood. The reign of terror was particularly ruthless at Rome. Rank, wealth and office, whether surrendered or retained, provided grounds for accusation, and the reward for virtue was inevitable death. The profits made by the prosecutors were no less odious than their crimes. Some helped themselves to priesthoods and consulships as the prize of victory. Others acquired official posts and backstairs influence, creating a universal pandemonium of hatred and terror. Slaves were suborned to speak against their masters, freedmen against their patrons, while those who had not an enemy in the world were ruined by their friends.

3   However, the period was not so barren of merit that it failed to teach some good lessons as well. Mothers accompanied their children in flight, wives followed their husbands into exile. There were resolute kinsmen, sons-in-law who showed steadfast fidelity, and slaves whose loyalty scorned the rack. Distinguished men driven to suicide faced the last agony with unflinching courage, and there were death-scenes not inferior to those held up to our admiration in the

2   history of early Rome. In addition to manifold tragedy on

the human plane, signs and wonders occurred in heaven and earth, premonitory lightnings and tokens of things to come, auspicious or ominous, doubtful or manifest. In short, Rome's unparalleled sufferings supplied ample proof that the gods are indifferent to our tranquillity, but eager for our punishment.

4 However, as a preliminary to my history proper, a retrospective survey seems in order, covering the state of affairs in Rome, the intention of the troops, the attitude of the provinces, and the areas of strength and weakness across the world. In this way one can discover not only the outcome and consequences of events, which are generally fortuitous, but also their background and reasons.[4]

One of the curiosities of the preface, which has attracted scholarly attention, is its very first sentence, where Tacitus announces that his starting point is January AD 69 and not, as might perhaps have been expected, the death of Nero in June 68. 'The decision Tacitus took', says the latest commentator, G.E.F. Chilver, 'was surely influenced by his determination to open his work on the lines laid down by his main model.'[5] The reference is to Sallust, whose *Histories* had begun with the names of the consuls for 78 BC. 'It is as if Tacitus implicitly announces a work in the grand manner of Sallust', says A.D. Leeman.[6] 'Like Sallust, too', adds Chilver, 'he proceeds straight to a comparison between himself and earlier historians, and then to an assertion of his own impartiality.'[7] Yet the matter is not quite as straightforward as these and other scholars allow.

It is true that the first fragment of Sallust's *Histories*, in addition to its annalistic rendering of consular names, contains the phrase *res populi Romani*, which recurs in Tacitus' second sentence;[8] and the phrase *magna ... ingenia* in his third sentence, though found in other authors too, is borrowed from Sallust's *Bellum Catilinae* (8.3). But Tacitus' references to his predecessors and to his own impartiality contain none of the striking verbal reminiscences by which Livy, when referring to the same topics, makes his debt to Sallust's *Histories* unmistakably clear (see above, p. 131). It is also true that Tacitus introduces his retrospective survey in 4.2-11.3 with phraseology at 4.1 which seems to echo that with which Sallust had introduced his own retrospective surveys in the *Bellum Catilinae* (5.9 'res ipsa hortari *uidetur* ... supra *repetere* ac paucis ... quomodo rem publicam habuerint ... disserere') and *Bellum Iguru-*

thinum (5.3 'sed priusquam huiuscemodi rei initium expedio, pauca supra *repetam*, quo ad *cognoscendum* omnia illustria magis magisque in aperto sint').[9] But though the echoes themselves seem clear enough, it has been argued by Syme that the actual survey owes little to the technique of Sallust: 'The survey ... is not merely a marvellous device. It appears to lack precedent or parallel in ancient historiography'.[10]

In fact many of Tacitus' allusions in the first section of his preface are either to phrases which are found first in Cicero (thus 2 *foedum crimen* ~ *Sull.* 90, 4 *uberiorem ... materiam* ~ *Fin.* 4.12)[11] or, more strikingly, to passages which seem exclusively Ciceronian. Thus the contrast between *amore* and *sine odio* in 3 recalls a famous passage of the *Pro Marcello*, 'sine amore ... et rursus sine odio' (29), where Cicero's use of *rursus* seems also to be picked up by Tacitus earlier in 1: 'aut rursus odio'. Again, *uita suppeditet* in 4 occurs not only three times in the *Brutus* (105, 124, 245) but also in Cicero's third *Philippic* (15), a later section of which, dealing with freedom of thought and expression (36 'nimium diu teximus quid sentiremus; nunc iam apertum est: omnes patefaciunt in utramque partem quid sentiant, quid uelint'), seems also to be echoed by Tacitus in 4: 'ubi sentire quae uelis et quae sentias dicere licet'. Since Cicero's manner and style were the opposite of those of Sallust, as we have seen (pp. 117-26), it would therefore appear that the signals presented at least by the first chapter of Tacitus' *Histories* are unclear. On the evidence so far considered, it certainly cannot be assumed without qualification that Sallust is, in Chilver's words, Tacitus' 'main model'.

If we now turn to the second section of the preface (2-4.1), we shall find that Tacitus previews the content of his work in terms which are directly comparable with those laid down by Cicero, particularly in the *De Oratore* (see above, pp. 79-80) but also elsewhere. Cicero had required that historiography should contain descriptions of geographical regions and battles (pp. 79, 83-5, 88-9, 91, 95): Tacitus lists a large number of foreign countries and peoples which, by inference, he plans to describe;[12] he also promises that his work is 'terrible with battles', the transference of the adjective from *proeliis* to *opus* hinting that his work will reproduce the horror of the battles themselves and will thus engender in his readers the same kind of emotional response as was felt by the participants in the actual conflict.[13] This too was a Ciceronian requirement in the letter to Lucceius (5: above, p. 72). Cicero took it for granted that historiography would deal with important and memorable events ('in rebus magnis memoriaque dignis': p. 79), categories to which the episodes of Tacitus' promised narrative clearly belong; he also assumed that the spotlight would fall on great men ('qui fama ac nomine excellant': p. 79): Tacitus points out that four of his protagonists are emperors. Cicero emphasised that historians should deal with fluctuating and suspenseful events (pp. 72, 85, 90-1, 97): Tacitus isolates precisely this aspect of the foreign affairs with which he will be concerned (2.1 *prosperae ~ aduersae, nutantes, perdomita ~ statim missa, cladibus mutuis*). In the letter to Lucceius and elsewhere (pp. 72, 100) Cicero shows a partiality for dramatic death-scenes, particularly if they involve great men: Tacitus mentions that in his period four emperors perished by the sword, that distinguished men committed suicide, and that his death-scenes rival any of those in earlier history. Cicero referred to the emotional mileage to be gained from stories about exile (above, p. 72), a topic which Tacitus mentions twice (2.2 *plenum exiliis mare*, 3.1). Cicero had advocated that historians should acknowledge the role played by chance in human affairs (p. 79), an element to which Tacitus alludes at 3.2 ('praeter multiplices rerum humanarum casus caelo terraque prodigia et fulminum monitus'). Finally, Cicero said that the historian should reveal 'not only what was said or done but also in what manner, and in the case of consequences to explain all the reasons, whether they be of chance ...' (p. 79), which Tacitus seems to echo very closely at 4.1: 'not only the outcome and consequences of events, which are generally fortuitous, but also their ... reasons'.

Thus the second part of Tacitus' preface, so far from being the 'extensive and gloomy characterisation of the subject' described by Leeman,[14] reveals instead that the topics of his work, together with their detailed and emotional treatment, are in exact agreement with the recommendations for pleasurable historiography which were laid down by Cicero in the middle of the first century BC.[15] The implicit emphasis on pleasure is confirmed by a consideration of the other topics which Tacitus lists but which Cicero had happened not to mention. Sacrilege, adultery and throwing victims from rocks (2.2 'pollutae caerimoniae, magna adulteria ... infecti caedibus scopuli') are known to have been popular subjects with the auditors of declamation.[16] Claims that one's material is novel (2.2 *nouis cladibus*) are standard in all branches of literature in the ancient world.[17] And the capturing and laying waste of cities were, as we have already seen, topics whose popularity stretches back through Thucydides to Homer (above, pp. 29-30). Indeed the whole of the second section of Tacitus' preface clearly performs exactly the same function as the third part of Thucydides' own preface (especially 1.23.1-3) in that it heralds a 'disaster narrative' of the most vivid and dramatic type (see above, pp. 28-30).[18]

But whereas Thucydides' work, like that of his imitator Sallust, is characterised by a pervasive pessimism which is well suited to the theme of decline and fall (above, pp. 44 and 124-6), Tacitus goes out of his way at 1.1.4 to remark that the disasters of AD 69-96 were followed by 'a period of rare delight' which will constitute the subject of a later work. Such declarations of future intent become common under the empire and are not to be taken too seriously, since they often amount to little more than conventional formulae by which the present régime is praised.[19] Yet the mere act of referring to the happy present means that Tacitus denies in advance that any permanent damage was done to the Roman constitution by the disasters which he is about to catalogue. By thus depriving events of their potentially tragic significance, Tacitus introduces a note which is absent from Thucydides and entirely antithetical to the unrelieved disillusionment of Sallust. His reference to the reigns of Nerva and Trajan not only provides further confirmation that his interest in the disasters centres primarily on their capacity to furnish gripping narrative material, but also indicates the extent to which we must qualify any statement alleging that Sallust is his 'main model'.

Book 1 of the *Annals*

Preface (Chapter 1)

The later work, when it came, did not in fact provide an encomiastic treatment of the contemporary world in the early second century AD but instead was devoted to the Julio-Claudian period which had begun a century earlier on the death of Augustus. Just as an Horatian ode will sometimes start by alluding to lines of whichever Greek poet was Horace's chief inspiration, so the famous first sentence of Tacitus' *Annals* ('Urbem Romam a principio reges habuere') alludes simultaneously and unmistakably to two of the prefaces of Sallust: *Bellum Catilinae* 6.1 '*Urbem*

Romam ... habuere initio Troiani' (the introduction to Sallust's account of early republican history), and *Histories* 1.8 '*a principio urbis*'. From these allusions, the striking nature and prominence of which seem to give them a significance denied to those in the preface of Tacitus' *Histories*, a reader might well have inferred that Tacitus was proposing to write history in the manner and style of Sallust. Such an inference would of course prove to be correct, since Sallust's brevity, abruptness, *uariatio* and phraseology are successfully reproduced on almost every page of the *Annals*. Yet since there had been no Sallustian historian of Rome for more than a hundred years, as we have seen (above, pp. 140-6), Tacitus' deviation from the style of his immediate predecessors is remarkable. As Perret has well said, 'le choix que Tacite fait de Salluste comme modèle est un fait significatif, lourd d'intentions, expressif d'un goût personnel'.[20] Yet it was only by rejecting the style of Cicero and Livy that Tacitus could fully express his antagonism towards the encomiastic historiography with which that style was associated; and it was only by embracing the alternative style of Sallust that he could portray himself fully as the historian of disenchantment. In the same way Tacitus' own style was imitated by Gibbon more than one and a half thousand years later (see above, p. 46).

The remainder of the preface to the *Annals* is enigmatic in its brevity, and, in comparison with that to the *Histories*, notable for what it omits rather than for what it says. Gone is the promise of a future encomiastic work, and gone too is the detailed listing of representative topics of the narrative. Instead, after surveying republican history and early imperial historiography in roughly a dozen lines (1.1-2), Tacitus merely says (1.3): 'So my intention is to record Augustus briefly, and his final days, then the principate of Tiberius and its sequel, without animosity and partiality, for which I have no grounds'.[21] From this laconic statement the reader is left to draw what further conclusions he can about the narrative which begins with the very next sentence.

The German campaigns of AD 15

Book 1 of the *Annals* deals principally with the first seventeen months of Tiberius' reign, two thirds of the book being devoted to foreign affairs: mutinies in Pannonia and Germany in AD 14 (chapters 16-30, 31-52) and campaigns against the Germans in AD

15 (chapters 55-71). It is with an episode in the last of these that I am concerned (60.3-68).[22]

The story. Six years earlier, in AD 9, Quintilius Varus and three legions had been lured by the German chieftain Arminius into the Teutoburg Forest in the heart of Germany and massacred. It was a disaster of the first magnitude, which remained mourned but unavenged. For months afterwards Augustus is said to have shouted out repeatedly 'Quintilius Varus, return the legions!' and the date of the disaster was observed as a day of mourning each year thereafter.[23] Now, six years later, Germanicus, the nephew and adopted son of the emperor Tiberius, was operating on the northern frontier and found himself 'not far from the Teutoburg Forest in which the remains of Varus and his legions were said to lie unburied [*insepultae dicebantur*]' (60.3). With *insepultae* we are reminded that lack of burial was a supreme misfortune in the ancient world, the constant source of inspiration to poets and prose-writers alike;[24] and as for *dicebantur*, its very imprecision, as Soubiran remarks, 'jette sur ce champ de bataille une sorte de brouillard, il donne à ce coin perdu dans les marais et la forêt … une véritable atmosphère d'irréel'.[25] Indeed the very mention of the Forest, where for six years no Roman had set foot, establishes from the outset the interplay of present and past which is one of the hallmarks of the episode. In this respect Tacitus greatly resembles Virgil, from whose masterly handling of time (perhaps influenced by that of Catullus in Poem 64) the *Aeneid* derives much of its power to stimulate the imagination. And indeed we shall see evidence that Virgil was on Tacitus' mind as he wrote.

The first phase of the episode is described by Tacitus as follows (61-2):

> Igitur cupido Caesarem inuadit soluendi suprema militibus ducique, permoto ad miserationem omni qui aderat exercitu ob propinquos, amicos, denique ob casus bellorum et sortem hominum. praemisso Caecina ut occulta saltuum scrutaretur pontesque et aggeres umido paludum et fallacibus campis imponeret, incedunt maestos
> 2 locos uisuque ac memoria deformis. primo[26] Vari castra lato ambitu et dimensis principiis trium legionum manus ostentabant; dein semiruto uallo, humili fossa accisae iam reliquiae consedisse intellegebantur. medio campi albentia

ossa, ut fugerant, ut restiterant, disiecta uel aggerata.
3 adiacebant fragmina telorum equorumque artus, simul
truncis arborum antefixa ora. lucis propinquis barbarae
arae, apud quas tribunos ac primorum ordinum cen-
4 turiones mactauerant. et cladis eius superstites, pugnam
aut uincula elapsi, referebant hic cecidisse legatos, illic
raptas aquilas; primum ubi uulnus Varo adactum, ubi
infelici dextera et suo ictu mortem inuenerit; quo tribunali
contionatus Arminius, quot patibula captiuis, quae scrobes,
utque signis et aquilis per superbiam inluserit.

62   igitur Romanus qui aderat exercitus sextum post cladis
annum trium legionum ossa, nullo noscente alienas
reliquias an suorum humo tegeret, omnes ut coniunctos, ut
consanguineos aucta in hostem ira maesti simul et infensi
condebant. primum exstruendo tumulo caespitem Caesar
posuit, gratissimo munere in defunctos et praesentibus
2 doloris socius. quod Tiberio haud probatum, seu cuncta
Germanici in deterius trahenti, siue exercitum imagine
caesorum insepultorumque tardatum ad proelia et formi-
dolosiorem   hostium   credebat;   neque   imperatorem
auguratu et uetustissimis caerimoniis praeditum adtrectare
feralia debuisse.

Germanicus was therefore overwhelmed by a desire to pay
his last respects to the soldiers and their commander; and
the army there present was moved to pity for their relatives
and friends, for the fortunes of war and the fate of men.
Caecina had been sent ahead to reconnoitre the hidden
areas of forest, to bridge the flooded marshes and to shore
up any ground likely to prove treacherous. Then they
entered the melancholy site, which was gruesome to set
eyes upon and in the memories which it evoked. First there
was Varus' camp, a wide area with its headquarters marked
out, testifying to the strength of the three legions; next there
was the rampart, half-destroyed, and the shallow ditch
where the mortally wounded had evidently huddled
together. In the middle of a plain there were whitening
bones, lying scattered where soldiers had fled, and piled up
where they had made their last stand. Broken pieces of
weapons lay nearby, and horses' limbs, and skulls fixed to
the trunks of trees. In the surrounding woods there were
altars at which the barbarians had engaged in the ritual

slaughter of tribunes and first-rank centurions. And survivors of the disaster, who had escaped from the battle or from captivity, recalled where the legates had fallen and where the standards had been captured, where Varus had received his first wound and where he had died by his own doomed hand. They pointed to the mound where Arminius had held his victory rally and arrogantly mocked the military standards, to the number of gibbets for the prisoners of war, and to the pits.

And so the Roman army there present, six years after the disaster, started to bury the bones of the three legions: since no one knew whether they were covering over the remains of relatives or not, they treated everyone as if they were kith and kin, while their anger against the enemy mounted with their grief. It was Germanicus who, in sympathy with his men and as a welcome gesture towards the dead, laid the first turf for the burial mound. But Tiberius did not approve — either because he criticized everything Germanicus did, or because he believed that the sight of the unburied dead had deterred the army from fighting and increased their fear of the enemy; besides, a general empowered as an augur to celebrate the sacred rites ought not in his opinion to have come into contact with relics of the dead.

Tacitus begins with Germanicus' desire to bury the dead soldiers ('cupido ... inuadit soluendi suprema', cf. Sall. *BJ* 89.6 *cupido inuaserat*) and the reaction of the present army ('omni qui aderat exercitu'), before noting that Germanicus' lieutenant Caecina was sent ahead to reconnoitre 'the hidden areas of forest' (61.1 *occulta saltuum*). There then follows an account of the battle-site itself (2-3), from which we also learn something of the battle which had taken place there six years ago: note the pathetic contrasts between the width of the camp and the shallow ditch (cf. Virg. *Aen.* 7.157 *humili ... fossa*),[27] between the precision of the HQ and the half-destroyed rampart, between the legions when at full strength and their mortally wounded remains. The whitening bones in the middle of the plain (2) are Virgilian in inspiration (*Aen.* 9.230 'castrorum et campi medio',[28] 12.36 'campique ... ossibus albent'), while the skulls fixed to the trunks of trees (3) are a sign of barbarism employed both by Virgil (the victims of the monster Cacus at 8.196-7 'foribusque adfixa superbis / ora',

Nisus and Euryalus after being killed by the Latins at 9.471 'ora uirum praefixa mouebant') and other authors (e.g. victims of the Scythians at Amm. 22.8.34 'caesorum capita fani parietibus praefigebant').[29] The barbarism of the Germans is further underlined by the paronomasia of *barbārae ārae*, which in Soubiran's words suggests 'la barbarie des rites d'immolation et la répulsion du narrateur romain'.[30] Next (4) are introduced survivors of the disaster, who point out where Varus committed suicide, for which Virgilian phraseology is again deployed (10.850 'uulnus adactum', 2.645 'manu mortem inueniam'), and where Arminius gloated in victory, which also has a Virgilian tone (9.634 'uerbis uirtutem inlude superbis'). Finally (62.1) Tacitus draws the first phase of the episode to a close by repeating, in reverse order, the two themes with which he began (ring composition): the reaction to the scene of the present Roman army ('Romanus qui aderat exercitus'), whose anger towards the enemy increased (*aucta in hostem ira*), and Germanicus' laying of the first turf for the burial mound.

The opening words of the second phase (63.1 'But Germanicus followed Arminius as he withdrew into trackless territory') bring home to the reader forcibly that the Roman general is confronting the same man whose total and barbaric victory over Varus has just been so vividly described. Arminius gains an initial advantage with troops whom he has hidden in the forests (*quos per saltus occultauerat*), a development which induces in the reader the kind of suspense and fear which Cicero associated with historiography (above, pp. 73, 85, 90-1, 97). For had not Caecina at 61.1 been sent ahead precisely to reconnoitre the hidden areas of forest (*occulta saltuum*)? Has he not done his job properly? Will the present leadership turn out to be as incompetent as that of Varus? Is Germanicus in fact likely to go the same way as Varus? Soon Arminius has trapped the Romans in a treacherous marsh (63.2 *paludem ... iniquam*), but at the very last moment Germanicus avoids defeat.

At this point (63.3) Germanicus withdraws his army, leaving Caecina alone with his own troops to face Arminius. Uncertain (65.3 *dubitanti*) how to repair the marsh causeway and fight off the Germans at the same time, Caecina decides to make camp. But the Germans attack all the same (64.1-3):

Barbari perfringere stationes seque inferre munitoribus nisi lacessunt, circumgrediuntur, occursant: miscetur operantium

bellantiumque clamor. et cuncta pariter Romanis adversa,
locus uligine profunda, idem ad gradum instabilis, proceden-
tibus lubricus, corpora gravia loricis; neque librare pila inter
undas poterant. contra Cheruscis sueta apud paludes proelia,
procera membra, hastae ingentes ad vulnera facienda quamvis
procul. nox demum inclinantis iam legiones adversae pugnae
exemit. Germani ob prospera indefessi, ne tum quidem
sumpta quiete, quantum aquarum circum surgentibus iugis
oritur vertere in subiecta, mersaque humo et obruto quod
effectum operis duplicatus militi labor.

In their efforts to break through the guardposts and attack the
workers, the barbarians engaged in harassment, encircling
manoeuvres and charges. The shouts of the workers and
fighters were confused, and everything was equally unfavourable to the Romans: the place, with its deep mud, provided
unreliable footholds and was too slippery to allow any
progress; their bodies were weighed down by armour, and in
the waves they were unable to throw their javelins. On the
other hand, the Cherusci were long accustomed to fighting in
marshland: they had long limbs, and their huge spears were
effective at long-range wounding. Nightfall finally rescued the
now sagging legions from their losing battle, but the Germans,
tireless in success, did not rest even then: they diverted the
torrents which rise in the surrounding hills, and by flooding
the low ground destroyed what work had already been done
and thus doubled the task of the Roman soldiers.

Yet Caecina is undismayed (64.4): with his forty years' experience
as a fighting soldier he has seen it all before and is thus beyond
fear (*eoque interritus*). He thinks they stand a chance if only they
can reach the level ground (*planities*) which lies between the
mountain and the marsh. Our estimate of Caecina begins to be
revised: he seems not to be a second Varus.

But the night is still not over (65.1):

nox per diuersa inquies, cum barbari festis epulis, laeto cantu
aut truci sonore subiecta uallium ac resultantis saltus com-
plerent, apud Romanos inualidi ignes interruptae uoces,
atque ipsi passim adiacerent uallo, oberrarent tentoriis,
insomnes magis quam peruigiles.

It was a restless night, though for different reasons. The barbarians at their celebration feasts filled the valleys and echoing

forests with their victory or war songs. On the Roman side the
fires were fitful, and voices hesitant: they lay against the rampart, or wandered among the tents, unable either to sleep or
keep watch.

To add to the despondency of the Romans, with their fitful fires
and hesitant voices (cf. *Aen.* 9.239 *interrupti ignes*), Caecina has a
nightmare. He sees emerging from the marsh the figure of Varus
himself (65.2), foul with blood (for combinations of the words
sanguine . . . cernere cf. *Aen.* 2.667, 5.413, 6.87) and beckoning to
him (cf. *Aen.* 4.460-1 'hinc exaudiri uoces et uerba uocantis / uisa
uiri'). The reader's fear returns (see above, p. 172), and not
without reason: when the battle is resumed at dawn (65.3),
Arminius encourages his men with the shout 'Here's Varus and
more doomed legions!' With this identification of Caecina with
Varus, the present and past merge into one, as they do so often in
the *Aeneid,* and the battle seems to be going the way of its predecessor: the horses of the Romans keep slipping in their own
blood (cf. *Aen.* 2.551 'in multo lapsantem sanguine'), and
Caecina's own horse is wounded and the man himself on the
point of being taken (50-6). Yet the Romans are assisted by the
greed of the enemy (*hostium auiditas*), who are keener on looting
than killing (*omissa caeda praedam sectantium*). By nightfall, as
Tacitus quietly informs us, the Romans have manged to reach
open ground (*aperta et solida*). Caecina's plan of the previous night
(see p. 173) has worked.

In front of them, however, there stretches another night of
sheer hell (65.7 *miseriarum*). They must dig fortifications but have
lost their equipment; they are wounded but have no first aid;
they are hungry but running out of food (as *cibos diuidentes*
suggests). They might just as well be dead (*funestas tenebras*); the
next day will surely be their last (*unum iam reliquum diem*). Suddenly a horse breaks loose, causing panic (66.1); and though
Caecina immediately establishes that his men's fear is groundless
(2 *uanam esse formidinem*), he can only prevent hysteria by a
desperate act of personal courage. Thereupon his subordinates
reassure the men that their fear is mistaken (*falsum pauorem esse*), a
detail which underlines Caecina's experience: *he* had summed
up the situation long before. He next makes a speech (67.1),
saying that their only hope is to fight (cf. *Aen.* 2.354 *una salus* and
317 *in armis*): if the enemy can be lured close next day by the
hope of an assault (*expugnandi . . . spe*), the Romans can break

through to the Rhine.

Meanwhile the Germans are as restless as on the previous night (68.1 *inquies*, cf. 65.1: p. 173), their only problem being how to deliver the *coup de grâce*. Arminius, true to form, suggests luring the Romans out of their encampment, but Inguiomerus has a bolder plan which meets with the men's enthusiastic approval: a swift assault (*promptam expugnationem*) followed by looting (*praedam*). These words from the German chieftain mark the turning-point of the episode and guarantee the reader's suspense in exactly the way that Cicero had recommended (see the references on p. 172): for an assault was just what Caecina had been banking on, while the German greed for looting had let the Romans off the hook the day before (see p. 174).[31]

The Germans attack at dawn (68.2) by rushing the Roman ditches and grasping the top of the outer mound (cf. *Aen.* 2.444 'prensant fastigia dextris'). The Romans at first hang back invitingly but then take full advantage of the reliable and level ground (68.3 *aequis locis*) which, in contrast to the treacherous marsh of two days before (63.2 *paludem ... iniquam*: p. 172), Caecina had struggled so hard to gain the previous day: they sweep down on the German rear. Surprised and confused by the sound of the Romans' trumpets and the flash of their weapons (cf. Hor. *Odes* 2.1.17-19 *minaci murmure cornuum / ... fulgor armorum*),[32] and more accustomed to greedy looting than to caution under fire (*ut rebus secundis auidi, ita aduersis incauti*), the Germans fall back (68.4). Arminius and the badly wounded Inguiomerus escape (5), but their troops are slaughtered for as long as daylight and Roman anger last (*donec ira et dies permansit*). This is the day which at 65.7 the Romans thought would be their last (p. 174); this is the anger which has been waiting for release since 62.1, when they saw what Arminius had done to their predecessors six years before (p. 172). Another night falls. The Romans have more wounded than on the previous night, the same scarcity of food, and Arminius has lived to fight again. But for the moment there is strength and health in victory (*uim sanitatem ... in uictoria*).

This episode shows Roman historical writing at its dramatic best. It consists of two complementary phases, the first (61-2) rooted deep in memories of the past and marked off by ring composition (above, pp. 171-2), the second (63-8) a series of present engagements from which the past is never far away and is at times indistinguishable (above, p. 174). During the course of these engagements, which are carefully divided into three days and nights,[33] the Romans are in desperate straits during the first forty-eight hours (63-5) and even suffer from mass hysteria on the night before their victory (66). That the victory is achieved at all is due in no small measure to Caecina, who is at first portrayed in ambiguous terms and regarded by Arminius as a reincarnation of Varus (p. 174); but he nevertheless realises his intermediate objectives (65.6) and then has the experience to anticipate the Germans' weakness and capitalise on it (67.1). Thus the contrast between the increasingly desperate Roman troops and their increasingly astute commander forms a sub-plot which increases the suspense of the major engagements. The various ironies and reversals of the narrative are underlined by the significant repetition of words or phrases, as I have indicated, and the epic quality of the encounter is brought out by the constant allusions to Virgil's *Aeneid*, which I have quoted.[34] Tacitus' account of the German campaign has all the qualities of which Cicero would have approved.

The 'inuentio' of the story. The detailed nature of Tacitus' narrative can be appreciated most fully if we compare his account of the first phase of the episode (61.2: above, pp. 169-71) with that of Suetonius, who describes the same series of events in a single sentence.[35] From where did Tacitus derive such detail about events which had taken place a full century before he came to write? Though scholars have suggested various sources such as the *Bella Germaniae* of the elder Pliny and Aufidius Bassus, both of which are now lost,[36] I believe that he was re-using his own account, which he had given in *Histories* 2.70 only a few years before, of Vitellius' visit to the site of the first Battle of Cremona in AD 69.[37] That account reads as follows:

> Inde *Vitellius* Cremonam flexit et spectato munere Caecinae insistere Bedriacensibus campis ac uestigia recentis uictoriae lustrare oculis *concupiuit*. foedum atque atrox spectaculum: intra quadragensimum pugnae diem lacera corpora, *trunci artus*, putres uirorum *equorumque* formae, infecta tabo humus,
> 2 protritis arboribus ac frugibus dira uastitas. nec minus inhumana facies uiae, quam Cremonenses lauru rosaque construerant, *exstructis altaribus caesisque uictimis* regium in morem; quae laeta in praesens mox perniciem ipsis fecere.
> 3 *aderant* Valens et Caecina *monstrabantque* pugnae *locos*: hinc

inrupisse legionum agmen, *hinc* equites coortos, *inde* circum-
fusas auxiliorum manus; iam tribuni praefectique, sua
quisque facta extollentes, falsa uera aut maiora uero misce-
bant. uolgus quoque militum clamore et gaudio deflectere uia,
spatia certaminum recognoscere, *aggerem* armorum, *strues*
corporum intueri mirari; *et erant quos uaria sors rerum lacrimaeque et*
4 *misericordia subiret.* at non Vitellius flexit oculos nec tot milia
insepultorum ciuium exhorruit: laetus ultro et tam propin-
quae sortis ignarus instaurabat sacrum dis loci.

From there Vitellius deviated to Cremona, and having seen
Caecina's gladiatorial exhibition, he desired to set foot on the
plain at Bedriacum and see with his own eyes the traces of the
recent victory. It was a macabre and horrifying sight: less than
forty days had elapsed since the battle, and there were
mutilated corpses, trunks, limbs, and the shapes of decom-
posed men and horses; the ground was stained with gore, and
the flattened trees and crops presented a scene of terrible
devastation. Equally barbaric was the view of the road, where
the people of Cremona had strewn laurel and roses, and built
altars for the victims whom they slaughtered: such tyrannical
behaviour, however satisfying at the time, was soon to be the
cause of their own destruction. Valens and Caecina were
present, and they pointed out the various important areas of
the battle-site: where the legionary column had burst out,
where the horsemen had massed, and where the auxiliaries
had completed their encirclement. Already the tribunes and
prefects were each boasting of their own achievements, adding
fabrications and exaggerating the truth; and the ordinary
soldiers too, shouting happily as they left the road, re-traced
the battle-field and proudly examined the pile of weapons and
heaps of corpses. Some were affected by the variability of fate,
by tears and by pity; but not Vitellius, who gazed impassively
on the many thousands of unburied citizens. Unable to
restrain his delight, and unaware of the fate that was so soon to
befall him, he sacrificed to the gods of the place.

It will be seen from the italicised words and phrases that there are
numerous and noteworthy similarities between this account and
that already quoted above (pp. 169-70). Naturally Tacitus has
introduced some changes in the *Annals*, such as his reference to
the vicissitudes of fortune, which now comes at the start of his

description whereas in the *Histories* it had come at the end; but the general similarity of the two accounts, and in particular the strikingly parallel introductions of the survivors of each disaster,[38] strongly suggest that the main outline of the story in *Annals* 1.61-2, together with many of its details, are derived directly from *Histories* 2.70. To anyone familiar with the theory of classical historiography as it is to be inferred from such key texts as Thucydides' preface or Cicero's *De Oratore* (see above, pp. 27-8 and 83-90), Tacitus' procedure will seem entirely natural. Given that he had some hard core of information about Germanicus' visit to the forest (and he need have had no more than that provided by Suetonius' single sentence), he was merely required to elaborate it in a manner which was plausible and true to life. Both he and his readers knew, from *Histories* 2.70 if from nowhere else, what visits to battle-sites were like: his readers would have been disappointed in their expectations if he had described Germanicus' visit any differently.[39]

Confirmation of Tacitus' technique in the first phase of the episode is provided by its being repeated in his account of the second phase, where the encounter with the Germans in 64.1-65.1 is borrowed from another encounter with Germans which Roman soldiers had experienced in AD 70 and which Tacitus had already described in *Histories* 5.14.2-15.2:[40]

> Ea loci forma, incertis uadis subdola et *nobis aduersa*: quippe miles Romanus *armis grauis* et nandi pauidus, Germanos *fluminibus suetos* leuitas armorum et *proceritas corporum*
> 15 attollit. igitur *lacessentibus* Batauis ferocissimo cuique nostr-orum coeptum certamen; deinde orta trepidatio, cum *praealtis paludibus* arma equi haurirentur. Germani notis uadibus persultabant, omissa plerumque fronte latera ac terga *circumuenientes*. neque ut in pedestri acie comminus certabatur, sed tamquam nauali pugna uagi *inter undas* aut, si quid *stabile* occurrebat, totis illuc corporibus *nitentes* ...
> 2 eius proelii euentus utrumque ducem *diuersis animi motibus* ad maturandum summae rei discrimen erexit: Ciuilis instare fortunae, Cerialis abolere ignominiam; *Germani prosperis feroces*, Romanos pudor excitauerat. *nox apud barbaros cantu aut clamore, nostris* per iram et minas acta.

> Such was the appearance of the place, treacherous with hidden swamps and unfavourable to us: for the Roman soldiers were weighed down by weapons and terrified of

swimming, whereas the Germans, long accustomed to the rivers, took advantage of their light armour and tall bodies. While the Batavi therefore engaged in harassment, our most intrepid men all began to fight; but panic struck when weapons and horses started to be swallowed up in the unusually deep marshes. But the Germans fairly ran through their native swamps, and disregarding the opposing front-line they encircled the flanks and rear. Contrary to what you would expect in an infantry battle, there was no close fighting, but the men wandered in the waves as if during a naval encounter; or else, if a reliable patch of ground showed up, they strove towards it with all their might ... The result of that particular battle encouraged each commander to bring the whole operation to a decision, although for different reasons: Civilis wished to press home his good fortune, Cerialis to redeem his disgrace. Thus the Germans were fierce on account of their success, while the Romans were spurred on by shame: night on the barbarian side was spent in singing or shouting, on ours in anger and threats.

Once again it will be clear from the italicisations, and particularly from the close similarity of the night scenes and from the precise repetition of the unusual phrase *inter undas*,[41] that this passage provided the outline and many of the details for the story which Tacitus tells in the *Annals* (above, pp. 172-3). Further details were available not only in Virgil, as we have seen, but also in Livy, whose work may have suggested both the incident in which the horse breaks loose and Caecina's speech which immediately follows (above, p. 174).[42]

Thus Tacitus' account of the German campaigns of AD 15 provides a striking example of Roman historiographical *inuentio* in operation. But the fact that Tacitus has derived much of his material from his own *Histories* will have encouraged his readers to believe that in the *Annals*, despite the lack of any such promise in the preface (above, pp. 167-8), they were being given the same kind of content which, as we know from his contemporary the younger Pliny, had proved so successful in the earlier work (*Ep.* 7.33.1). As the *Annals* progress, however, it becomes gradually clear to the reader that any such belief is entirely mistaken. The re-working of earlier material serves only to emphasise the extent to which the reader's expectation is eventually thwarted.[43]

Book 4 of the *Annals*

Programmatic elements

With *Annals* 4 Tacitus begins the second part of his account of Tiberius' reign,[44] and at the very start he reaffirms the relationship with Sallust which he had already established in the opening to Book 1 (see p. 167). His statement that in AD 23 'fate suddenly turned disruptive and the emperor himself savage' (4.1.1 'repente turbare *fortuna coepit, saeuire* ipse') is borrowed from Sallust's description of an earlier occasion on which Roman history had taken a decisive turn for the worse (*Bell. Cat.* 10.1 '*saeuire fortuna* ac miscere omnia *coepit*'). Tacitus attributes the change in Tiberius to his henchman Sejanus, who is duly described as if he were the reincarnation of the republican traitor Catiline (4.1.2-3, cf. Sall. *BC* 5).[45] Yet references to fate and to the malign influence of Sejanus are not the only means by which Tacitus underlines the change which now took place in Tiberius' reign.

Several chapters later in Book 4 Tacitus concludes his account of the year AD 24 by interposing a digression in which he explains the nature of the history which he is now writing (32-3):

> Pleraque eorum quae rettuli quaeque referam parva forsitan et levia memoratu videri non nescius sum; sed nemo annalis nostros cum scriptura eorum contenderit qui veteres populi Romani res composuere. ingentia illi bella, expugnationes urbium, fusos captosque reges, aut si quando ad interna praeverterent, discordias consulum adversum tribunos, agrarias frumentariasque leges, plebis
> 2 et optimatium certamina libero egressu memorabant; nobis in arto et inglorius labor: immota quippe aut modice lacessita pax, maestae urbis res et princeps proferendi imperi incuriosus erat.
>
> non tamen sine usu fuerit introspicere illa primo aspectu levia ex quis magnarum saepe rerum motus oriuntur. nam
> 33 cunctas nationes et urbes populus aut primores aut singuli regunt. (delecta ex iis et conflata rei publicae forma laudari
> 2 facilius quam evenire, vel si evenit, haud diuturna esse potest.) igitur ut olim plebe valida, vel cum patres pollerent, noscenda vulgi natura et quibus modis temperanter

haberetur, senatusque et optimatium ingenia qui maxime perdidicerant, callidi temporum et sapientes credabantur, sic converso statu neque alia re Romana quam si unus imperitet, haec conquiri tradique in rem fuerit, quia pauci prudentia honesta ab deterioribus, utilia ab noxiis discernunt, plures aliorum eventis docentur.

3   ceterum ut profutura, ita minimum oblectationis adferunt. nam situs gentium, varietates proeliorum, clari ducum exitus retinent ac redintegrant legentium animum; nos saeva iussa, continuas accusationes, fallaces amicitias, perniciem innocentium et easdem exitii causas coniungimus, obvia rerum similitudine et satietate.

4   tum quod antiquis scriptoribus rarus obtrectator, neque refert cuiusquam Punicas Romanasne acies laetius extuleris; at multorum qui Tiberio regente poenam vel infamias subiere posteri manent. utque familiae ipsae iam extinctae sint, reperies qui ob similitudinem morum aliena malefacta sibi obiectari putent. etiam gloria ac virtus infensos habet, ut nimis ex propinquo diversa arguens. sed ad inceptum redeo.

[a¹] I am well aware that many of the events which I have been describing, and will proceed to describe, perhaps seem insignificant and too trivial to mention. [b¹] But no one should try to compare my *Annals* with the work of republican historians. Their uninhibited narratives dealt with great wars, sieges of cities, the routing and capture of kings, or (on the domestic front) disputes between consuls and tribunes, agrarian and supply legislation, and power struggles between aristocracy and people. [a²] My work, on the contrary, is limited and mundane, since peace reigned almost completely undisturbed, life in Rome was grim, and the emperor uninterested in imperialist expansion.

[a³] Yet there is some point in focusing on what at first sight are trivialities, since great events often originate from them. [c] Let me explain what I mean. All governments, whether national or civic, are either democracies, oligarchies or monarchies. (A mixed constitution is more of an ideal than a reality, and if it becomes a reality cannot last very long.) Now when the government of Rome was democratic, as was once the case, it was essential to understand the character of the people and the appropriate methods of controlling it. Again, in the days of oligarchy, men achieved reputations as politicians and statesmen if they had acquired a thorough knowlege of the character of the senate and aristocracy. [a⁴] Similarly, with the change in constitution and Rome's survival depending on monarchy, it is useful to investigate and record topics such as mine. Few people have the capability of making moral or practical judgements in the abstract, but many of them can learn from reading about the experiences of others.

[a⁵] Yet for all their usefulness these topics provide hardly any pleasure. [b²] Geographical descriptions, fluctuating battles and generals' glorious deaths are what hold the attention of readers and stimulate their imagination. [a⁶] My narrative, on the other hand, is a series of savage edicts, repeated accusations, treacherous friendships, and innocent people slaughtered, always for the same reasons — an obstacle course of monotony and saturation.

[b³] Then there is the fact that hardly anyone objects to ancient historians, and no one now cares if your treatment of the Carthaginians or Romans is too encomiastic.[a⁷] But many who suffered punishment or disgrace during Tiberius' reign have descendants alive today; and in cases where the families themselves have died out, you will find people whose own analogous behaviour leads them to assume that another's crimes are being imputed to themselves. Even distinction and excellence invite hostility since they constitute too harsh an indictment of their opposites merely by coexisting with them. But I return to my main theme.

This digression is of immense importance because in it Tacitus explains that his own work, which I have denoted by [a] in the above translation, is now significantly different from earlier historiography, which I have denoted by [b].[46] Let us consider his various statements in turn.

Tacitus begins at [a¹] by stating that much of his material may seem insignificant and too trivial to mention, an exact reversal of Cicero's assumption in the *De Oratore* that the material of history would be significant and worthy of being recorded ('in rebus *magnis memoriaque dignis*': above, pp. 79-80). Indeed the importance of one's material was a commonplace of historiography, to be found particularly in prefaces,[47] and the full force of Tacitus' statement of the opposite can be appreciated if it is compared with the remarks with which Dionysius began his *Roman Antiquities* (above, pp. 41-2). Some authors actually claimed that their material increased in significance as their work progressed. Thus Virgil, to quote a classic example, begins the second half of the *Aeneid* by announcing that the more weighty part of his epic is under way (7.44-5 '*maior* rerum mihi nascitur ordo, / *maius* opus moueo').[48] Here Tacitus, at the equivalent point in *Annals* 1-6, does precisely the opposite: henceforward his material will apparently be less, not more, important than hitherto.[49]

Tacitus next at [b¹] discourages his readers from comparing his *Annals* with republican historiography. This in itself constitutes a reversal, since historians in their prefaces often claimed that their work was superior to those of their predecessors.[50] Tacitus sees his own inferiority in terms of content, which for earlier historiography consisted of precisely the topics which Tacitus himself had been so glad to advertise in the preface to his *Histories*: great wars, city sieges and the tragedies of famous men (see above, pp. 165-6).[51] Since the topics which now offer themselves are the opposite of these [a²], his present work is correspondingly mundane: the Latin word *inglorius* perhaps suggests an inability on Tacitus' part to achieve the *gloria* which Sallust sought (above, p. 121)[52] and hence also the readership amongst posterity for which Tacitus himself expressed concern in the *Histories* (1.1.1).[53]

Although the second paragraph of the digression contains a defence of his work based on the grounds of utility [a³⁻⁴], which is also one of the standard topics in historical prefaces,[54] this defence is effectively undermined by the paragraph which follows and in which Tacitus denies the pleasurableness of his work [a⁵]. Pleasure was regarded not only as an essential ingredient if literature in general was to be useful,[55] but also as a vital requirement for historiography in particular: Cicero refers to it no fewer than seven times in a single paragraph of his letter to Lucceius (above, pp. 72-3), while whole sections of the prefaces of Thucydides and of Tacitus' own *Histories* are devoted to it (see pp. 25-30 and 165-6).[56] Tacitus illustrates his point, as in the first paragraph, by comparing the pleasurable topics of conventional historiography [b²]. Geographical descriptions were singled out as essential by Cicero in the *De Oratore* and *Orator* (above, pp. 79, 83-5, 88-9, 91, 95) and by Tacitus himself in the preface to the *Histories* (p. 165);[57] and the same two authors also emphasise the importance of suspenseful battles and the glorious deaths of famous men (references on p. 165 above). Indeed Tacitus' description of the effect of these topics here (*retinent ... legentium*) perhaps recalls Cicero's account of their importance in the letter to Lucceius (5 *in legendo ... retinetur*):[58] if so, Tacitus' argument is all the more telling. Finally, the third paragraph of the digression ends, as again did the first, with a depreciatory account of Tacitus' present work [a⁶]. The number of words suggesting monotony emphasises that his work lacks the variety at which authors conventionally aimed and to which the word *uarietates*, just above, perhaps alludes.[59] Lacking as it does so many of the elements of which pleasurable historiography normally consists, his narrative at this point in the *Annals* presents an obstacle course to those readers who might otherwise have derived at least some profit from it.

In the fourth and last paragraph Tacitus engages in a final contrast between the indifference with which ancient historians are read and the hostility which he himself risks as he writes the *Annals*. He then concludes the digression with a standard 'signing-off' formula which itself is significant, as we shall see below.

It is therefore clear that in this digression Tacitus has comprehensively reversed a representative sample of the statements which we would expect to find in a historical preface and which are in fact found in the preface to his own *Histories*. In consequence it may reasonably be asked why he did not place his statements at the very beginning of Book 4, forming a kind of 'second preface' such as is found in some other historians,[60] but instead chose to reserve them for a digression in the body of the narrative. One answer to this question is that he would then have been deprived of his dramatic opening, with its Sallustian references to fate and Sejanus (above, p. 180); but there is also another consideration.[61] Rhetorical convention dictated that when a writer's material was unattractive, as Tacitus now claims his to be, he should not use a direct opening but instead should adopt the technique of *insinuatio*, or the 'disguised opening'.[62] By adhering to rhetorical convention Tacitus has successfully underlined the unpleasantness of the material with which he is now dealing.

That his disguised opening takes the form of a digression, which is clearly identified as such by its signing-off formula (*sed ad inceptum redeo*),[63] is also of significance. We know from Cicero that digressions were regarded as a traditional means of entertaining one's readers;[64] and we know from Quintilian and Pliny that by Tacitus' time digressions were particularly associated with the genre of historiography.[65] Thus, by using a digression specifically to *deny* that his work contains any of the pleasurable elements of which conventional historiography was thought to consist, Tacitus could hardly have chosen a more ironically appropriate medium in which to emphasise the changed nature of his work.

That change will have seemed particularly striking to those readers of the *Annals* who were already acquainted with the *Histories*. The latter work, as we have seen (above, pp. 160-7), was equipped with an elaborate preface in which Tacitus explained fully the conventional nature of the narrative on which he was embarking. The preface to the *Annals*, on the other hand, is enigmatic in its brevity (above, pp. 167-8) and designedly, as it now appears, left readers guessing what line its author was going to take. From the narrative of Book 1, with its concentration on foreign fighting and some of its episodes actually borrowed from the *Histories* (above, pp. 168-79), readers might reasonably have expected that the *Annals* would be a similar work to its predecessor. But it now transpires that Tacitus has capitalised on his *inuentio* there in order to frustrate those expectations in Book 4 and so emphasise the completely different kind of historiography which is appropriate for the second half of Tiberius' reign.[66]

Tacitus could hardly have written the digression in Book 4 if he and his readers had not regarded historiography as primarily a literary activity. It is because classical historiography functions as a genre like poetry (see above, pp. 98-100), having its own conventions and generating its own expectations, that Tacitus is able to capitalise on his alleged reversal of them. In just the same way his contemporary, the poet Juvenal, begins his very first satire with an introductory paragraph in which he promises to drive like a charioteer across the open plain (1.19-21); and he concludes the same satire by saying that he is opening up his sails to their full extent in the wind (149-50). These metaphors of the charioteer, the plain and the open sea, are conventional ways of describing the elevated style of epic poetry, whereas satire was traditionally a self-consciously humble genre. But Juvenal's claim now to be writing satire in the hitherto unacceptable style of epic is explained by his statement (149) that vice is now at its peak. Faced with such unprecedented material, the satirist is compelled to adopt an unprecedented style.[67] A similar position is adopted in the second volume, which consists entirely of the long sixth satire and which Juvenal concludes by suggesting that only the elevated style of tragedy can tackle appropriately the theme of modern women (634-7).[68]

These programmatic allusions to breaking the conventions of the genre resemble those of Tacitus, who, after signifying his unfashionable following of Sallust at the start of Book 1, claims in Book 4 to be unable to write conventional historiography at all. It is true that Juvenal's movement is from the basic to the elevated, whereas that of Tacitus is in the opposite direction;[69] but each writer is adopting the same technique of claiming to pervert generic convention in order to reflect and do justice to abnormal events.[70]

Metahistory

It is a commonplace that events are at their most abnormal during civil war,[71] and Tacitus in the *Annals* resorts to various devices to suggest that the Julio-Claudian era already displayed many of the symptoms of internecine strife long before the civil war actually broke out on Nero's death in AD 68 (the point at which the *Annals* closes).[72] One such device is the suggestion that first-century AD society was peopled by characters who, like Sejanus at the start of Book 4 (above, p. 180), have republican counterparts.[73] In this way Tacitus implies that the period is nothing other than a re-run of the late republic, an implication which serves as a constant reminder that, like its predecessor, it too will end in disaster.

Another device is the suggestion, which emerges in the second half of Book 4, that after his self-imposed withdrawal from Rome the emperor Tiberius made war on his own people. This intensified version of the civil war motif, most appropriate to the second half of Tiberius' reign, is first used during Tacitus' account of the year AD 26, when astrologers predicted that the emperor, having left the city, would never return (58.2-3):

unde exitii causa multis fuit properum finem vitae coniectantibus vulgantibusque; neque enim tam incredibilem casum providebant ut undecim per annos libens patria careret. mox patuit breve confinium artis et falsi veraque quam obscuris tegerentur. nam in urbem non regressurum haud forte dictum: ceterorum nescii egere, cum propinquo rure aut litore

et saepe moenia urbis adsidens extremam senectam com-
pleverit.

This resulted in the downfall of many who made no secret of
their assumption that his death was imminent. They did not
foresee the incredible development that he would willingly
abandon his native land for eleven full years. But soon the
narrow dividing-line between that science and falsehood was
revealed, and with what obscurities the truth is disguised.
Although theirs had been no idle statement that he would
never re-enter Rome, they were unaware of its ramifications:
he lived out the last years of his life in the neighbouring countryside or littoral, and on frequent occasions took up a position
by the city walls.

Here Tacitus depicts Tiberius as a voluntary exile (*libens patria
careret*)[74] who, since the verb *adsidere* can mean 'besiege',[75]
regularly returned to assault the very city from which he was
supposed to govern. And the same image is used later, as a
dramatic opening to Book 6 (1.1-2):

He entered the gardens on the Tiber bank, but again returned
to his lonely cliffs by the sea, ashamed of the criminal lusts
with which he burned unchecked to such an extent that like
an oriental monarch he assaulted the virginity of free-born
youngsters ... Slaves were detailed to search out suitable
victims and produce them for the emperor; the willing were
rewarded, the unwilling threatened; and if relatives or parents
clung on to their charges, the slaves simply kidnapped them
and themselves had their way with them as though they were
prisoners of war [*uelut in captos*].

Not only is the scene here very like that of a sacked city, but the
final phrase *uelut in captos* shows that this is what Tacitus was
thinking of. It is as if Tiberius were the commanding officer of the
siege, directing it from a distance, while his subordinates exact
from their victims the traditionai penalties of the victors. Later in
Book 6 there is a similar scene (39.2): 'Tiberius heard this news
from just outside the city ... as if able to see the blood flowing
through the houses and the executioners at work'.[76] In the light of
this evidence from Books 4 and 6 of the *Annals* it is likely, but not
of course provable, that Tacitus also exploited the same image at

strategic points in Book 5, which is now lost.

The alienation of Tiberius, which we have hitherto seen expressed on a metaphorical level, is further emphasised in Book 4 when, during the account of AD 27, Tacitus describes the island of Capri to which Tiberius then retired (67.1-3):

> The island is separated from the tip of the promontory at Surrentum by a strait which is three miles wide. I am inclined to think that its isolation held a particular attraction for him since its entire coastline lacks any proper harbour and its few anchorages are scarcely adequate even for small sailing-craft. In any case no one could land there without alerting the guard. In winter the climate is mild, since a mountain protects it from the worst of the prevailing winds; but it catches the west wind during the summer, when the surrounding sea is seen to its best advantage. There also used to be a fine view across the bay towards the mainland, until the eruption of Mt Vesuvius altered the landscape. Tradition has it that the Greeks took possession of the island and that the Teleboae colonised it; but now it was Tiberius who had settled there in twelve individual and substantial villas, secretly dissipating his energies in depravity and idleness in sharp contrast to the conscientiousness with which he had previously carried out his public duties.

Now it has recently been pointed out that when ancient writers were describing a foreign country, there were five standard elements to which reference was conventionally made: (i) the physical geography of the area; (ii) climate; (iii) agricultural produce and mineral resources; (iv) the origins and features of the inhabitants; (v) the political, social and military organisation.[77] And it will be seen that four of these five elements are present in Tacitus' description of Capri: its geography, its climate, its original inhabitants, and the social and military organisation of its present incumbent. In other words, Tacitus has here employed a kind of metonymy, by applying to Capri the form of geographical description which was normally reserved for foreign countries. The effect is to suggest that the island really was a foreign country, thus emphasising further the alienation of the emperor who inhabited it.[78]

A similar tactic is used by Tacitus earlier in his account of the same year in order to increase the horror even of those events for which Tiberius was not directly responsible (chapters 62-3):

In the consulships of M. Licinius and L. Calpurnius an unexpected disaster took place. Though over almost as soon as it began, its effects rivalled those of a major military defeat [*ingentium bellorum cladem aequauit*]. An ex-slave called Atilius had started to build an amphitheatre near Fidenae for gladiatorial displays, but he failed to sink the foundations in solid ground and failed also to lock the wooden superstructure together with reliable brackets. His behaviour was just what one would expect of someone who was intent on making an unacceptable profit without the proper capital or any sense of civic pride.

Deprived of their sport during Tiberius' reign, fans flocked in, men and women of all ages, their numbers swollen because it was so close to the town. That increased the scale of the disaster. The building was packed, and when it gave way it collapsed both internally and externally: a large crowd of people, spectators and bystanders alike, were hurled through the air and buried by the falling structure. Those who were killed outright in the initial collapse (which is what happens when fate strikes like this) escaped further suffering; more to be pitied were those who clung on to life despite terrible mutilation and whose only contact with husband, wife or children were glimpses during the day and wailing at night. Soon others, alerted by the news, came to mourn a brother, a relative, or parents; even those whose friends or relatives were only away on business became apprehensive: since it had not been established exactly who had perished in the catastrophe, uncertainty magnified the panic.

As people began to move away the rubble, there was a general rush to embrace and kiss the dead; and often quarrels arose when disfigured corpses, but of the right stature and age, led to cases of mistaken identity. Forty thousand people were maimed or killed in that disaster ... but ... the aristocracy opened up their houses to provide first aid and doctors. Throughout the period, although the city was in mourning, one was reminded of the customs of our ancestors, who in the aftermath of every great battle [*magna post proelia*] tended the wounded with selfless devotion.

Now this account can be compared, almost point by point, with the advice given by Quintilian on how to describe the fall of a besieged city (8.3.67-70).[79] According to Quintilian you should mention the crash of falling roofs, the confusion, people clinging to relatives, the wailing of women and children, and the cruelty of fate. It is as if Tacitus has described the collapse of the amphitheatre in terms which are appropriate to the fall of a besieged city. Indeed he actually invites the comparison himself since he begins and ends his account by likening the disaster to a military catastrophe of major proportions — and the type of military disaster most likely to involve the collapse of a building is of course the fall of a besieged city. On this occasion the disaster cannot strictly be laid at the emperor's door; but since the amphitheatre would not have been overcrowded if Tiberius had encouraged public spectacles, as Tacitus notes, he is portrayed as indirectly responsible for its collapse: indeed, suggestions of his responsibility are encouraged by the very use of a metaphor which, as we have seen, is elsewhere associated with Tiberius himself.[80]

Thus numerous episodes in the second half of *Annals* 4 can be interpreted metonymically or metaphorically. But although these interpretations have the effect of heightening Tacitus' critical treatment of Tiberius, they also cause the digression earlier in Book 4 to be seen in a different light. In the digression Tacitus claimed that he could do justice to the changed nature of Tiberius' reign only by adopting an alternative form of historiography from which such conventional elements as the besieging of cities and the description of foreign countries were excluded (see above, pp. 180-4). Yet in the subsequent narrative Tacitus comes to terms with the change in Tiberius' reign by providing, through the further alternative of 'metahistory',[81] precisely the elements which he earlier professed to exclude. This latter procedure, while not strictly at variance with the former,[82] is nevertheless intended to elicit an opposite reaction from his readers, whose attention is expected to be engaged by the metonymic or metaphorical presentation of elements whose absence they had been asked previously to deplore. Yet such ambivalence is entirely characteristic of a narrative in which we are warned repeatedly about the deceptiveness of first impressions by a writer whom we are often required to read 'very closely indeed to perceive that he has in fact denied what one thought he had said'.[83]

Notes

1. We owe the figure thirty to Jerome. Since substantial portions of both works have been lost, the original number of volumes in each work is uncertain. It is often suggested that the *Histories* consisted of twelve books and the *Annals* of eighteen, but this is no more than speculation.

2. The *Histories* were in progress in AD 106 (cf. Plin. *Ep.* 7.33) and perhaps completed by 109 (so Syme). The dating of the *Annals* is disputed: 109-18, according to Goodyear (1981) pp. 387-93; 114-20, according to Syme (1979a) pp. 274-7.

3. *opimum* has been questioned on the grounds (i) that it does not correspond to *casibus* as does *atrox* to *proeliis* and *discors* to *seditionibus*, (ii) that it is never used without special reference to richness of soil. (i) seems to me insubstantial since in the fourth element of the list *saeuom* too not only fails to correspond to *pace* but also produces a similar oxymoron. As for (ii), *opimum* seems defensible as contributing to a sustained agricultural metaphor which begins with *uberiorem . . . materiam* at 1.1.4 and continues with *non . . . uirtutum sterile* at 1.3.1. Tacitus will have in mind the relatively common image of the writer's or speaker's 'territory' (*terra, solum* etc.).

4. The translation of 1.1-2 and 4.1 is my own; that of 2.1-3.2 is by K. Wellesley.

5. Chilver p. 34.

6. Leeman (1973) p. 176.

7. Chilver p. 33, referring to Sall. *H.* 1.4 and 6.

8. This point is not actually noted by Chilver p. 35.

9. Only the latter is quoted by Chilver p. 45. My italicisations indicate words which Tacitus has taken over directly; dots indicate synonyms and the like.

10. Syme (1958) p. 147.

11. The former recurs in Val. Max. 4.2.5 and Mart. 2.56.2; the latter in Quint. 3.1.3.

12. Much of *Hist.* is of course now lost, but one of these full-scale descriptions (of Jerusalem and its inhabitants) survives at 5.2-13.

13. *atrox proelium* is a standard phrase.

14. Leeman (1973) p. 174, an extraordinary misreading — and instructive.

15. This is not the impression given by Syme (1958) pp. 146-7.

16. For sacrilege cf. Sen. *Contr.* 1.2; for adultery, Sen. *Contr.* 2.7 (where Winterbottom compares Sen. *Ben.* 1.9.4, 3.16.3, Juv. 6); for victims from rocks, Sen. *Contr.* 1.3, Quint. 7.8.3, 5-6. Similarly, some of the topics which Cicero had mentioned were equally popular declamatory themes: e.g. torture at *Contr.* 2.5, exile at 6.4.

17. See Lausberg 1.244-5 § 270, Herkommer p. 167 n. 4. For its particular application to historiography see esp. Vitruv. 5 *praef.* 1 'habent enim [sc. historiae] nouarum rerum uarias exspectationes'; Heubner quotes Liv. 5.51.7 'urbis nostrae clades noua', and cf. also Sall. *C.* 4.4 'periculi nouitate'.

18. Compare also Vell. 67.2, App. *BC* 4.12.

19. See Woodman (1975) pp. 287-8.

20. Perret p. 97. Michel's study of 'le style de Tacite et sa philosophie de l'histoire' is not especially helpful, despite its promising title.

21. This is effectively a list of (very unequal) contents: (a) *pauca de Augusto* ▬ 1.2.1-1.4.1; (b) *extrema* ▬ 1.4.2-1.5.4; (c) *Tiberii principatum* ▬ 1.6.1-6.51.3; (d) *et cetera* ▬ Books 7 and following.

22. For reasons of space I cannot provide a full text of the episode, though I quote some extended passages.

23. Suet. *Aug.* 23.2.

24. See Soubiran p. 56, who refers to the *Antigone* and *Aen.* 6.305-30; cf. also Woodman (1983) p. 102 on Vell. 53.3.

25. Soubiran p. 56.

26. For a defence of Koehler's *primo* see Woodman (1979) p. 232 n. 2.

27. This parallel with Virgil, like almost all the others I proceed to quote, may be found in Baxter, although often he is not the first to have spotted them. I have quoted only those passages which Tacitus may reasonably be thought to have had on his mind (see e.g. n. 28 below). I am not suggesting that Tacitus was conscious of all of them, but their very presence seems to me to contribute to the Virgilian *color* of the whole. Goodyear (1981) seems to me excessively sceptical on this matter.

28. At first sight an unpromising parallel, and not mentioned by Baxter, but Tacitus does seem to have the passage on his mind (see *Aen.* 9.239, quoted on p. 174).

29. Used also of the Gauls by Strabo.

30. Soubiran p. 60.

31. 'During May and June the Germans advanced to great effect near the rivers Lys and Marne. But unwittingly they were engaged in demonstrating the most ironic point of all, namely, that successful attack ruins troops. In this way it is just like a defeat ... The spectacular German advance finally stopped largely for this reason: the attackers, deprived of the sight of "consumer goods" by years of efficient Allied blockade, slowed down and finally halted to loot, get drunk, sleep it off, and peer about' (Fussell pp. 17-18, of the great German attack of 1918).

32. I mention this parallel because, in this ode to Pollio, Horace is rightly thought to be singling out the details of dramatic historiography which Pollio's *Histories* typified: see Ullman pp. 50-1 and Nisbet and Hubbard ad loc.

33. This principle of division is rightly adopted by Goodyear (1981) pp. 105-6.

34. Compare Thucydides' narrative of the funeral speech and plague (above pp. 33-5), and note the novelistic technique mentioned on p. 64 n. 199.

35. Suet. *Calig.* 3.2 'Intending to bury in a mass grave the old and scattered remains of those who died in the Varian disaster, he [Germanicus] was the first to gather them into a pile with his own hand'.

36. Pliny's work is mentioned by name at 1.69.1.

37. For a fuller statement of this case see Woodman (1979) pp. 147-9.

38. I have been unable to discover a parallel elsewhere for this motif.

39. To repeat a parallel from another medium which I have used already (p. 111 n. 106), the Romans thought nothing of decorating the

fourth-century Arch of Constantine with second-century reliefs and sculptures.

40. For a fuller argument see again Woodman (1979) 151; also Goodyear (1981) 106-8.

41. On which see also Goodyear (1981) p. 110.

42. For the former Goodyear (1981) pp. 118-19 follows Andresen in quoting Liv. 37.20.11 'equi ... territi, cum uincula abrupissent, trepidationem et tumultum inter suos fecerunt'; for the latter, Liv. 7.35 (and note how Tacitus' *expugnandi ... spe ... succederent* echoes also Liv. 7.7.2 'ad castra Romana cum haud dubia expugnandi spe succedentes'). In other words, almost any of the literary allusions which Tacitus makes can be used to *build up* even the most meagre *hard core elements* of genuine information (*exaedificatio* and *monumenta* in Cicero's terminology: above, pp. 78 and 83ff.) into a full-scale narrative. (This is quite apart from any emotive resonances which such allusions may convey.) Other potentially useful parallels with Livy are cited by Goodyear on 61.3-4, 64.2 and 66.2; and with Sallust on 61.2, 64.3 and 65.1. We should also remember the conventional nature of much of what Tacitus says, e.g. the characterisation of the Germans at 61.3 (above, p. 171 with parallels cited there) and 64.2 (see Woodman (1977) on Vell. 106.1), and nightfall bringing the end of battle at 68.5 (cf. e.g. Hdt. 1.76.4, 82, Plaut, *Amph.* 255, Virg. *Aen.* 11.912-15, Liv. 4.39.6, 6.32.6, 9.23.4, 21.59.8, Plin. *Ep.* 4.9.9 etc.). Nor should we discount the possibility of further imitation by Tacitus of other sections of his own narrative: indeed it was the thesis of Bacha that much of the *Annals* is composed on precisely this principle. It is therefore easy to appreciate how quickly and successfully an episode can be constructed by resorting to these various techniques.

43. See further p. 185 and n. 66.

44. Since the first hexad of books is devoted to Tiberius' reign (above, n. 21), the break between Books 3 and 4 is the half-way point.

45. This character sketch early in Book 4 balances that of Tiberius himself early in Book 1 (4.3-5), thus further emphasising the division of the hexad into two. (The sketch of Sejanus also contains an echo of Sall. *J.* 48.1.)

46. [c] at 33.1-2 is different in that there Tacitus points to political circumstances in earlier Roman history with which his present narrative might have some affinity; but he still does not suggest an affinity with the historiography of those earlier periods. (Note that our digression is not mentioned in Hahn's discussion of Tacitean digressions.)

47. See Avenarius pp. 128-9, Herkommer pp. 164ff.

48. Cf. also *Ecl.* 4.1 'paulo maiora canamus'; Herkommer p. 169 n. 4 [p. 170].

49. It is of course true that Tacitus twice says that the insignificance of his material is only apparent (32.1 *uideri*, 2 *primo aspectu*), thus strictly preserving his historiographical self-respect. But no one, on reading the digression, could fail to derive the *impression* that his material is *actually* insignificant. He does the same at [a³⁻⁴] below (see p. 183), and creating such impressions is one of his most characteristic techniques (see p. 190).

50. See above, pp. 6-7, 49 nn. 24, 131; in general, Herkommer pp. 102ff., especially 109.

51. Tacitus also mentions domestic issues, which, though they perhaps seem uninteresting to us, were presumably not so to his readers. We should remember that Livy regularly dressed up archaic Roman history in an exciting, late-republican guise (Ogilvie (1965) pp. 10-16, 19). Since Tacitus refers to the *liber egressus* of earlier historians, it is possible that he is alluding to the topic of free speech, to which he devotes the last paragraph of the digression; but most scholars simply (and probably rightly) see a contrast with *in arto*, immediately following.

52. That is, there is perhaps a suggestion that because the author cannot describe exploits which win *gloria*, he will not achieve *gloria* himself. Such a connection between the author and his material lies behind the notion of a hierarchy of genres (on which see D'Alton pp. 413-14). Since Tacitus couples *inglorius labor* with *in arto*, commentators naturally quote Virg. *G.* 4.6 'in tenui labor', which is immediately followed by 'at tenuis non gloria'. But Virgil is manipulating generic conventions in just the same way as Tacitus, and in any case he makes it clear in lines 4-5 that the bees can be treated like epic heroes.

53. Concern for posterity is the touchstone by which Lucian judges the ideal historian: see e.g. 61 'do not write with your eye only on the present ...; aim at eternity and prefer to write for posterity', 63 'history should be written ... with truthfulness and an eye to future expectations ...; there is your rule and standard for impartial history'.

54. See Herkommer pp. 128ff.

55. The classic expression of this view is Hor. *AP* 343 'omne tulit punctum qui miscuit utile dulci': see D'Alton pp. 483-8. Admittedly some theorists maintained that pleasure and usefulness were mutually exclusive, but such a stance is inapplicable in the case of historiography (see my next remarks).

56. Cf. also Duris (above, p. 25), Cic. *De Or.* 2.59, *Or.* 37, *Fin.* 5.51, Vitr. 5 *praef.* 1, Plin. *Ep.* 5.8.4; also above, p. 113 n. 125 and reference there to Fornara. Though it is often stated that Thucydides denied any pleasurable aspect to his work, I have argued above that this is not the case (pp. 28-31). Polybius thought that some of his writing might appear austere and have a restricted appeal since he had excluded from it mythical, genealogical and foundation history; but since he also professes to deal with the activities of nations, cities and monarchs, topics which are 'novel in themselves and demand novel treatment', it seems clear that his apologia is greatly qualified (9.1-2). Livy (*praef.* 4) suggests that readers might derive less pleasure from his account of early Roman history than from that of more recent times; but since it was precisely the earlier, mythical material to which readers were conventionally attracted, Livy's diffidence is somewhat disingenuous (cf. 5).

57. Their absence here is underlined by Tacitus' use of the technical term *situs* (see Woodman (1977) on Vell. 96.3).

58. Cf. also *H.* 2.50.2 'fictis oblectare legentium animos'.

59. For variety see above, p. 106 n. 51.

60. E.g. Dion. *Ant. Rom.* 11.1, Liv. 21.1.1. Hdt. 7.20.2-21.1 and Thuc. 5.26 are early examples of the same phenomenon. See Herkommer p. 10.

61. Note also that, by ending on the topic of free speech, he leads neatly into the episode of Cremutius Cordus at 4.34-5.

62. See Lausberg 1.255-6 §§ 280-1.

63. For which see Woodman (1983) on Vell. 68.5.

64. See above, p. 106 n. 51.

65. Quint. 10.1.33 'licet tamen nobis in digressionibus uti uel historico nonnumquam nitore', Plin. *Ep.* 2.5.5 'descriptiones locorum ... non historice tantum sed prope poetice prosequi fas est'.

66. For this technique of surprise elsewhere see Cairns (1979) Chapter 7.

67. See Bramble pp. 164ff., Rudd p. 108.

68. Rudd pp. 106-8.

69. Juvenal does, however, adopt a technique analogous to Tacitus' at 4.11 'sed nunc de factis leuioribus'.

70. Though their relative chronologies are problematical (see Syme (1979a)), there are numerous other striking similarities between Tacitus and Juvenal. Some involve matters of simple technique: thus just as Tacitus notoriously uses elevated circumlocutions to describe the commonplace (Syme (1958) p. 343), so Juvenal consistently employs 'the dignified to intensify the squalid' (Rudd p. 109). But others are more fundamental. For example, the well known 'credibility gap' between the obsolescence of Juvenal's material and his *persona* of the savage satirist (Rudd pp. 70-81, 187-90) is paralleled by Tacitus' savage treatment of a still earlier period in the *Annals.* The explanation in both cases would seem to be that the authors wished to criticise the imperial system but, unable to do so by attacking contemporary society directly, chose an indirect method instead. This is a familiar ploy in both ancient and modern times (see, respectively, Bonner (1949) p. 43 and Balfour p. 112), although the genuineness of Juvenal's and Tacitus' criticism is in my opinion highly disputable.

71. See Jal (1963) *passim.*

72. See Keitel pp. 312-17. As she notes (p. 316), following Koestermann, a key passage for this interpretation is 3.28.1-3.

73. Keitel pp. 322-3. It follows from the observations in n. 70 above that Tacitus' characters can also prefigure those of his own lifetime: this two- or three-dimensional aspect of character is another area in which Tacitus resembles Virgil, whose epic heroes look both backwards to those of Homer and forwards to the men of his own day.

74. For *patria carere* ▬ 'live in exile' cf. e.g. Cic. *Att.* 3.26, Val. Max. 3.8.4.

75. See Koestermann ad loc., followed by Woodman (1972) p. 155 and Keitel p. 307 n. 2. See *OLD* s.v. 2.

76. See Keitel p. 307.

77. See R.F. Thomas pp. 1ff.

78. R.F. Thomas p. 128.

79. See Woodman (1972) pp. 155-6. For Quint, see also above, p. 89.

80. Such continuity of metaphor is a regular Tacitean technique: see e.g. Walker p. 159.

81. This term is borrowed from the title of Hayden White's well known book on the 'historical imagination in nineteenth-century Europe'.

82. That is, the narrative remains metonymic or metaphorical. It

cannot be denied, however, that the fighting in Thrace in AD 26, which Tacitus describes in 4.46-51, does indeed contradict the programmatic statements made in the digression only a dozen or so chapters earlier. I have no other explanation for this than that it is a large-scale example of the technique mentioned in the following note.

83. Irving Kristol (*Encounter* 6 (May 1956) 86). Tacitus, as is well known, regularly uses such words as *species* or *imago* to suggest that in political life things are rarely what they seem to be (see e.g. Walker pp. 240-1). This suggestion is so characteristic of his narrative that it almost constitutes a warning to view the narrative itself in that light. Certainly Tacitus, as I have tried to illustrate with reference to Book 4, likes to manipulate his readers in contrary directions. For example, at 1.73.1-3 the impressively sinister introduction to the trials of Falanius and Rubrius would lead one to think that they were found guilty and punished; but they are in fact acquitted. At 1.74.3 Granius Marcellus is arraigned on a charge of treason 'from which there was no escape' (*ineuitabile crimen*); yet he too is acquitted. At 1.74.4 when the emperor speaks Tacitus comments bitterly about the state of freedom; but at 1.77.3 when the emperor remains silent he comments equally bitterly about the state of freedom. (These two passages form a neat inversion of the scene described at Sen. *Contr.* 6.8 *fin.*) Finally, the account of foreign affairs at 6.31-7 is used to suggest at 38.1 both that domestic events are frightful and that there are no foreign affairs worth the name to be described. This is, of course, only a selection from a much greater number of cases and types. See also above, n. 49.

5

Epilogue

From the arguments and illustrations put forward in these Studies it will be clear that in my view classical historiography is different from its modern namesake because it is primarily a rhetorical genre and is to be classified (in modern terms) as literature rather than as history. But since the mere expression of this view involves questions of definition and nomenclature, some further clarification is perhaps called for.

The classical historians wrote narrative, and narrative history is currently said to be experiencing a revival in its fortunes.[1] Now the question whether Thucydides' narrative should be regarded as history or rather as literature has been discussed recently by K.J. Dover.[2] That he is able to make this distinction is due to the perception of many modern historians that in the nineteenth century history became dissociated from literature and established self almost as a science (above, p. ix).[3] But since Dover argues that Thucydides is to be regarded not as literature but as history, it seems to follow, despite the apparent anachronism, that he sees little or no difference between Thucydides and modern historians. His position is therefore close to that of P.A. Brunt, who has expressly stated that the theory of classical historiography as formulated by Cicero is no different from that of its modern namesake (above, p. 80). Thus the view of these scholars seems to be that the narratives of classical and modern historiography are similar because they are both in some sense 'scientific'.[4]

Now it has been pointed out by Hayden White that 'the most recent turn in historical theory [is] from an analysis of the epistemological status of historical knowledge to a consideration of the rhetoric of historical discourse'.[5] In other words, students of historical theory are responding to the realisation that (in White's own words) 'narrative discourse is much more than an assemblage of facts and arguments about the facts':

> It is also a performance in which meanings are produced by a writer's mastery of such ... strategies as those displayed in story-telling and legal disputation. If we are reluctant to call such performances 'oratorical', it is because both modern science and modern literature have condemned all oratory as mere eloquence — and obscured to themselves the rhetorical dimensions of their own discursive practices in the process.[6]

Yet Cicero himself expressly tells us that classical historiography is *opus oratorium maxime*, 'a particularly rhetorical activity' (above, pp. 98-9), and earlier I argued that the narrative practices of the historians were analogous to those used precisely in judicial oratory (above, pp. 83-8). It therefore seems possible to arrive at *the same conclusion* as that in the preceding paragraph but for a different reason: *the narratives of classical and modern historiography are similar because they are both in some sense 'rhetorical'.*

Further, it might be argued that these two ways of regarding classical historiography, so far from being alternatives, are complementary. White elsewhere refers, without apparent dissent, to the view that 'historical events can be plotted in a number of ways with equal plausibility and without in any way doing violence to the factual truths derived from study of the documentary record'.[7] His use of the word 'plot' suggests that in his view a work of modern narrative history can be seen in terms of a play or novel and that 'historical events' or 'factual truths derived from ... the documentary record', like the 'facts' to which he referred in the preceding paragraph, are manipulated by the historian for dramatic purposes. Now it is true that Dover assimilates Thucydides' narrative to works of modern historiography by *differentiating* it from the same two genres of drama and the novel:

> The matter of a tragedy, a novel, or a poem is not there until the author's imagination has created it, and never outside him in the sense in which the matter of historiography is outside ... Any attempt to deal with Thucydides solely as a powerful and

interesting writer is repeatedly drawn into consideration of his relation to a subject-matter which was irrevocably *there*.[8]

Yet at the same time Dover also acknowledges that 'Thucydides is an extremely *dramatic* writer',[9] a choice of words which suggests that there may nevertheless be an area of agreement between himself and White.

Thucydides' narrative is seen by Dover as dramatic in much the same way as modern historiography is seen by White as dramatic — a term which, in White's case, is apparently synonymous with 'rhetorical' (above, p. 198). The difference between the two scholars is evidently one of emphasis. Dover, reacting to recent work in which the literary aspects of Thucydides' narrative have been stressed, emphasises his relation to his subject-matter; White, reacting to generations of historians who have seen their handling of factual truths as in some sense scientific, emphasises their manipulation of their subject-matter. Yet there is common ground between the scholars to the extent that in their view the narratives of Thucydides and of modern historiography each deal with a subject-matter which consists of 'factual truths' and that those factual truths are handled 'rhetorically' in the sense of 'dramatically'.[10] It looks, therefore, as though one might be able *to conclude that classical and modern historiography are similar* because both are *simultaneously* rhetorical and scientific. Yet such a conclusion would of course be at odds with the view adopted in this book.

It will be clear from my analyses of episodes in Thucydides and Tacitus that in my view classical historians, like their modern namesakes, are indeed rhetorical in the sense that they manipulate factual truths for dramatic purposes. But the conclusion mentioned above would be possible only if one were to agree with such scholars as Dover and Brunt that classical historiography, like modern, 'differs from imaginative literature in offering ... not what might or could have happened, but what did'.[11] I have argued, on the contrary, that Cicero understood the word 'rhetorical' to include also the narrative of 'what might or could have happened' and that the very same episodes of Thucydides and Tacitus actually illustrate narrative of this type. It will therefore be clear that it is the role of *inuentio*, a concept which is naturally the antithesis of the 'scientific', which distinguishes my position and prevents me from accepting the conclusion mentioned above.

The distinction between 'what might or could have happened' and 'what did happen' raises the question of what is meant by 'historical truth', a matter on which White has recently and conveniently summarised the position adopted by McCullagh:

> Historical interpretations ... are not properly assessed by the criteria of truth and falsity which are honoured in the physical sciences. They are to be assessed in terms of their adequacy or inadequacy, with respect to their concomitance with the scholarly practices and standards prevailing among the community of professional historians. Interpretations which satisfy these standards may for practical purposes be regarded as true in a correspondence sense. This links historical truth to the conventions, rules and beliefs prevailing in a given society at a given time and place ... rather than to some universal standard of veracity.[12]

As a statement of principle this seems unexceptionable. Consider, for example, what historical truth means to the Gola, who live on the Liberian coast:[13]

> The test of validity is not the consistency or 'fit' of a given version of past events, but whether or not the ancestors of the spokesman would be in agreement with the version ... It is taken for granted that the view of the past put forward by an elder will be the view which is most advantageous to him, his family, and his ancestors. Regardless of what may appear to the outsider as inconsistencies between rival family versions of the pasts, all is taken as the truth until that situation arises in which the past must be entered as evidence in a matter of honor or litigation. Then one's own version is held up as the truth and all others are characterised as incompetent ... The ramifications of this approach to what is 'true', or 'fact', are great ... On one occasion, when the investigator had pressed for an explanation of the discrepancy between the genealogies of two families, an old man shook his head and said: 'You *kwi* [strangers from over the seas] want everything to be one way. We Gola see things in different ways ... A country man does not ask what is true by talking to the words, but he asks "Who is it that said the words", and from that he decides what is right. But if the grandfather and the King say different, then it is not different to a country man. Both are true, but one must

wait a while to understand that. No one can know everything at once.'

Or take the case of medieval historiography, which was greatly influenced by the conventions of epic poetry and which Fleischman sums up as follows:[14]

> There was a concept of history which was distinct from fiction, and which was linked to a particular criterion of truth. But historical truth did not imply, as it does for us, the authenticity of facts and events ... History was what was willingly believed ... For the Middle Ages and even well beyond, historical truth was anything that belonged to a widely accepted tradition.

Such views of historical truth are clearly very different from that of our own society, and many more examples could of course be produced to demonstrate the validity of the above statement that opinion on historical truth is linked to 'the conventions, rules and beliefs prevailing in a given society at a given time and place'.

Since classical historiography is the product of a society which is also very different from our own, it might be thought that its view of historical truth is likely to have been correspondingly different.[15] Certainly Brunt is aware that, when we study Roman historical narrative, cultural differences must be taken into account:[16]

> In relation to Cicero, we have to ask not whether he had any notion of historical investigation that would satisfy a scholar today, but only whether his standards would have been the best accepted in antiquity.

It is, however, clear from the rest of Brunt's discussion that this is merely the statement of a theoretical position which he consistently fails to adopt in practice.[17] Dover for his part, while acknowledging that 'in some respects much that is written now about Thucydides revives the spirit of what was written about him in the ancient world',[18] nevertheless purposely rejects the implications of this remark and maintains that some modern scholars, by treating Thucydides' narrative as literature rather than as history, make the writer out to be 'a liar'.[19] Having earlier stated his belief that 'the Greeks in general had more sense than to call a pretentious kind of falsehood "ideal truth"',[20] Dover says:

> It is perfectly possible to read Thucydides as if he had written a work of creative fiction, ... but only at the price of pretending we do not know that historiographers and scientists tried to do something different from what poets tried to do.[21]

But this statement of course assumes that our view of historiography is the same as that of the ancients, an assumption Dover makes explicit by introducing his discussion with an account of his own experiences as a historiographer and by maintaining that

> All classicists, whether they know it or not, are historians ... This fact creates a special relationship between classicist and ancient historiographer, which we ought to exploit. In trying to say about the past only what is best reconcilable with the evidence available up to the time of utterance, we are doing what ancient historiographers, much of the time, professed to be doing.[22]

Yet any similarity between ancient and modern remains no more than an assumption. The ancients themselves, like Dover, debated the exact nature of Thucydides' work in antiquity; but the debate was not between 'literature' and 'history', which is how Dover sees it, but between rhetoric and (precisely) poetry.[23] The terms of this debate therefore underline the importance of the cultural differences which exist between ancient and modern society, and suggest very strongly that the classical view of historical truth was indeed different from our own.

Why do scholars not contemplate the possibility that we perceive historical truth differently from the ancients? One reason is that the difference is incapable of being proved to their general satisfaction. That certain elements in Thucydides' description of the plague may derive from contemporary medical literature, as I have suggested (above, pp. 38-9), rather than from personal observation, as is usually assumed, is not susceptible of proof because of the lack of the appropriate evidence and of the time-span involved. Indeed it is ironical that precisely these considerations are used to explain the potentially awkward fact that despite Thucydides' detailed description we cannot now identify the plague. As M.I. Finley has rightly observed, modern historians of the ancient world are 'often seduced' into the 'unexpressed proposition ... that statements in the literary or documentary sources are to be accepted unless they can be disproved (to the satisfaction of the individual historian)'.[24]

In the case of Tacitus' *Annals*, however, we considered an instance of *inuentio* where the evidence is perhaps capable of convincing all but the most prejudiced scholar (above, pp. 176-9).[25] It is of course true that the episode in Book 1 is only a single item from a work of several volumes; but since Tacitus' technique on this occasion corresponds so closely with the theory of *inuentio* which Cicero expressed, we are entitled to infer that it is by no means exceptional but rather the reverse and that Tacitus resorted to *inuentio* on numerous other occasions which we cannot now identify.[26] To quote M.I. Finley again: 'the ability of the ancients to invent and their capacity to believe are persistently underestimated'.[27] If such *inuentio* is indeed regular in Tacitus,[28] it means that when we are using his narrative as historical evidence, we should not regard it as the privileged document of a superior historian but should treat it with the utmost scepticism as a typical example of classical historiography.[29] But, as T.S. Jerome aptly remarked, 'scepticism about a matter on which the evidence is insufficient to justify a definite opinion is impossible for the vulgar and appears to be exceedingly difficult for the erudite'.[30] And the truth of this remark is well illustrated by the following 'case study'.

Two of our sources for the career of the emperor Tiberius are Velleius Paterculus and Tacitus himself. The latter's account, written at least a century after the events it describes, takes up six volumes and is replete with circumstantial detail. Tacitus refined the mannerisms of Thucydides and Sallust to produce a style which is remarkable for its difficulty and obtuseness (above, p. 168). He likewise followed Thucydides and Sallust in adopting towards his subject matter, and particularly towards Tiberius himself, a critical attitude which is heightened by the deployment of various rhetorical and dramatic devices (above, pp. 180-90). Tacitus is thus the antithesis of Velleius in almost every respect. Velleius' account takes up a mere thirty-eight chapters[31] and deals with events of which he was often a contemporary and sometimes a participant. His style, though often criticised for its rhetoric and awkwardness, is clearly an attempt at reproducing the inflated eloquence of Cicero (above, pp. 141-3). Like Cicero too, and Livy, he adopted towards his subject matter, and particularly towards Tiberius himself, an encomiastic attitude which is heightened by the deployment of various devices derived from panegyric proper.[32] Which of these two writers, it may be asked, has been perceived as the more reliable guide to the career of Tiberius Caesar?

The answer to this question may be found in the writings of Sir Ronald Syme, who throughout his career has accepted the general reliability of Tacitus' work and has never ceased to express his contempt for that of Velleius.[33] Syme's preferment of Tacitus to Velleius represents (if it has not been responsible for actually forming) the opinion of the majority of scholars during the last fifty years.[34] Yet is Velleius' contemporary account likely to be quite so inferior to that written by Tacitus a century or so later? We have seen that in his use of *inuentio* Tacitus is a typical product of the mainstream of classical historiography; yet this is not true of Velleius, who belongs to a sub-genre known as the historical summary, which of its very nature eschews most forms of rhetorical elaboration and aims instead at brevity.[35] Of course no one would wish to deny the rhetorical trappings of a work which has been attacked consistently for its rhetoric; but such features as the apostrophe and the exclamation are entirely superficial and quite different from Tacitus' employment of *inuentio*, which, as Cicero makes clear (above, pp. 83-94), is concerned with content (*res*).[36] Velleius' style, no matter how rhetorical, cannot divert attention from the fact that his content is relatively free from the *inuentio* which Tacitus necessarily espoused.[37] It might be objected that the residual history provided by Velleius, in comparison with the detail of Tacitus, is hardly worth having; but how can we be sure that in the twentieth century we are able to know much more about Tiberius' career than the information provided by Velleius? We certainly should not allow the mere presence of detail to persuade us that an account is true, although few scholars seem to have heeded so obvious a warning.[38] As Jerome has again remarked, 'the very paucity of material regarding Roman conditions seems often to produce a distinct unwillingness to discard any part of the evidence save where it is manifestly absurd or incredible'.[39]

If in the light of these cautionary observations it is asked why scholars have nevertheless persisted in preferring the late testimony of Tacitus to the contemporary evidence of Velleius, one need only refer to the opening pages of Syme's first book, *The Roman Revolution*:[40]

> In narrating the central epoch of the history of Rome I have been unable to escape from the influence of the historians Sallust, Pollio and Tacitus, all of them Republican in sentiment. Hence a deliberately *critical* attitude towards Augustus. If Caesar and Antonius by contrast are treated rather leniently, the reason may be discovered in the character and opinions of the historian Pollio — a Republican, but a partisan of Caesar and of Antonius. This also explains what is said about Cicero and about Livy ... The style is likewise direct and even abrupt ... Much that has recently been written about Augustus is simply *panegyric*, whether innocuous or edifying ... The example of Pollio ... may encourage the attempt to record the story of the Roman Revolution and its sequel, the Principate of Caesar Augustus, in a fashion that has now become *unconventional*, from the Republican and Antonian side. The *adulatory* or the *uncritical* may discover in this design a *depreciation* of Augustus.

No doubt it was Sir Ronald's personal hatred of autocracy which first attracted him to the historians who had criticised its existence at Rome. (His book was written as Hitler's Third Reich was extending its shadow over Europe, and published in 1939 three days after war with Germany was declared.) But it is clear from the words which I have italicised that Syme valued Sallust, Pollio and Tacitus as historians precisely because of the critical attitude which they adopted towards their subject matter. And if in that first book it was Pollio who above all received Syme's stamp of approval, the subsequent publication of *Tacitus* (1958) and *Sallust* (1964) performed the same service for their eponymous historians and did much to confirm their reputations in the eyes of the majority. Yet a critical attitude is no guarantee of historical reliability:

> Readers are automatically resistant to blatant canvassing on the part of an historian, whereas they will readily lend their ears to denigration and spite: adulation is open to the loathsome accusation of servitude, but *malice gives a false impression of free speech.*

It is ironical that, while explaining Velleius' continued unpopularity, Tacitus' words also highlight a fallacy on which his own reputation has been built (*Histories* 1.1.2).

In *The Roman Revolution* Syme also drew attention to his dismissal of Cicero and Livy and to his adoption of an 'abrupt style', programmatic statements which are perhaps elucidated by remarks made almost twenty years later:[41]

> Sallust ... wrecked the rhythm, balance, and elaboration of the long and convoluted sentence. The ample oratorical manner which had recently been brought to perfection by Cicero was admirably designed to beguile and persuade an audience ... When Roman history came to its maturity ..., it sought ruthlessly to get at the facts behind the words. Smooth phrases were suspect, their authors in discredit. A plain, hard, and broken style seemed to convey a serious guarantee of incorruptible veracity. Next to native models among the annalists it was Thucydides who appealed most to Sallust.

It would seem from these remarks that Syme associated historical excellence with an anti-Ciceronian style, an association which has served further to condemn Velleius and to promote Sallust and his successors, Pollio and Tacitus.

It is of course no accident that attitude and style are the same factors which, as I argued earlier (pp. 45-7), have contributed to the generally good opinion in which Thucydides is held by scholars. Sallust, Pollio and Tacitus are the 'Thucydidean' historians of Rome, and they share with their predecessor (the only Greek historian to whom Syme has devoted an article)[42] a critical attitude to their subjects and an idiosyncratic style. Yet the presence of these factors is no more a guarantee of the authors' reliability than is their absence from Velleius a sign of his 'mendacity'.[43]

Syme's desire that his work should be seen in terms of the ancients' is not simply an inversion (characteristic of its author) of the more usual syndrome by which classical historiography is seen in modern terms; it also illustrates another reason why scholars are reluctant to accept that our view of historical truth is different from that of the Greek and Roman historians.

Syme is a modern historian, and it will not be denied that modern historiography has the status and attributes of a specialist professional discipline. Thus Hayden White (above, p. 200) refers quite naturally to 'the community of professional historians'. Yet this exclusivity tends to promote a uniform response to genres which, while in one sense historical, cannot be classed as 'pure' or 'specialist history'. In what follows I shall provide examples of three different types of such genres.

First, the historical film 'The Birth of a Nation' (1915), which portrayed the formative period of the United States:

> The people who made it, and most of the people who saw it, regarded it as exact history. Lilian Gish, one of the stars of the film, said that the makers had 'restaged many moments of history with complete fidelity to them'; a reviewer wrote: 'History repeats itself upon the screen with a realism that is maddening'. At last, history was revealed ... For them, obviously, pictures, unlike words, could not lie. Griffith, the director, asserted that in the libraries of the future, history books would be replaced by films: 'Instead of consulting all the authorities ... and ending bewildered ... you will actually see what happened. There will be no opinions expressed. You will merely be present at the making of history.' Speaking of historical film, he said: 'In the film play we show the actual occurrence ... If your story traverses to a battlefield we show an actual battlefield ... We show you the scene as realistically as if you were looking down from a hilltop and watching an engagement of contending forces.'[44]

But the response of the professional historian is very different:[45]

> After having spent many hours of careful work in archives in search of historical evidence, historians often think that their conception of history is the only valid one. Very few of them accept that what they regard as historical truth has nothing in common with what other people think of as truth ... An historical film can be puzzling for a scholar: everything that he considers history is ignored; everything he sees on the screen is, in his opinion, pure imagination. But at the same time it is important to examine the difference between history as it is written by the specialist and history as it is received by the non-specialist.

It will of course be pointed out that, although widely perceived to be 'true', the film was an early product of that medium, was intended primarily as entertainment, was aimed at spectators who were perhaps largely naive, and cannot really be called 'historical' in any meaningful sense at all. In response to these objections we must bear in mind that 'film reality is so powerful as to be almost self-authenticating, to the point that we sometimes judge the authenticity of a moment or place by relating it to a visual memory from a film':[46]

> The journalist A.J. Liebling, for example, once reported in a dispatch from the German front that a battle never seemed more 'real' than when it evoked the memory of scenes from Hollywood war movies.

Nevertheless, let us pass on to a different and more recent category of genre.

Twenty years ago George Steiner suggested that realism, on which the novel had depended throughout the nineteenth century, had become redundant in the face of twentieth-century reality, which modern methods of communications made instantly and vividly available to all:[47]

> Being committed to secular reality, the novel made factual information one of its principal devices ... The guns of Waterloo sound to the ears of Fabrice and Amelia Sedley. But they are the same guns as those of the historian or writer on strategy. This equivalence gave to the novel its strong grip on life. And for long periods, reality was such that fiction could master it and give it expressive form. It became a commonplace of criticism to assert that historical and social events as mirrored in the plots of Stendahl, Dickens or Tolstoy, had a realness, an authenticity deeper than that conveyed by the journalist or professional historian (a distinction which echoes Aristotle's famous comparison of poet and historian). But is this still the case? Is prose fiction able to match or surpass the claims made on the life of the imagination by the new media of direct knowledge and graphic reproduction? The world is at our breakfast table, its ceremonies and disasters rendered with fantastic completion and intensity. Why turn to fiction — unless it be to escape? But that is the crux. By its very nature and vision, the art of the novel is realistic ... Fiction falls silent

before the enormity of the fact, and before the vivid authority
with which that fact can be rendered by unadorned report.

As a result of this process, he argued, there was a 'decline in
fiction, a turn of the literate public to history, biography, science
and argument':

> In western culture, with its urban and technological character,
> the representative transitional genre seems to be a kind of
> documentary poetic or 'post-fiction' ... Though it is itself no
> longer a very interesting medium, the novel has developed and
> made available to other literary modes a large range of ideals
> and technical resources. We can now see these at work
> throughout the varieties of non-fiction. In modern biographies
> and historical writing there is a wide measure of collaboration,
> one might almost say collusion, between factual material and
> a particular rhetoric of vivid presentation. Colourful setting,
> dramatic psychology, imaginary dialogue — devices derived
> from the novel — are put at the service of the archive. The
> problem is not one of stylistic liveliness, but of the inevitable
> manipulations which the idiom and psychology of the novel
> bring to the historical evidence ... In that characteristic
> contemporary genre which might be called 'high journalism',
> techniques inherited from the novel play a decisive role. The
> eye of the political and social reporter is direct heir to that of
> the novelist. Hence the obvious stylisation, the deceptive
> dramatic or sentimental gloss on so much that passes itself off
> as scrupulous witness. Much of the interpretation and record
> offered us of the causes of political actions, of the behaviour of
> great persons, comes in the dramatic conventions of the
> realistic novel, conventions now worn to cliché ... In short:
> there is at this point in western culture a mass of non-fiction
> whose particular qualities of vividness, dramatic pace and
> psychological appeal derive from the fact that it has behind it
> the major epoch of the novel.[48]

More recently, it is true, the novel has experienced a resurgence in popularity, due, at least in part, to the publicity
surrounding the various literary prizes for which novels may now
compete; but Steiner's remarks about the prevalence of 'documentary poetic or "post-fiction"' remain valid, as can be seen from

the number of drama-documentaries on television and of 'factoids' in bookshops.[49] That such products are believed by the general mass of 'consumers' to be historically true is clear from the anxiety they cause in anyone who claims to have some special knowledge of the subject in question and believes that the public is being grievously misinformed;[50] but the products are not, of course, regarded as true by professional historians. Thus the television series 'Winston Churchill — The Wilderness Years' (1981), which dealt with the great leader's career between the wars, was based on the official biography of Churchill by Martin Gilbert, who observed that 70 per cent of the production was 'accurate' and 'good history', while 30 per cent was 'good television'.[51] Although this is a markedly different ratio from that in 'The Birth of a Nation', its significance for our purposes is that it could be expressed at all.[52] And if it is again objected that television is too entertaining a medium to produce a valid example of the comparison with professional history, let us consider a third and final case.

Newsreels do not declare themselves as drama or as the entertaining re-enactment of historical events but purport to be a factual record. Yet their producers quickly

discovered that one burning house or one smoking gun muzzle looked so much like another that it made no difference at all whether it had been filmed at the place or at the time in which the sequence of the finished film made the audience imagine it ... In addition, many of the producers also learned the exciting possibilities of intermixing 'real' shots of the exterior of buildings etc. with re-enactments of what might have been happening inside. They also learned the use of models, from battleships in Manila Bay to rubber figures 'leaping' from a burning hotel and from firework volcanoes to panoramic models of earthquake-stricken Los Angeles, which was based on the realisation that both perspective and scale are in any case an artificial product of camera optics. Some of these techniques were later known in the newsreel industry as 'faking', and there had been always a good deal of debate amongst newsreelmen where the line ought to be drawn ... Models and re-enactments were always regarded by some newsfilm producers as unacceptable; by the majority as only to be used in the very last resort; and by some as quite legitimate techniques, because truth, in their view, resided in the truthfulness of the *story* told by the film *as a whole* and not in the photographic credentials of any one shot.[53]

It is hard to imagine a professional historian in sympathy with this last group of newsreelmen; theirs is not the uniform view of historical truth which is taken for granted by 'the community of professional historians'. One recalls Dover's sarcastic remark about those who 'call a pretentious kind of falsehood "ideal truth"' (above, p. 202).[54]

It will be observed, however, that the newsreelmen's 'intermixing of "real" shots ... with re-enactments of *what might have been happening*', like Martin Gilbert's distinction between 'good history' and 'good television', refers to the building-up of hard-core elements by means of *inuentio* — precisely the process which is described by Cicero in theory and put into practice by Thucydides and Tacitus. The result in each case, both modern and classical, is a product which, like medieval history, is 'willingly believed' and in which historical truth does not imply 'the authenticity of facts and events'. Such parallels with classical historiography extend even to the details of passages I have quoted in this Epilogue. The ability of the Gola to accept as true two versions of the 'same' event recalls the bi-focal capacity of the ancients to accept two versions of the 'same' speech (above, p. 14). The film-director's belief that 'in the film play we show the actual occurrence' is paralleled by Plutarch's contention that readers of Thucydides' narrative are turned into 'spectators' of the original action (p. 25). And the newsreel producers' discovery that 'one burning house or one smoking gun muzzle looks much like another' recalls Tacitus' exploitation in the *Annals* of material which he had already used once in the *Histories* (pp. 176-9).

Against these parallels it cannot be argued that the Gola or medieval historians are too culturally remote from classical historiography to render any comparison valid, since the same argument would also invalidate the contention that classical historiography is similar to its modern namesake. Nor, conversely, can it be argued against the parallels with film or television that they are modern, since that would contradict the assumption that classical historiography itself can be seen in modern terms. (On the contrary, if Steiner's analysis above is correct, we stand today in relation to the techniques and conventions of the novel, from which those of the visual media are derived, very much as classical historiography once stood in relation to those of epic.) And while it is true that the visual media have entertainment as one of their aims, we have seen ample evidence that the classical historians were expected to provide entertainment for their readers.

The argument which can be brought against all of these parallels, whether ancient or modern, literary or visual, is that they do not come from history at all in our sense of the word. But that, of course, is precisely the point. As the late Sir Moses Finley observed, 'We start from the wrong premise by assuming that Greeks and Romans looked upon the study and writing of history essentially as we do'.[55]

Notes

1. This was argued in 1979 by Stone; see also the subsequent discussion by K. Thomas (1982).
2. Dover (1983).
3. See further, for example, Gossman's discussion.
4. I apologise for using a term with which many professional historians may disagree, but Dover himself pairs historiography and science: (1983) pp. 61 (quoted on p. 202), 62-3.
5. H. White (1986) p. 109, in a discussion of the works of Veyne, McCullagh and others.
6. H. White (1986) p. 109, expressed more fully in (1984). Compare the trend described by Steiner on pp. 208-9.
7. H. White (1986) p. 109.
8. Dover (1983) pp. 55-6 (his italics), though it should be pointed out that the matter at least of a Greek tragedy was also 'there', in the form of myth.
9. Dover (1983) p. 57 (my italics).
10. This would seem to be the position of Momigliano also: see e.g. (1984) p. 59.
11. Atkinson p. 6. See above, p. 61 and nn. 159 and 160.
12. H. White (1986) p. 109. My abbreviation of the passage has changed its syntax but not, I hope, its meaning.
13. W.L. D'Azevedo, 'Tribal history in Liberia', in Neisser pp. 267-8. See also Finnegan for some general observations.
14. Fleischman p. 305. See also the excellent discussion of Ray, and the very pertinent remarks of Gossman p. 11 on Voltaire.
15. H. White himself would no doubt be prepared to accept this conclusion since he has elsewhere maintained that only in the nineteenth century did it become conventional among historians to identify truth with fact and to regard fiction as the opposite of truth. See e.g. (1978) p. 123, (1980) p. 10.
16. Brunt p. 316.

17. Exactly the same could be said of Momigliano. For example, in the first chapter of his recent *Contributo* he warns 'against assuming *a priori* that there are universal psychological constants' but in the third chapter himself assumes that historiography and historical truth have been just such universal constants from the time of Herodotus through to the present day (Momigliano (1984) pp. 31 and 49-59).

18. Dover (1983) p. 56.

19. Dover (1983) p. 55 ('I shall argue ... that it is salutary, now and again, to discuss issues of Thucydidean scholarship in very simple terms'), 61, 63.

20. Dover (1981) p. 396 n. 2. I am not of course maintaining that the Greeks did not distinguish between truth and falsehood (see above, p. 4 and n. 26), although it has in fact been argued that they had different ideas about these concepts from ours and that they placed less value on 'objective truth' (Starr (1968) pp. 107-11, 142-6 and (1968a) 348-59). What I am concerned with is the nature and role of truth as they are perceived in historical writing at different times and by different societies.

21. Dover (1983) p. 61.

22. Dover (1983) p. 55.

23. Marc. *Vit. Thuc.* 41. See also above, pp. 98-100.

24. M.I. Finley (1985) p. 21. See above, pp. 16-17; also below, n. 29.

25. It has convinced Goodyear (1981) pp. 94-113, especially pp. 106-8, normally the most sceptical of commentators.

26. That we cannot identify them is not in itself an objection since *inuentio* depends upon verisimilitude, which is by definition almost indistinguishable from truth. See also above, p. 92 and n. 99.

27. M.I. Finley (1985) p. 9.

28. For two further examples (in the *Histories*) see Woodman (1983a) pp. 116-19; for the *Annals* note Bacha's hypothesis of regular examples of self-imitation (above, p. 193 n. 42).

29. M.I. Finley (1985) p. 10 rightly refers to 'the widespread sentiment that anything written in Greek or Latin is somehow privileged, exempt from the normal canons of evaluation'.

30. Jerome p. 426, with a good quotation from Ihne.

31. 2.94-131.

32. See Woodman (1977) pp. 285-6, Index 1 s.v. 'panegyric'.

33. For some examples see Woodman (1975) p. 289.

34. Velleius is conspicuous by his absence from, for example, C. Wells, *The Roman Empire* (1984) p. 318 (under 'Sources') and B. Levick, *The Government of the Roman Empire: a Sourcebook* (1985). See also Woodman (1975) p. 289.

35. See Woodman (1975) pp. 273-87.

36. This is analogous to the distinction drawn by Steiner between 'stylistic liveliness' and 'the inevitable manipulations [of] historical evidence' (above, p. 209).

37. I hope this will go some way towards meeting the criticism of Moles (1984) p. 242.

38. It is remarkable how often in scholarly writings the word 'detail' is accompanied by the adjective 'authentic'; yet detail is of course also the trademark of *inuentio* in the ancient world — and of the historical forger

in the modern. The classic case of the latter is Sir Edmund Backhouse's 'history' of China: see Trevor-Roper p. 277.

39. Jerome p. 426.

40. Syme (1939) pp. vii-viii, 6-7.

41. Syme (1958) p. 135.

42. *PBA* 48 (1960) pp. 39-56.

43. Syme's own word: see, recently, 'Mendacity in Velleius', *AJPh* 99 (1978) pp. 45-63.

44. Sorlin pp. viii-ix.

45. Sorlin pp. viii-ix.

46. W. Hughes, 'The evaluation of film as evidence' in Smith p. 52.

47. Steiner pp. 420-1.

48. Steiner pp. 103 and 105-7. For some further remarks on the nature and development of this genre see e.g. Foley.

49. I use 'factoid' to denote a product of the genre of writing known as 'faction' (which is not quite the meaning adopted by F.G. Maier, 'Factoids in ancient history', *JHS* 105 (1985) pp. 32-9). 'Faction' is in fact an excellent equivalent to what we know as classical 'historiography', but I have refrained from using the term because the Latin word *factio*, whatever it means, has nothing to do with historical narrative.

50. For the outcries which greeted drama-documentaries on T.S. Eliot and Captain Scott see *The Observer* for 24.2.1985; for that involving Aneurin Bevan see Woodman (1983b) p. 24.

M.I. Finley and Fleischman, as we have seen, have drawn attention to the capacity of classical and medieval societies to believe what they read in works of history. But we should not underestimate the same capacity of our own society. Steiner p. 104 has remarked that 'by absurd but unassailable logic, the mass-circulation magazines which purvey sentimental romances or tales of contrived terror, now call themselves "True Fiction"'. And consider also what are known as 'urban legends':

> Urban legends belong to the subclass of folk narratives, legends, that — unlike fairy tales — are believed, or at least believable, and that — unlike myths — are set in the recent past and involve normal human beings rather than ancient gods or demigods. Legends are folk history, or rather quasi-history. As with any folk legends, urban legends gain credibility from specific details of time and place or from references to source authorities ... In the world of modern urban legends there is usually no geographical or generational gap between teller and event. The story is *true*; it really occurred, and recently, and always to someone else who is quite close to the narrator ... The legend's physical settings are often close by, real, and sometimes even locally renowned for other such happenings ... Tellers of these legends, of course, are seldom aware of their roles as 'performers of folklore'. The conscious purpose of this kind of storytelling is to convey a true event, and only incidentally to entertain an audience ... Legends can survive in our culture as living narrative folklore if they contain three essential elements: a strong basic story-appeal, a foundation in actual belief, and a meaningful message or 'moral' ... Legends survive by being as lively and 'factual' as the television

evening news, and, like the daily news broadcasts, they tend to concern deaths, injuries, kidnappings, tragedies and scandals. (Brunvand pp. 16-17, 21-2.)

Of course, urban legends are not true and their origins can never be traced (see Brunvand pp. 17, 42), yet they nevertheless thrive in a society as developed and sceptical as our own, and indeed they often appear as genuine stories in newspapers (Brunvand pp. 30, 101-2, 107-8, 117-31). I myself heard a version of one of the most famous legends, 'The Vanishing Hitchhiker' itself, apparently reported as fact on the radio during the summer of 1985. Such is the persuasive power of emphasising the 'truth' and of referring to 'eyewitnesses'.

51. Interview in *The Sunday Times* for 13.9.1981. (His observation was intended as praise.)

52. For another example of the same distinction see Woodman (1983a) p. 111.

53. N. Pronay, 'The newsreels: the illusion of actuality', in Smith p. 100.

54. Note, however, the words of Voltaire: 'We have to make distinctions among the errors of historians. A false date, a wrong name, are only material for a volume of *errata*. If the main body of the work is otherwise true, if the interests, the motives, the events have been faithfully unfolded, we have a well made statue which can be faulted for some slight imperfection of a fold in the drapery' (quoted by Gossman p. 23).

55. M.I. Finley (1985) p. 14.

Abbreviations and Bibliography

In the course of this book I have usually referred to works of modern scholarship by author's name alone, adding the date of publication where an author is responsible for several works: full details can be found in the Bibliography. (Occasionally I have referred to standard commentators on ancient texts without providing full details in this way.)

When referring to Lucian's *How to write history* I have invariably omitted the title. When referring to the *Letter to Pompeius* by Dionysius of Halicarnassus I usually provide a reference in the form '2.372 Usher': this means the appropriate page of Volume 2 of S. Usher's Loeb edition of Dionysius (1985).

Abbreviations

Periodical abbreviations normally follow the system used in *L'Année philologique*. Other abbreviations are as follows:

ANRW   *Aufstieg und Niedergang der röm. Welt*, Vols 1- , ed. H. Temporini and W. Haase, Berlin-New York, 1972-

CHCL   *Cambridge history of classical literature*, Vols 1-2, ed. P.E. Easterling and E.J. Kenney, Cambridge, 1982-5

LSJ   *A Greek-English lexicon*, ed. H.G. Liddell, R. Scott, H. Stuart Jones and R. McKenzie, 9th edn, Oxford 1940

OLD   *Oxford Latin dictionary*, ed. P.G.W. Glare, Oxford, 1968-82

ORF³   *Oratorum Romanorum fragmenta*, Vol. 1, ed. H. Malcovati, 3rd edn, Turin, 1967

RE   *Paulys Real-Encyclopädie der classischen Altertumswissenschaft*, ed. G. Wissowa *et al.*, Stuttgart, 1893-

RRC   M.H. Crawford, *Roman Republican coinage*, Cambridge, 1974

TLL   *Thesaurus linguae latinae*, Leipzig, 1900-

Bibliography

Ackroyd, P.R. and Evans, C.F. (1970) *Cambridge History of the Bible*, vol. 1, Cambridge

Adams, J.N. (1974) 'The Vocabulary of the Later Decades of Livy', *Antichthon 8*, 54-62

Adkins, A.W.H. (1972) *Moral Values and Political Behaviour in Ancient Greece*, London

——(1972a) 'Truth, ΚΟΣΜΟΣ and ΑΡΕΤΗ in the Homeric Poems', *CQ* 22, 5-18

Aili, H. (1979) *The Prose Rhythm of Sallust and Livy*, Stockholm

Allen, W. (1955) 'The British Epics of Quintus and Marcus Cicero', *TAPA 86*, 143-59

Allison, J.W. (1983) 'Pericles' Policy and the Plague', *Historia 32*, 14-23

André, J. (1949) *La Vie et l'oeuvre d'Asinius Pollion*, Paris

Armayor, O.K. (1977-8) 'The Homeric Influence on Herodotus' Story of the Labyrinth', *CB 54*, 68-72

—— (1978) 'Did Herodotus ever go to the Black Sea?', *HSCP 82*, 45-62

—— (1978a) 'Did Herodotus ever go to Egypt?', *JARCE 15*, 59-73

—— (1978b) 'Herodotus' Persian Vocabulary', *Anc. World 1*, 147-56

—— (1978c) 'Herodotus' Catalogues of the Persian Empire in the Light of the Monuments and the Greek Literary Tradition', *TAPA 108*, 1-9

—— (1980) 'Sesostris and Herodotus' Autopsy of Thrace, Colchis, Inland Asia Minor, and the Levant', *HSCP 84*, 51-74

—— (1985) 'Herodotus' Influence on Manethon and the Implications for Egyptology', *CB 61*, 7-11

Atkinson, R.F. (1978) *Knowledge and Explanation in History*, Ithaca, N.Y.

Avenarius, G. (1956) *Lukians Schrift zur Geschichtsschreibung*, Meisenheim am Glan

Bacha, E. (1906) *Le Génie de Tacite: la création des Annales*, Brussels and Paris

Badian, E. (1966) 'The Early Historians' in *Latin Historians* (ed. T.A. Dorey), 1-38, London

—— (1985) 'A Phantom Marriage Law', *Philologus 129*, 82-98

Balfour, M. (1979) *Propaganda in War 1939-45*, London

Bann, S. (1984) *The Clothing of Clio*, Cambridge

Bardon, H. (1952-6) *La Littérature latine inconnue*, vols 1-2, Paris

Barthes, R. (1970) 'Historical Discourse' in *Structuralism: a Reader* (ed. M. Lane), 145-55, London

Bartlett, F.C. (1932) *Remembering: a Study in Experimental and Social Psychology*, Cambridge

Baxter, R.T.S. (1972) 'Virgil's Influence on Tacitus in Books 1 and 2 of the *Annals*', *CP 67*, 246-69

Bayet, J. (1947) *Tite-Live. Histoire romaine*, Tome 1, Livre 1, Paris

Bianchi Bandinelli, R. (1971) *Rome: the Late Empire (Roman Art AD 200-400)*, London

Bloch, M. (1979) *The Historian's Craft*, repr. Manchester

Börner, F. (1952) 'Naevius und Fabius Pictor', *SO 29*, 34-53

Bonner, S.F. (1949) *Roman Declamation*, Liverpool

—— (1977) *Education in Ancient Rome*, London

Bosworth, A.B. (1972) 'Asinius Pollio and Augustus', *Historia 21*, 441-73

Boyer, J.W. (1977) 'A.J.P. Taylor and the Art of Modern History', *Journ. Mod. Hist. 49*, 40-72

Bramble, J.C. (1974) *Persius and the Programmatic Satire*, Cambridge

Breisach, E. (1983) *Historiography: Ancient, Medieval and Modern*, Chicago and London

Brunt, P.A. (1979) 'Cicero and Historiography' in *Miscellanea di studi classici in onore di Eugenio Manni*, 1.311-40, Rome

Brunvand, J.H. (1983) *The Vanishing Hitchhiker: American Urban Legends and Their Meanings*, Pan, London

Buckhout, R. (1974) 'Eyewitness Testimony', *Scientific American 231*, 23-31

Cagnazzi, S. (1977) 'Tre note tucididee', *SIFC 49*, 197-208

Cairns, F. (1979) *Tibullus: a Hellenistic Poet at Rome*, Cambridge

—— (1982) 'Cleon and Pericles: a Suggestion', *JHS 102*, 203-4

Cameron, A. [D.E.] (1968) 'The First Edition of Ovid's *Amores*', *CQ 18*, 320-33

Cameron, A. (1970) *Agathias*, Oxford

—— (1985) *Procopius and the Sixth Century*, London

—— (1988) 'Between True and False' in *History as Text*, London

Canary, R.H. and Kozicki, H. (1978) *The Writing of History: Literary Form and Historical Understanding*, Madison, Wisconsin

Carr, E.H. (1970) *What is History?* Penguin, Harmondsworth (1st publ. 1961)

Chausserie-Laprée, J.-P. (1969) *L'Expression narrative chez les historiens latins*, Paris

Chilver, G.E.F. (1979) *A Historical Commentary on Tacitus'* Histories *I and II*, Oxford

Clark, E.G. (1973) *Augustus and the Historians*, unpubl. diss. Oxford

Classen, J. and Steup, J. (1963) *Thukydides*, vol. 1, 6th edn., repr. Berlin

Collingwood, R.G. (1946) *The Idea of History*, Oxford

Connor, W.R. (1977) 'A Post Modernist Thucydides?', *CJ 72*, 289-98

—— (1984) *Thucydides*, Princeton

Cornford, F.M. (1907) *Thucydides mythistoricus*, London

Croll, M.W. (1966) *Style, Rhetoric and Rhythm*, Princeton

Crump, C.G. (1928) *History and Historical Research*, London

D'Alton, J.F. (1931) *Roman Literary Theory and Criticism*, New York

De Groot, A.W. (1921) *Der antike Prosarhythmus*, Groningen

Denniston, J.D. (1952) *Greek Prose Style*, Oxford

—— (1959) *The Greek Particles*, 2nd edn., Oxford

De Romilly, J. (1963) *Thucydides and Athenian Imperialism*, Eng. tr., Oxford

—— (1967) *Histoire et raison chez Thucydide*, Paris

—— (1977) *The Rise and Fall of States According to Greek Authors*, Michigan

De Ste Croix, G.E.M. (1972) *The Origins of the Peloponnesian War*, London

Detienne, M. (1967) *Les maîtres de vérité dans la Grèce archaïque*, Paris

Dickie, M.W. (1981) 'The Disavowal of *invidia* in Roman Iamb and Satire' in *Papers of the Liverpool Latin Seminar 3*, 183-208, Arca 7, Liverpool

Douglas, A.E. (1955) 'A Ciceronian Contribution to Rhetorical Theory', *Eranos 55*, 18-26

—— (1968) *Cicero. Greece and Rome*, New Surveys in the Classics 2, Oxford

Dover, K.J. (1970) *A Historical Commentary on Thucydides* (with A.W. Gomme and A. Andrewes), vol. 4, Oxford

—— (1973) *Thucydides. Greece and Rome*, New Surveys in the Classics 7, Oxford

—— (1981) *A Historical Commentary on Thucydides* (with A.W. Gomme and A. Andrewes), vol. 5, Oxford

—— (1983) 'Thucydides "as History" and "as Literature"', *History and Theory 22*, 54-63

Dray, W. (1980) *Perspectives on History*, London

Drews, R. (1973) *The Greek Accounts of Eastern History*, Washington, D.C. and Cambridge, Mass.

Drexler, H. (1972) *Herodot-Studien*, Hildesheim and New York

Dutoit, E. (1936) 'Le Thème de "la force qui se détruit elle-même"', *REL* *14*, 365-73

Earl, D.C. (1961) *The Political Thought of Sallust*, Cambridge

—— (1967) *The Moral and Political Tradition of Rome*, London

Eden, P.T. (1962) 'Caesar's Style: Inheritance Versus Intelligence', *Glotta* *40*, 74-117

Eissfeldt, O. (1966) *The Old Testament: an Introduction*, Eng. tr., Oxford

Elton, G.R. (1976) *The Practice of History*, Fontana, Glasgow (1st publ. 1967)

Erbse, H. (1970) 'Über das Prooimion (1,1-23) des thukydideischen Geschichtswerkes', *RhM 113*, 43-69

Evans, J.A.S. (1979) 'Herodotus and Athens: the Evidence of the *Encomium*', *Ant. Class. 48*, 112-18

Fairweather, J. (1981) *Seneca the Elder*, Cambridge

—— (1984) 'Traditional Narrative, Inference and Truth in the Lives of the Greek Poets' in *Papers of the Liverpool Latin Seminar 4*, 315-69, *Arca 11*, Liverpool

Fantham, E. (1972) *Comparative Studies in Republican Latin Imagery*, Toronto

—— (1978) 'Imitation and Evolution: the Discussion of Rhetorical Imitation in Cicero *De Oratore 2*, 87-97 and Some Related Problems of Ciceronian Theory', *CP 73*, 1-16

—— (1979) 'On the use of *genus*-terminology in Cicero's Rhetorical Works', *Hermes 107*, 441-59

Feeney, D.C. (1986) 'Epic Hero and Epic Fable', *Comp. Lit. 38*, 137-58

Fehling, D. (1971) *Die Quellenangaben bei Herodot*, Berlin

—— (1975) 'Zur Funktion und Formgeschichte des Proömiums in der älteren griechischen Prosa' in *ΔΩPHMA Hans Diller*, 61-75, Athens

Finley, J.H. (1942) *Thucydides*, Cambridge, Mass.

—— (1967) *Three Essays on Thucydides*, Cambridge, Mass.

Finley, M.I. (1985) *Ancient History: Evidence and Models*, London

Finnegan, R. (1970) 'A Note on Oral Tradition and Historical Evidence', *History and Theory 9*, 195-201

Flashar, H. (1969) *Der Epitaphios des Perikles*, *SHAW* Phil.-hist. Klasse 1, Heidelberg

Fleischman, S. (1983) 'On the Representation of History and Fiction in the Middle Ages', *History and Theory 22*, 278-310

Focke, F. (1923) 'Synkrisis', *Hermes 58*, 327-68

Foley, B. (1980) 'History, Fiction and the Ground Between: the Uses of the Documentary Mode in Black Literature', *PMLA 95*, 389-403

Fornara, C.W. (1983) *The Nature of History in Ancient Greece and Rome*, Berkeley, Los Angeles and London

Foxhall, L. and Davies, J.K. (1984) *The Trojan War: its Historicity and Context*, Bristol

Fraenkel, E. (1964) *Kleine Beiträge*, vols 1-2, Rome

Frier, B.W. (1979) *Libri annales pontificum maximorum*, Rome

Fussell, P. (1979) *The Great War and Modern Memory*, Oxford (1st publ. 1975)

Gabba, E. (1981) 'True History and False History in Classical Antiquity', *JRS 71*, 50-62

—— (1983) 'Literature' in *Sources for Ancient History* (ed. M. Crawford), 1-79, Cambridge

Gamberini, F. (1983) *Stylistic Theory and Practice in the Younger Pliny*, Hildesheim, Zurich and New York

Gay, P. (1975) *Style in History*, London

Gentili, B. and Cerri, G. (1978) 'Written and Oral Communication in Greek Historiographical Thought', in *Communication Arts in the Ancient World* (ed. E.A. Havelock and J.P. Hershbell), 137-55, New York

Gomme, A.W. (1945) *A Historical Commentary on Thucydides*, vol. 1, Oxford

—— (1954) *The Greek Attitude to Poetry and History*, Berkeley and Los Angeles

—— (1956) *A Historical Commentary on Thucydides*, vol. 2, Oxford

Goodyear, F.R.D. (1981) *The Annals of Tacitus*, vol. 2, Cambridge

Gordon, C.H. (1953) *Introduction to Old Testament Times*, Ventnor, N.J.

—— (1962) *Before the Bible: the Common Background of Greek and Hebrew Civilisation*, London

Gossman, L. (1978) 'History and Literature' in Canary and Kozicki, 3-40

Grant, J.R. (1974) 'Toward Knowing Thucydides', *Phoenix 28*, 81-94

Grenade, P. (1950) 'Le Mythe de Pompée et les Pompéiens sous les Césars', *REA 52*, 28-63

Griffin, J. (1977) 'The Epic Cycle and the Uniqueness of Homer', *JHS 97*, 39-53

Grimm, J. (1965) *Die literarische Darstellung der Pest in der Antike und in der Romania, Freiburger Schriften zur romanischen Philologie 6*, Munich

Guthrie, W.K.C. (1957) *In the Beginning*, London

—— (1971) *The Sophists*, Cambridge

Hahn, E. (1933) *Die Exkurse in den Annalen des Tacitus* (diss., Munich), Borner and Leipzig

Hammond, N.G.L. (1952) 'The Arrangement of the Thought in the Proem and in other Parts of Thucydides I', *CQ 2*, 127-41

Harriott, R. (1969) *Poetry and Criticism before Plato*, London

Häussler, R. (1965) *Tacitus und das historische Bewusstsein*, Heidelberg

Herkommer, E. (1968) *Die topoi in den Proömien der römischen Geschichts-werke*, diss., Tübingen

Heubner, H. (1963) *P. Cornelius Tacitus: Die Historien*, Band I, Erstes Buch, Heidelberg

Hinks, D.A.G. (1936) 'Tria genera causarum', *CQ 30*, 170-6

Holladay, A.J. and Poole, J.C.F. (1979) 'Thucydides and the Plague of Athens', *CQ 29*, 282-300

—— (1982) 'Thucydides and the Plague: a Footnote', *CQ 32*, 235-6

—— (1984) 'Thucydides and the Plague: a Further Footnote', *CQ 34*, 483-5

Horsfall, N. (1981) 'Some Problems of Titulature in Roman Literary History', *BICS 28*, 103-14

—— (1982) 'The Caudine Forks: Topography and Illusion', *PBSR 50*, 45-52

—— (1985) 'Illusion and Reality in Latin Topographical Writing', *GR 32,* 197-208

Howie, G. (1984) 'Thukydides' Einstellung zur Vergangenheit. Zuhörerschaft und Wissenschaft in der *Archäologie'*, *Klio 66,* 502-32

Hunter, I.M.L. (1978) *Memory,* Harmondsworth (1st publ. 1957)

Hunter, V. (1982) *Past and Process in Herodotus and Thucydides,* Princeton

Hunter, V.J. (1973) *Thucydides the Artful Reporter,* Toronto

Immerwahr, H.R. (1960) 'ERGON: History as a Monument in Herodotus and Thucydides', *AJPh 81,* 261-90

—— (1966) *Form and Thought in Herodotus,* Cleveland, Ohio

—— (1973) 'Pathology of Power and the Speeches in Thucydides' in Stadter (1973), 16-31

—— (1985) 'Historiography' in *CHCL 1,* 426-71

Jal, P. (1963) *La Guerre civile à Rome,* Paris

—— (1967) *Florus: Oeuvres,* vols 1-2, Paris

Jerome, T.S. (1923) *Aspects of the Study of Roman History,* New York and London

Kagan, D. (1975) 'The Speeches in Thucydides and the Mytilene Debate', *YCS 24,* 71-94

Katičič, R. (1957) 'Die Ringkomposition im ersten Buche des thukydideischen Geschichtswerkes', *WS 70,* 179-96

Kazazis, J.N. (1978) *Herodotos' Stories and History: a Proppian Analysis of his Narrative Technique,* diss., Urbana, Illinois

Keegan, J. (1978) *The Face of Battle,* Harmondsworth (1st publ. 1976)

Keitel, E. (1984) 'Principate and Civil War in the *Annals* of Tacitus', *AJPh 105,* 306-25

Kelley, A.P. (1969) *Historiography in Cicero,* diss., Pennsylvania

Kemmer, E. (1903) *Die polare Ausdrucksweise in der griechischen Literatur,* Würzburg

Kerferd, G.B. (1981) *The Sophistic Movement,* Cambridge

Kitto, H.D.F. (1966) *Poiesis: Structure and Thought,* Berkeley, Los Angeles and London

Kleingünther, A. (1933) ΠΡΩΤΟΣ ΕΥΡΕΤΗΣ : *Untersuchungen zur Geschichte einer Fragestellung, Philologus* Suppl. 26.1, Leipzig

Klingner, F. (1958) 'Tacitus und die Geschichtsschreiber des 1. Jahrhunderts n. Chr.', *MH 15,* 194-206

Knightley, P. (1978) *The First Casualty: from the Crimea to Vietnam,* Quartet, London (1st publ. 1975)

Knox, B.M.W. (1956) 'The Date of the *Oedipus Tyrannus* of Sophocles', *AJPh 77,* 133-47

Koestermann, E. (1965) *Cornelius Tacitus: Annalen,* Band II, Buch 4-6, Heidelberg

Lang, M. (1984) *Herodotean Narrative and Discourse,* Cambridge, Mass. and London

Lateiner, D. (1977) 'Pathos in Thucydides', *Antichthon 11,* 42-51

Latham, K.J. (1981) 'Hysteria in History: Some *topoi* in War Debates of Homer, Herodotus, and Thucydides', *Mus. Phil. Lond. 5,* 54-67

Laughton, E. (1951) 'The Prose of Ennius', *Eranos 49,* 35-49

Lausberg, H. (1975) *Manual de retórica literaria,* Sp. tr. by J.P. Riesco, vols 1-3, Madrid

Lebek, W.D. (1970) *Verba prisca, Hypomnemata 25*, Göttingen

Leeman, A.D. (1955) 'Le Genre et le style historique à Rome: théorie et pratique', *REL 33*, 183-208

—— (1963) *Orationis ratio*, Amsterdam

—— (1973) 'Structure and Meaning in the Prologues of Tacitus', *YCS 23*, 169-208

Leo, F. (1901) *Die griechisch-römische Biographie*, Leipzig

Lesky, A. (1966) *A History of Greek Literature*, Eng. tr., London

Lintott, A.W. (1972) 'Imperial Expansion and Moral Decline in the Roman Republic', *Historia 21*, 626-38

Littman, R.J. and M.L. (1969) 'The Athenian Plague: Smallpox', *TAPA 100*, 261-75

Lloyd, G.E.R. (1966) *Polarity and Analogy*, Cambridge

Lloyd-Jones, H. (1971) *The Justice of Zeus*, Berkeley, Los Angeles and London

Lockyer, J.C. (1971) *The Fiction of Memory and the Use of Written Sources: Convention and Practice in Seneca the Elder and Other Authors*, diss., Princeton

Longrigg, J. (1980) 'The Plague of Athens', *History of Science 18*, 209-25

Lucas, D.W. (1968) *Aristotle's Poetics*, Oxford

Luce, T.J. (1965) 'The Dating of Livy's First Decade', *TAPA 96*, 209-40

—— (1977) *Livy: the Composition of his History*, Princeton

Luschnat, O. (1978) *Thukydides der Historiker*, Munich [= *RE* 12A.1085-1354 and 14A.759-88]

Macleod, C. (1983) *Collected Essays*, Oxford

Marino, R. (1979) 'Livio storico del "dissenso"?' in *Miscellanea di studi classici in onore di Eugenio Manni 4*, 1406-23, Rome

Marwick, A. (1976) *The Nature of History*, repr. London and Basingstoke (1st publ. 1970)

McCullagh, C.B. (1984) *Justifying Historical Descriptions*, Cambridge

McDonald, A.H. (1957) 'The Style of Livy', *JRS 47*, 155-72

—— (1968) 'The Roman Historians' in *Fifty Years (and Twelve) of Classical Scholarship*, pp. 465-95, Oxford

Michel, A. (1981) 'Le Style de Tacite et sa philosophie de l'histoire', *Eos 69*, 283-92

Middlebrook, M. (1971) *The First Day on the Somme*, London

—— (1978) *The Kaiser's Battle*, London

Millar, F. (1981) Review of Syme (1979) in *JRS 71*, 144-52

Miller, N.P. (1956) 'The Claudian Tablet and Tacitus: a Reconsideration', *RhM 99*, 304-15

—— (1975) 'Dramatic Speech in the Roman Historians', *GR 22*, 45-57

Mink, L.O. (1978) 'Narrative Form as a Cognitive Instrument' in Canary and Kozicki, pp. 129-49

Mittelstadt, M.C. (1968) 'The Plague in Thucydides: an Extended Metaphor', *RSC 16*, 145-54

Moles, J.L. (1984) Review of Woodman (1983) in *JRS 74*, 242-4

—— (1985) 'The Interpretation of the "Second Preface" in Arrian's *Anabasis*', *JHS 105*, 162-8

Momigliano, A. (1966) *Studies in Historiography*, London

—— (1978) 'Greek Historiography', *History and Theory 17*, 1-28

—— (1984) 'The Place of Ancient Historiography in Modern Historiography' and 'The Rhetoric of History and the History of Rhetoric' in *Settimo contributo alla storia degli studi classici e del mondo antico*, pp. 13-36 and 49-59, Rome

Moxon, I.S., Smart, J.D. and Woodman, A.J. (1986) *Past Perspectives: Studies in Greek and Roman Historical Writing*, Cambridge

Müller, C.W. (1984) *Zur Datierung der Sophokleischen Ödipus, AAWM 5*, Wiesbaden

Murray, O. (1972) 'Herodotus and Hellenistic Culture', *CQ 22*, 200-13

Myres, J.L. (1914) 'Herodotus the Tragedian' in *A Miscellany. Presented to J.M. MacKay, LL.D.*, pp. 88-96, Liverpool and London

Nagy, G. (1979) *The Best of the Achaeans. Concepts of the Hero in Archaic Greek Poetry*, Baltimore and London

Neisser, U. (1982) *Memory Observed*, San Francisco

Nisbet, R.G.M. (1984) 'Horace's *Epodes* and History' in *Poetry and Politics in the Age of Augustus* (ed. Tony Woodman and David West), pp. 1-18, Cambridge

Norden, E. (1958) *Die antike Kunstprosa*, vol. 1, 5th edn., repr. Stuttgart

—— (1959) *Die germanische Urgeschichte in Tacitus' Germania*, 4th edn., repr. Darmstadt

North, H.F. (1956) 'Rhetoric and Historiography', *Quart. Journ. Speech 42*, 234-42

Ogilvie, R.M. (1965) *A Commentary on Livy Books 1-5*, Oxford

—— (1967) *Cornelii Taciti de Vita Agricolae* (with I. Richmond), Oxford

O'Mara, M. (1971) *The Structure of the* De Oratore: *a Study in Ciceronian Amplification*, unpubl. diss., N. Carolina

Page, D.L. (1953) 'Thucydides' Description of the Great Plague at Athens', *CQ 3*, 97-119

Parry, A. (1957) *'Logos' and 'ergon' in Thucydides*, diss. Yale (publ. New York 1981)

—— (1969) 'The Language of Thucydides' Description of the Plague', *BICS 16*, 106-18

—— (1972) 'Thucydides' Historical Perspective', *YCS 22*, 47-61

Paul, G.M. (1982) '*Urbs capta*: Sketch of an Ancient Literary Motif', *Phoenix 36*, 144-55

Pearson, L. (1939) 'Thucydides and the Geographical Tradition', *CQ 33*, 48-54

—— (1947) 'Thucydides as Reporter and Critic', *TAPA 78*, 37-60

Percival, J. (1971) 'Thucydides and the Uses of History', *GR 18*, 199-212

Perret, J. (1954) 'La Formation du style de Tacite', *RÉA 56*, 90-120

Peter, H. (1897) *Die geschichtliche Litteratur über die röm. Kaiserzeit*, vols 1-2, Leipzig

Petzold, K.-E. (1972) 'Cicero und Historie', *Chiron 2*, 253-76

Phillips, J.E. (1974) 'Form and Language in Livy's Triumph Notices', *CP 69*, 265-73

—— (1982). 'Current research in Livy's first decade' in *ANRW 2*, 30.2.998-1057

Pouncey, P.R. (1980) *The Necessities of War: a Study of Thucydides' Pessimism*, New York

Press, G.A. (1982) *The Development of the Idea of History in Antiquity*,

Kingston and Montreal

Pritchett, W.K. (1975) *Dionysius of Halicarnassus: On Thucydides*, Berkeley, Los Angeles and London

Puccioni, G. (1981) *Il problema della monografia storica latina*, Bologna

Rambaud, M. (1953) *Cicéron et l'histoire romaine*, Paris

Rawlings, H.R. (1981) *The Structure of Thucydides' History*, Princeton

Rawson, E. (1972) 'Cicero the Historian and Cicero the Antiquarian', *JRS 62*, 33-45

—— (1985) *Intellectual Life in the Late Roman Republic*, London

Ray, R. (1980) 'Bede's *Vera Lex Historiae*', *Speculum 55*, 1-21

Rhodes, P.J. (1985) *The Athenian Empire. Greece and Rome* New Surveys in the Classics 17, Oxford

Richardson, N.J. (1980) 'Literary Criticism in the Exegetical Scholia to the *Iliad*', *CQ 30*, 265-87

Ridley, R.T. (1980) 'Fastenkritik: A Stocktaking', *Athenaeum 58*, 264-98

Rittelmeyer, F. (1915) *Thukydides und die Sophistik*, Borna and Leipzig

Robinson, P. (1985) 'Why do we Believe Thucydides?' in *The Greek Historians: Literature and History* (ed. M.H. Jameson), pp. 19-23, California

Rosenmeyer, T.G. (1982) 'History or Poetry? The Example of Herodotus', *Clio 11*, 239-59

Rubincam, C.R. (1979) 'Qualification of Numerals in Thucydides', *AJAH 4*, 77-95

Rudd, N. (1986) *Themes in Roman Satire*, London

Russell, D.A. (1964) *'Longinus': On the Sublime*, Oxford

—— (1967) 'Rhetoric and Criticism', *GR 14*, 130-44

Sacks, K.S. (1983) 'Historiography in the Rhetorical Works of Dionysius of Halicarnassus', *Athenaeum 71*, 65-87

Scanlon, T.F. (1980) *The Influence of Thucydides upon Sallust*, Heidelberg

Schadewaldt, W. (1929) *Die Geschichtsschreibung des Thukydides*, Berlin

Scheller, P. (1911) *De hellenistica historiae conscribendae arte*, diss., Leipzig

Schmid, W. and Stählin, O. (1948), *Geschichte der griechischen Literatur*, part 1, vol. 5, 2.2, Munich

Schneider, C. (1974) *Information und Absicht bei Thukydides*, Hypomnemata 41, Göttingen

Schultze, C. (1986) 'Dionysius of Halicarnassus and his Audience' in Moxon, Smart and Woodman, pp. 121-41

Schwartz, E. (1929) *Das Geschichtswerk des Thukydides*, 2nd edn., Bonn

Seager, R. (1980) *'Neu sinas Medos equitare inultos*: Horace, the Parthians and Augustan Foreign Policy', *Athenaeum 58*, 103-18

Shackleton Bailey, D.R. (1965) *Cicero's Letters to Atticus*, vol. 1, Cambridge

—— (1980) *Cicero: Select Letters*, Cambridge

Skard, E. (1942) 'Die Bildersprache des Sallust' in *Serta Eitremiana*, pp. 141-64. *SO* Suppl. 11, Oslo

Smith, P. (1976) *The Historian and Film*, Cambridge

Sontag, S. (1983) *Illness as Metaphor*, Penguin, Harmondsworth

Sorlin, P. (1980) *The Film in History*, Oxford

Soubiran, J. (1964) 'Thèmes et rhythmes de l'épopée dans les *Annales* de Tacite', *Pallas 12*, 55-79

Stadter, P.A. (1972) 'The Structure of Livy's History', *Historia 21*, 287-307

—— (1973) *The Speeches in Thucydides*, Chapel Hill

Stahl, H.-P. (1966) *Thukydides: die Stellung des Menschen im geschichtlichen Prozess*, Munich

Stambler, S. (1982) 'Herodotus' in *Ancient writers* (ed. T.J. Luce), *1*, 209-32, New York

Starr, C.G. (1968) *The Awakening of the Greek Historical Spirit*, New York

—— (1968a) 'Ideas of Truth in Early Greece', *PP 23*, 348-59

Steiner, G. (1967) *Language and Silence*, London

Stone, L. (1979) 'The Revival of Narrative: Reflections on a New Old History', *Past and Present 85*, 3-24

Strasburger, H. (1972) *Homer und die Geschichtsschreibung, SHAW 1*, Heidelberg

—— (1975) *Die Wesensbestimmung der Geschichte durch die antike Geschichtsschreibung, SBWG Goethe Univ. Frankfurt/Main* 5.3 (1966), 3rd edn., Wiesbaden

Strebel, H.G. (1935) *Wertung und Wirkung des thukydideischen Geschichtswerkes in der griechisch-römischen Literatur*, diss., Munich, Speyer

Sussman, L.A. (1978) *The Elder Seneca*, Leyden

Syme, R. (1939) *The Roman Revolution*, Oxford

—— (1958) *Tacitus*, Oxford

—— (1959) 'Livy and Augustus', *HSCP 64*, 27-87

—— (1964) *Sallust*, Berkeley and Los Angeles

—— (1964a) 'The Historian Servilius Nonianus', *Hermes 92*, 408-24

—— (1979) *Roman Papers*, vols 1-2, Oxford

—— (1979a) 'Juvenal, Pliny, Tacitus', *AJPh 100*, 250-78

Thomas, K. (1982) Review of L. Stone, *The Past and the Present* (London, 1982) in *TLS* 30 April (p. 479)

Thomas, R.F. (1982) *Lands and Peoples in Roman Poetry: the Ethnographical Tradition, Camb. Philol. Soc.* Suppl. 7, Cambridge

Thompson, P. (1978) *The Voice of the Past: Oral History*, Oxford

Trencsényi-Waldapfel, I. (1960) 'Poésie et réalité historique dans la théorie et la pratique littéraire de Cicéron', *Ann. Univ. Scient. Budap.* (Sect. Philol.), *2*, 3-18

Trevor-Roper, H.R. (1976) *A Hidden Life: the Enigma of Sir Edmund Backhouse*, London

Trompf, G.W. (1979) *The Idea of Historical Recurrence in Western Thought*, Berkeley, Los Angeles and London

Ullman, B.L. (1942) 'History and Tragedy', *TAPA 73*, 25-53

Usher, S. (1969) *The Historians of Greece and Rome*, London

Valesio, P. (1980) *Novantiqua: Rhetorics as a Contemporary Theory*, Bloomington

Veyne, P. (1984) *Writing History: Essay on Epistemology*, Eng. tr., Manchester

Vretska, K. (1976) *C. Sallustius Crispus. De Catilinae Coniuratione*, vols 1-2, Heidelberg

Walbank, F.W. (1955) 'Tragic History: a Reconsideration', *BICS 2*, 4-14

—— (1957) Review of Avenarius in *Gnomon 29*, 416-19

—— (1960) 'History and Tragedy', *Historia 9*, 216-34

—— (1965) *Speeches in Greek Historians*, J.L. Myres Memorial Lecture, Oxford

—— (1972) *Polybius*, Berkeley, Los Angeles and London
Walcot, P. (1973) 'The Funeral Speech: a Study of Values', *GR 20*, 111-21
—— (1978) *Envy and the Greeks: a Study of Human Behaviour*, Warminster
Walker, B. (1968) *The Annals of Tacitus. A Study in the Writing of History*, repr., Manchester
Wallace, W.P. (1964) 'Thucydides', *Phoenix 18*, 251-61
Walsh, P.G. (1955) 'Livy's Preface and the Distortion of History', *AJPh 76*, 369-83
—— (1961) *Livy: his Historical Aims and Methods*, Cambridge
—— (1961a) 'Livy and Augustus', *PACA 4*, 26-37
—— (1974) *Livy. Greece and Rome* New Surveys in the Classics 8, Oxford
Walters, K.R. (1981) '"We fought at Marathon": Historical Falsification in the Attic Funeral Oration', *RhM 124*, 204-11
Wardman, A.E. (1960) 'Myth in Greek Historiography', *Historia 9*, 403-13
Weidauer, K. (1954) *Thukydides und die hippokratischen Schriften*, Heidelberg
Weinbrot, H.D. (1978) *Augustus Caesar in 'Augustan' England*, Princeton
Weinstock, S. (1960) 'Pax and the "Ara Pacis"', *JRS 50*, 44-58
—— (1971) *Divus Julius*, Oxford
Weissenborn, W. and Müller, H.J. (1885) *Titi Livi ab urbe condita. Liber I*, Berlin
West, M.L. (1978) *Hesiod. Works and Days*, Oxford
West, S. (1985) 'Herodotus' Epigraphical Interests', *CQ 35*, 278-305
Westlake, H.D. (1969) *Essays on the Greek Historians and Greek History*, New York
—— (1977) 'ΛΕΓΕΤΑΙ in Thucydides', *Mnem. 30*, 345-62
White, H. (1973) *Metahistory. The Historical Imagination in Nineteenth Century Europe*, Baltimore
—— (1978) *Tropics of Discourse*, Baltimore
—— (1980) 'The Value of Narrativity in the Representation of Reality', *Crit. Inquiry 7*, 5-27
—— (1982) 'The Politics of Historical Interpretation: Discipline and Desublimation', *Crit. Inquiry 9*, 113-37
—— (1984) 'The Question of Narrative in Contemporary Historical Theory', *History and Theory 23*, 1-33
—— (1986) Review Discussion of Veyne, McCullagh and others in *TLS* 31 January (109-10)
White, T.H. (1979) *In Search of History*, London
Wiedemann, T.E.J. (1983) 'ἐλάχιστον ... ἐν τοῖς ἄρσεσι κλέος: Thucydides, women, and the limits of rational analysis', *GR 30*, 163-70
Wilkes, J. (1972) 'Julio-Claudian Historians', *CW 65*, 177-203
Wilkins, A.S. (1881) *Cicero: De Oratore II*, Oxford
Williams, G. (1968) *Tradition and Originality in Roman Poetry*, Oxford
—— (1980) *Figures of Thought in Roman Poetry*, New Haven and London
Williamson, G. (1951) *The Senecan Amble*, London
Wilson, J. (1982) 'What does Thucydides claim for his Speeches?', *Phoenix 36*, 95-103
Winter, D. (1979) *Death's Men: Soldiers of the Great War*, Harmondsworth (1st publ. 1978)

Winterbottom, M. (1974) *The Elder Seneca: Declamations*, Cambridge, Mass. and London

Wiseman, T.P. (1974) *Cinna the Poet and Other Roman Essays*, Leicester

—— (1979) *Clio's Cosmetics*, Leicester

—— (1981) 'Practice and Theory in Roman Historiography', *History 66*, 375-93

—— (1985) *Roman Political Life 90 BC-AD 69*, Exeter

—— (1985a) *Catullus and his World*, Cambridge

—— (1986) 'Monuments and the Roman Annalists' in Moxon, Smart and Woodman, 87-100

Wolff, L. (1979) *In Flanders' Fields*, Harmondsworth (1st publ. 1959)

Woodman, A.J. (1968) 'Sallustian Influence on Velleius Paterculus' in *Hommages à M. Renard, 1*, 785-99, Brussels

—— (1972) 'Remarks on the Structure and Content of Tacitus, *Annals* 4.57-67', *CQ 22*, 150-8

—— (1973) 'A Note on Sallust, *Catilina* 1.1', *CQ 23*, 310

—— (1975) 'Questions of Date, Genre and Style in Velleius: Some Literary Answers', *CQ 25*, 272-306

—— (1977) *Velleius Paterculus: the Tiberian Narrative*, Cambridge

—— (1979) 'Self-imitation and the Substance of History', in *Creative Imitation and Latin Literature* (ed. David West and Tony Woodman), 143-55, Cambridge

—— (1983) *Velleius Paterculus: the Caesarian and Augustan Narrative*, Cambridge

—— (1983a) 'From Hannibal to Hitler: the Literature of War', *Univ. Leeds Review 26*, 107-24

—— (1983b) 'Reading the Ancient Historians', *Omnibus 5*, 24-7

Wylie, J.A.H. and Stubbs, H.W. (1983) 'The Plague of Athens 430-428 BC: Epidemic and Epizoötic', *CQ 33*, 6-11

Zanker, G. (1981) 'Enargeia in the Ancient Criticism of Poetry', *RhM 124*, 297-311

General Index

Aeschylus 27, 33, 60, 64
Agathias 100, 116
annals (*annales*) 72, 88-9, 107-8
Antonius, M. (cos. 99 BC), speaker in
    the *De Oratore* 75-8, 81-9, 92-9,
    101-6, 108-9, 115-16
Arch of Constantine 111, 192-3
archaising 141, 146, 158 *see also*
    Sallust, style
Archilochus 67
Aristophanes 66
Aristotle 41, 60, 62, 67, 99, 108, 115,
    208
Arminius, German chieftain 169, 172,
    174-6
Arruntius, L. (cos. 22 BC) 140-1, 146,
    158
Atticus, T. Pomponius 92, 98-100
attitude (διάθεσις) of historian to
    subject matter 40-5, 67, 69, 102,
    125-8, 130-2, 136-7, 139-40, 140-6,
    150-1, 156-7, 168, 203-6
Aufidius Bassus 143, 158, 176
Augustus, emperor 127-8, 134, 136-9,
    150, 156-7
autopsy 18-20 *see also* Herodotus,
    Thucydides

Backhouse, Sir E. 214
Bede 110
'Birth of a Nation', film 207, 210
blame or criticism (ψόγος,
    uituperatio) 40-4, 67, 74, 95, 125-8,
    134, 185-6, 190, 203, 205-6 *see also*
    historiography, ancient
blessings and sufferings 33, 35
Bloch, M. 100
Brunt, P.A. 197, 199, 201

Caecina Severus, A. (cos. suff. 1 BC)
    169, 171-6, 179
Calpurnius Piso, L. (cos. 133 BC) 99,
    148
Cassius Hemina, L. 99
Cato the Elder 13, 54
Catullus 169
causae (ὑποθέσεις) 90, 109
Chladenius, theologian 102
Churchill, Sir W.S. 53-4, 210
    'Winston Churchill — the

Wilderness Years',
    drama-documentary 210
Cicero 70-120, 165-6, 182-4
    and early Roman historians 76-8,
        88-9
    clausulae *see* clausulae
    encomiastic historiography 124-5,
        148
    historical narrative, content of
        83-94
        exaedificatio of 83-95, 193
        hard core of 88-9, 91-3
    impartiality 73-4, 82-3
    inuentio 87-8, 88-94, 199, 203, 211
    leges historiae see historiography,
        ancient, laws of
    ring composition 78, 81, 82,
        94-5, 112
    sees historiography in terms of
        judicial oratory 78-80, 84-8,
        92-4, 95-9, 112
    of epideictic oratory 95-8
    style 45, 83, 94, 112, 117-20, 124,
        126, 128, 139, 144, 146, 150,
        165, 168, 203-4, 206
Cicero, Q. Tullius, brother of the
    orator 90-1, 109, 113
clausulae in Cicero 119-20, 147-8, 150
    Florus 158
    Pollio 150
    Sallust 122-3, 147-8, 149-50
    Thucydides 9-10, 52, 147-50
    Velleius 158
Clitarchus 30
Coelius Antipater, L. 78, 103
Collingwood, R.G. 46-7, 55
colores 125, 149
commentarius 90, 92, 110-11
comparison (σύγκρισις), literary
    critical 40-1, 43, 45, 68, 76, 78
    magnifying 2-3, 29, 37
content (*res*) of historical narrative
    battles (*descriptio pugnae*) 3, 89, 91,
        95, 165, 183, 189-90
    besieging and capture of cities
        29-30, 89, 166-7, 183, 186-90
    deaths 72, 166, 183-4
    exile 72, 166, 187, 191
    geographical descriptions
        (*descriptio regionum*) 78-80,

228

Index of Passages